THE ART OF THE LINE IN DRAWING

THE ART
OF
THE LINE
IN
DRAWING

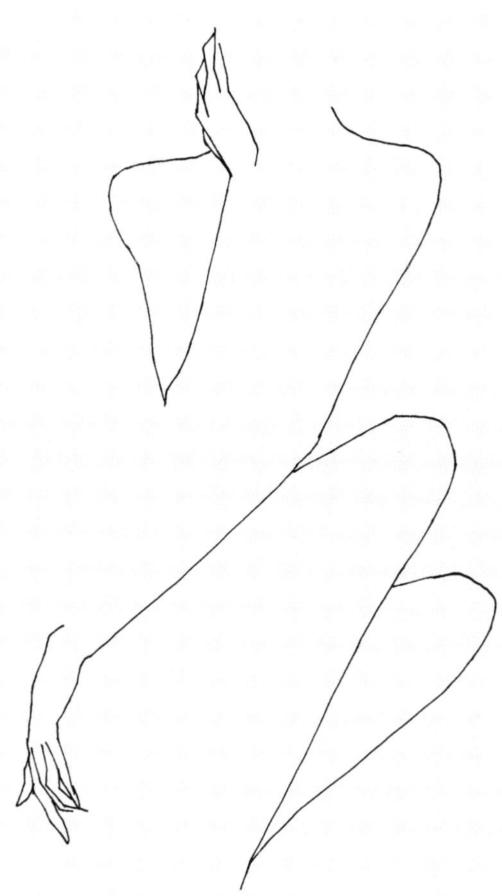

Frédéric Forest

*A Step-by-Step Guide to Creating
Simple, Expressive Drawings*

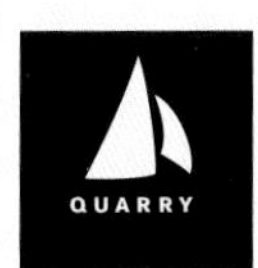

To my mother,
who introduced me to art instruction books in 1984.
Thirty-nine years later, this one is dedicated to her.

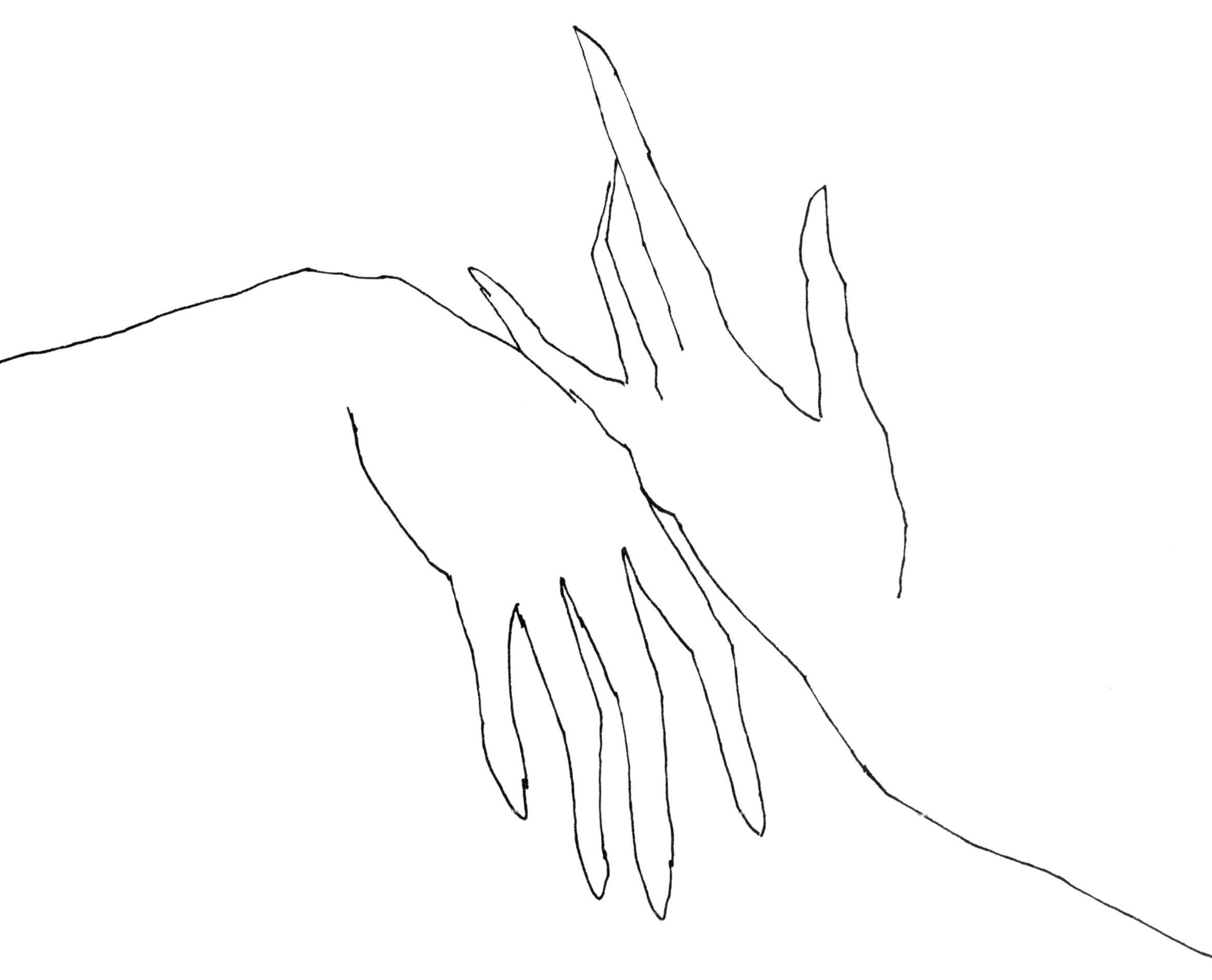

CONTENTS

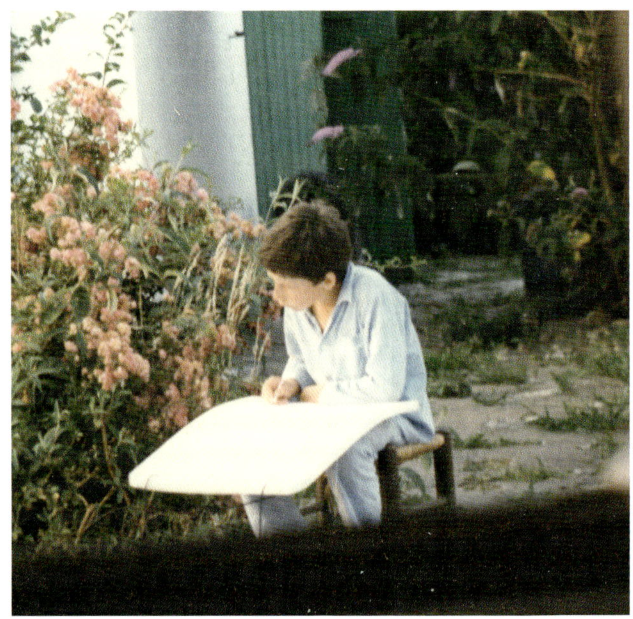

Frédéric Forest at age 8, Isle of Oléron in France, 1984

PREFACE

I've been drawing for as long as I can remember. All the time. Every day. Drawing is constantly on my mind.

Sometimes people ask me what schools I attended, which professors or teachers I pursued and what courses helped me the most and so on. To be completely honest, I did none of those things. I started out by studying industrial design. Sometimes, there were a few live model sessions during my ID studies, but that's it! I drew every day, but I never thought of being an artist. I never had that aspiration and yet here I am today. I've been drawing since I was a kid and I simply never stopped. In a way, I attended my very own art school.

On the other hand, I have always been surrounded by a lot of visual inspiration: my mother's and sisters' fashion magazines, my comic books, but also art books at the library. In Annecy, in the French Alps, there is no art school, so I just learned to look for and show what I wanted to express. I drew what I didn't have. I drew what I longed for. I also drew for the sake of drawing.

When I was eight years old, my mother gave me two books she had found in an art store to learn how to draw the human body, with all of the basic muscles, proportions, hand details, eye placements and shadows. If I close my eyes, I can still describe each page to you because I know these books by heart. They constituted the foundation of my drawings. They were, in a way, the teachers I never had. When Quarry Books invited me to create a book on how I draw, it felt like the perfect opportunity to remind myself of the importance of such books.

The idea of this one is not to teach you how to draw like me, but to share with you the pure pleasure of drawing and of each aspect that surrounds this skill. Always draw and paint for yourself first. Keep it fun. Never give up. Never stop.

This book is for you, to pursue the thrill and develop the creative pleasure of drawing.

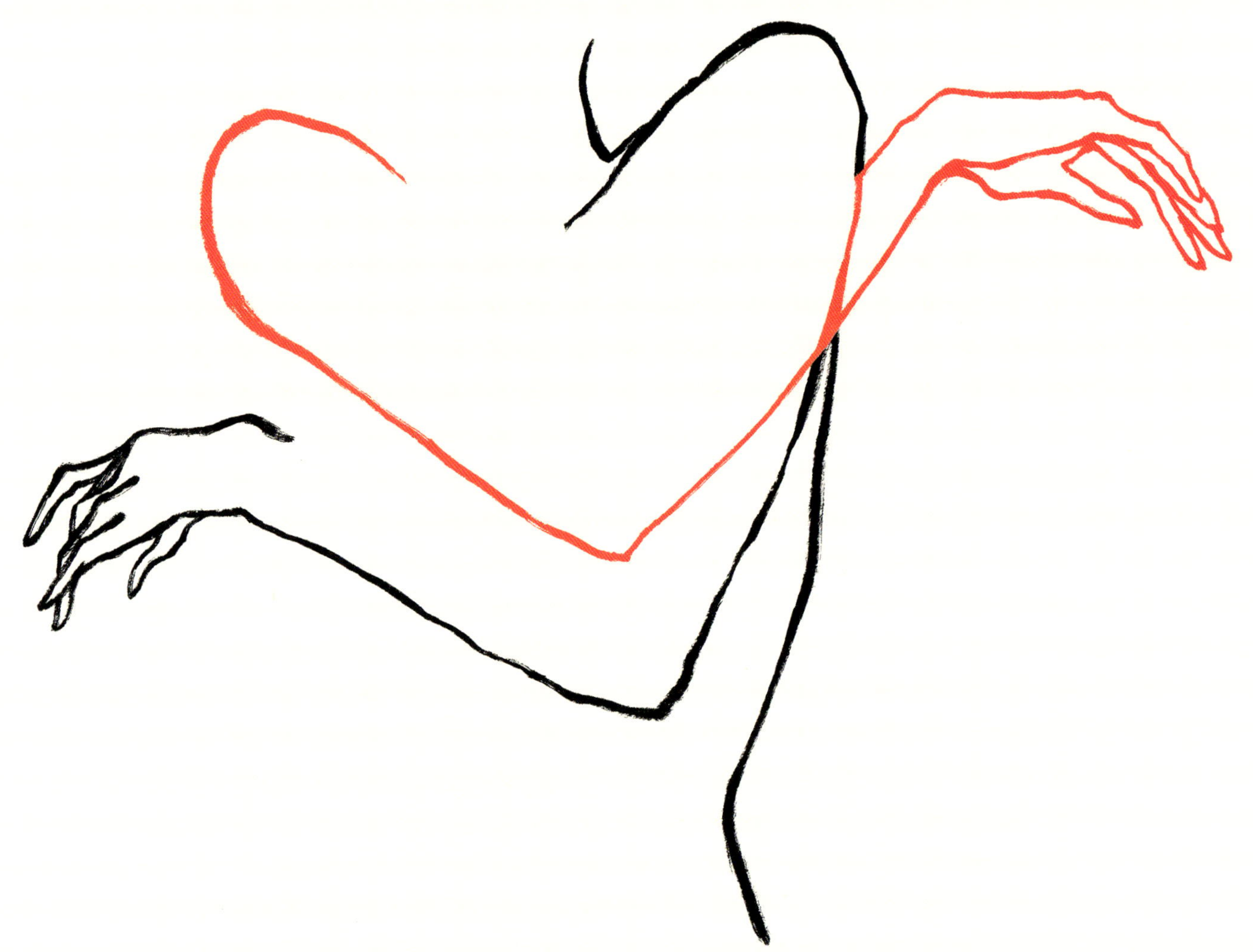

PORTFOLIO

In the traditional sense, an artist's portfolio is an edited collection of an artist's best artwork, compiled to showcase their style or method of work. A portfolio showing different samples of current work can have many uses, depending on the persons you present it to (art galleries, commercial clients, editors, and so on).

I feel that the best way to display the many facets of my career is to share with you the different types of artworks that I create for commercial clients (Chanel, *Cereal* magazine, Maison Kitsuné, Lancôme, or Massimo Dutti, for example), for art exhibitions (solo shows in galleries in France and abroad, art fairs such as Art Basel Miami Beach) and personal artworks I create on my own in the comfort of my home or in the studio.

On the following pages, I showcase examples of these different types of creations so that you can grasp the differences that exist among them while hopefully also seeing that they all form a coherent body of work.

For commercial works, I try to keep the drawings as pure as possible so that they can take on the identity of the brand's image and the subject of the commission while still functioning on their own as artworks. All of these works are hand-drawn in my sketchbooks or on paper, scanned and prepared as high-definition digital files so that clients can use them as they see fit, create animations, and so on, but the original work is always done with simple ink and paper.

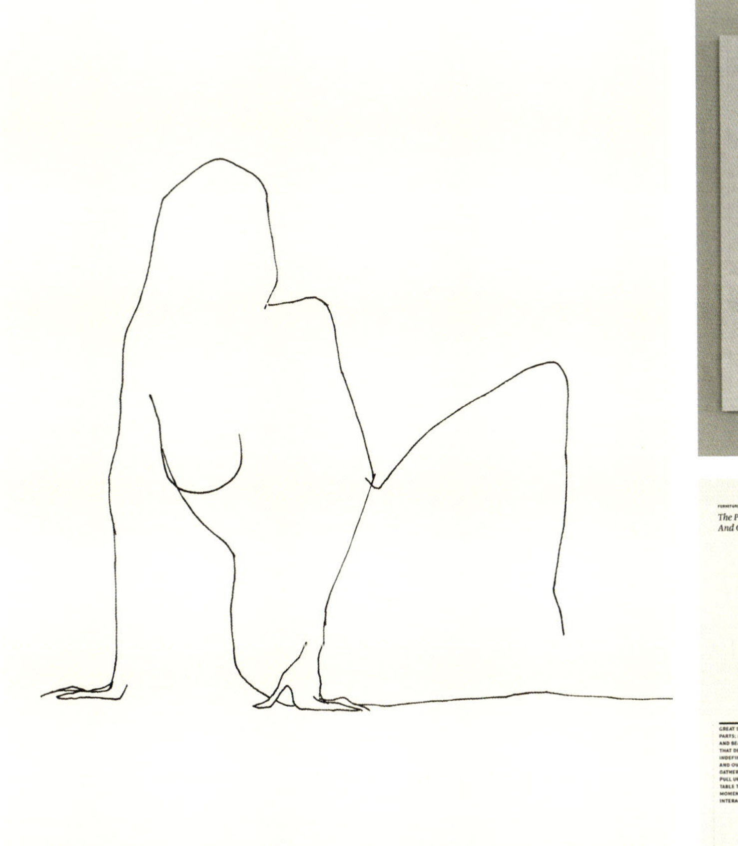

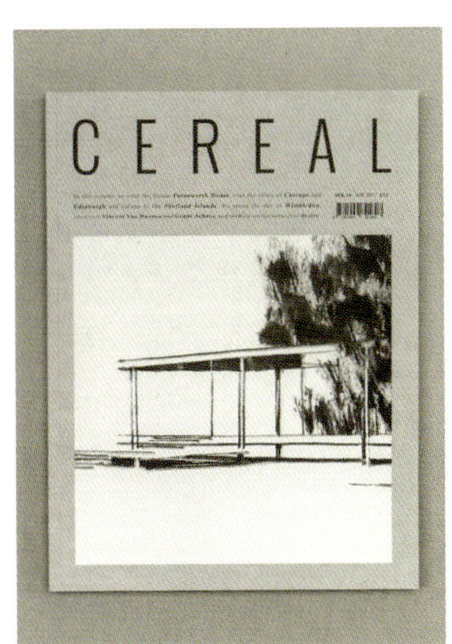

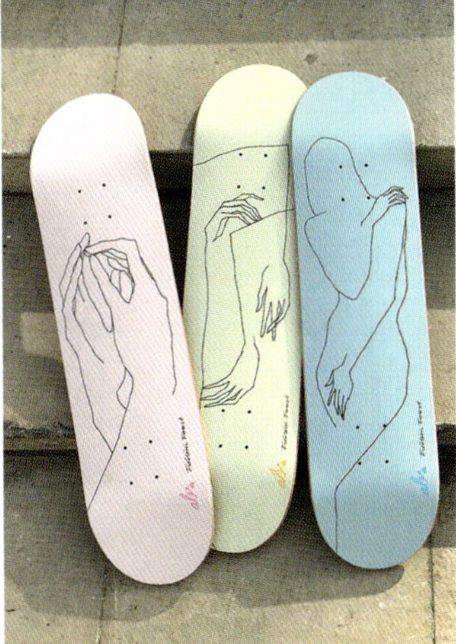

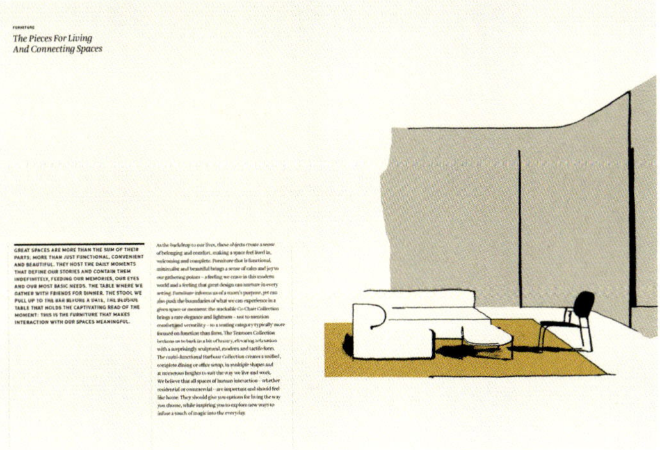

Opposite page: Women's Day campaign for Lancôme. This page, clockwise from left: Campaign for SKIMS with Kim Kardashian / Limited-edition cover for Cereal *Magazine / Limited-edition skateboards for ABS / Catalog illustrations for Menu Space*

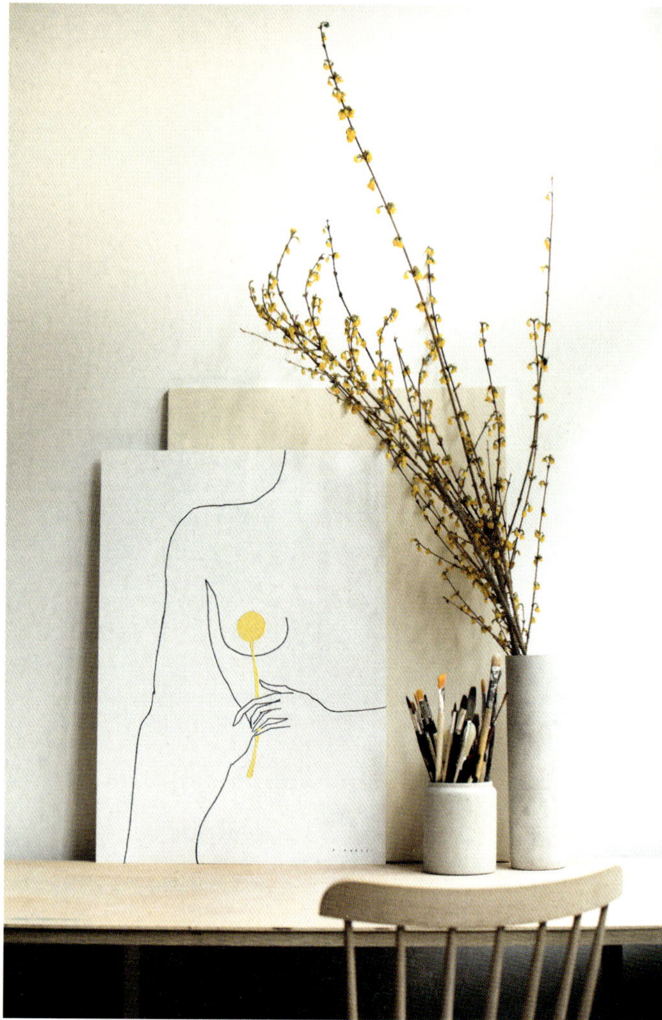

When preparing works for exhibitions of any kind, I like to create the works on-site so that I can be inspired by my surroundings and truly craft the pieces for a specific space, thus giving them a certain sense of belonging.

Finally, my personal works take on many forms and are generally more geared toward experimenting and discovering new ways of capturing my subjects, adding new color techniques, or testing abstract compositions.

These works can sometimes develop into commercial collaborations because I occasionally post the finalized works I'm happy with or my creative process on social media and future clients reach out to discuss a potential project, a commissioned series of drawings, or the purchasing of the work itself.

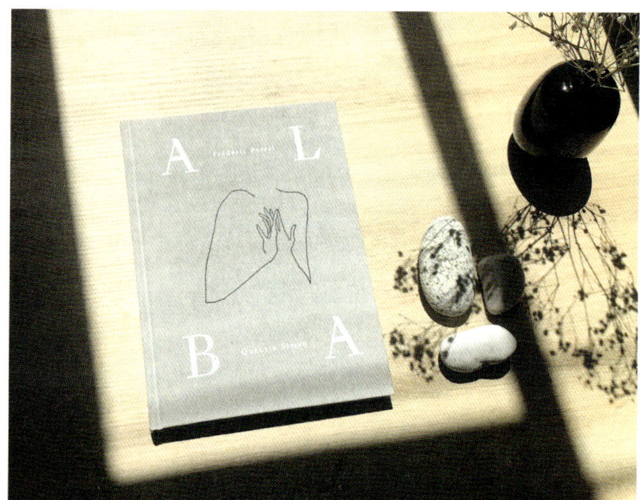

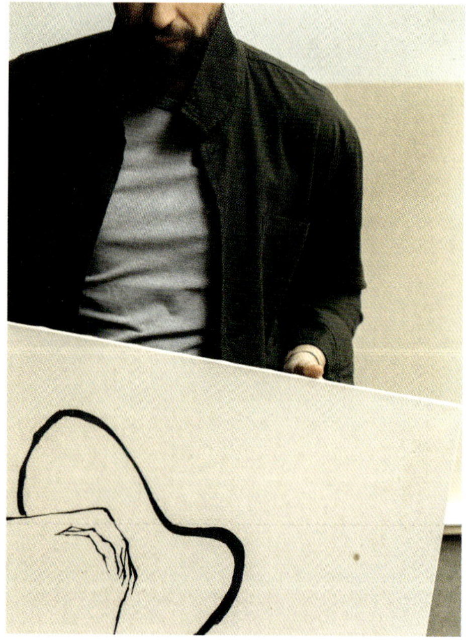

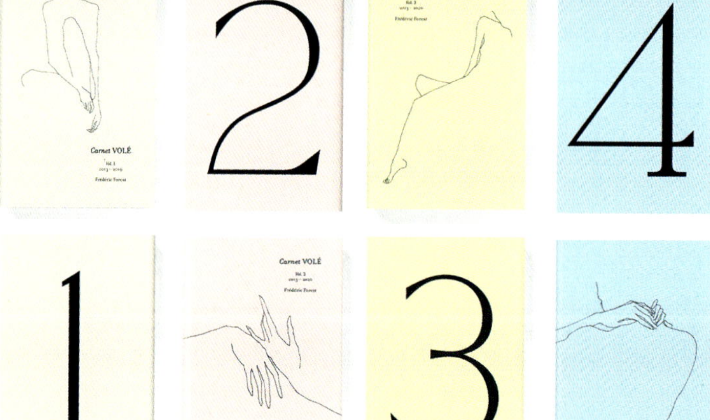

Top and bottom left: Tu es mon Jour, *Eleven House Gallery, Spain*
Top right: Alba, *exhibition and book, Paris*
Bottom right: Carnets Volés, *book collection, published by Grammatical*

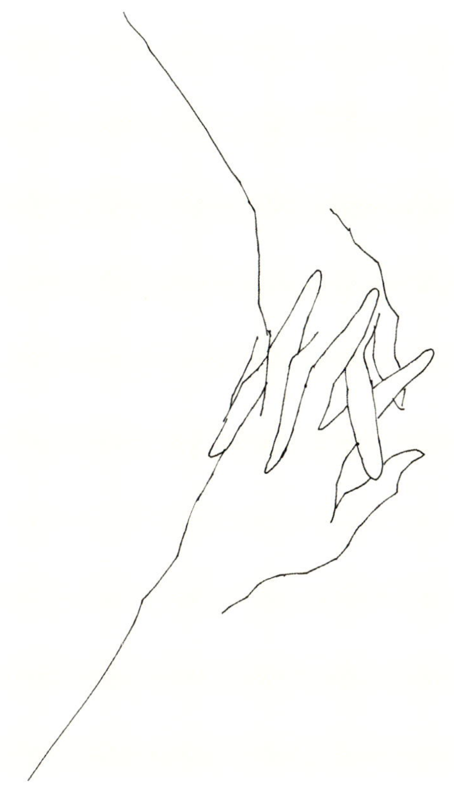
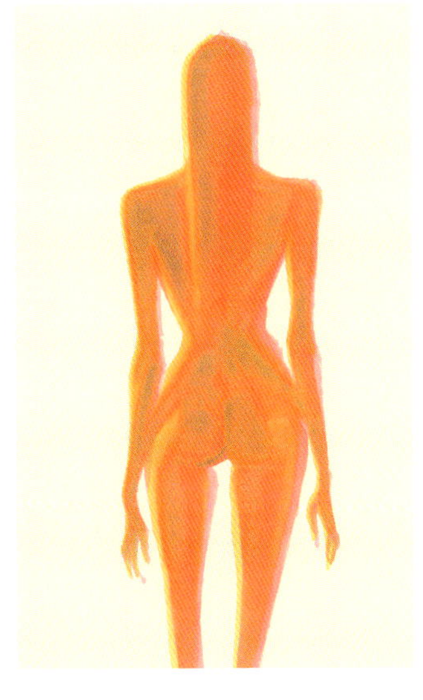
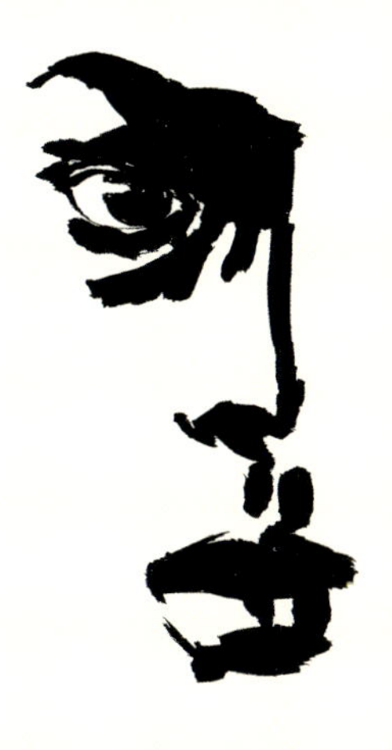
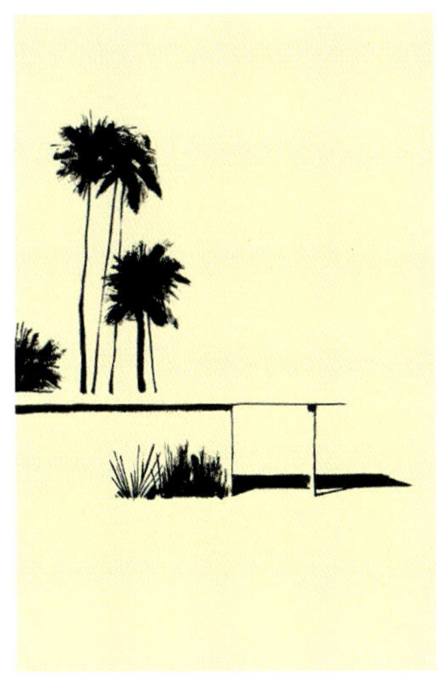
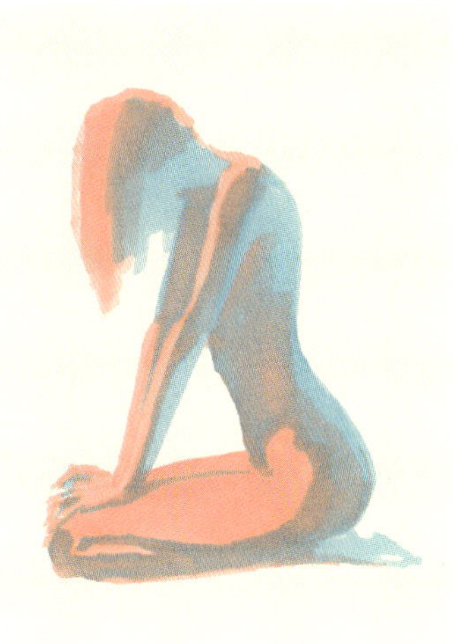
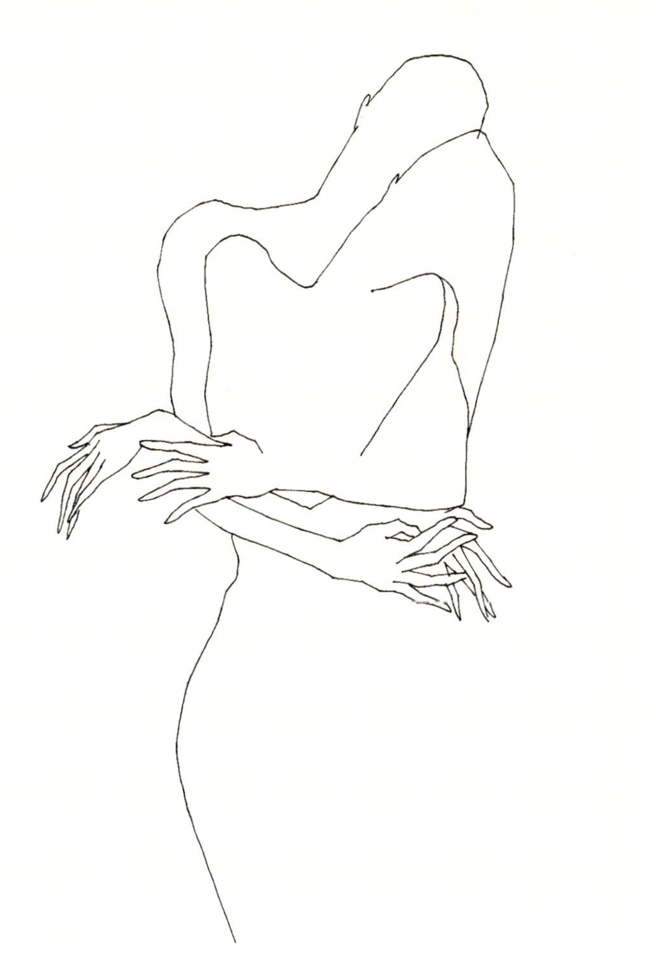

Clockwise from top left:
Just Us
Sun on her Skin
Portrait
Dancing Together
Spring
Palm Springs

LINE ART

DEFINITION AND ORIGINS

Line is considered one of the earliest forms of mark-making in human history. In fact, as one of the seven visual elements of art, along with form, shape, color, value, texture, and space, the line is deemed to be a hallmark of the arts.

Line as an element of art can be defined as the path that is formed between two points, usually a straight line, but not always. At its core, line drawing consists of creating distinct lines against a primarily solid background. Line art is often black and white, but as we will see later in this book, it can also be colorful. Elements like shading and color gradients are, however, absent, allowing the viewer's focus to rest firmly on the lines themselves. Line in art can vary in color and width and length to evoke different responses in the viewer or to illustrate a visual illusion. Many of the world's most famous portraits make use of lines, alongside other art elements, to define the sitter, characterize the drawing, and bring it to life.

Let's quickly go back to the origins of the art form. Line art dates back nearly seventy-five thousand years. In fact, the first recognized drawing made by a human was discovered on a rock flake in South Africa and is estimated to be seventy-three thousand years old. The design on the rock, made using red ocher (a type of reddish-brown clay), consists of several intersecting strokes.

Over time, line art has evolved considerably from this rather primitive example. Some of today's most famous artists, including Pablo Picasso and Leonardo da Vinci, created powerful line drawings. These works are often seen as "studies" or precursors to painted masterpieces that the artists would later create. For example, the Picasso Museum in Barcelona, Spain, houses several early works by the Spanish artist as well as very constructed sketches that helped him design his later greatest works. These line drawings have also often become highly prized masterpieces.

Fashion designers past and present use line art alike to materialize on paper what they have in mind before bringing it to life through their desired textiles. Watch an episode of Project Runway or check out your favorite designer's Instagram account, and you'll see the designers making line art of their own.

The use of line can also become an artist's key signature or art style. Many artists make use of lines in a variety of ways, such that it is associated with their characteristic visual aesthetic. Iconic American pop artist Keith Haring, who reached the height of his fame while living in New York in the 1980s, is one of the most well-known and celebrated line artists of the modern world. Did you know that he became famous for his line drawings, created with chalk, which appeared on the New York City subway and in other public spaces? Later in his life, Haring was commissioned to create murals. The juxtaposition of his simple designs and the provocative themes he addressed—including AIDS and homosexuality—made his work particularly powerful.

French artist Henri Matisse, who led the Fauvism movement in the 1900s, increasingly incorporated throughout his career the quick, expressionistic touch of his drawings into his paintings. One of his most famous pieces, The Dance, relies heavily on the contours he created. With bold, flat colors and striking outlines, viewers perceive the power and movement of the dancers through Matisse's lines.

Today, lines are as important as ever in contemporary art. From sculpture to painting, the tradition of line art continues through the work of cutting-edge artists.

So why is line art a technique appreciated by artists? There is indeed a reason why so many artists are drawn to line drawing as a practice and form of personal expression. Line art allows you to explore and understand the world around you. It can be used as a stepping stone to more advanced methodologies, such as painting or digital art, or it can simply be a means (perhaps even the main one) you choose to channel your creativity. In this book, you will learn the basic techniques and notions of line art to then choose the purpose you will want to give to this newly acquired artistic skill. In my case, line art is present in all areas of my life and work: as a preliminary sketch for object design or in preparing an event, as a creative outlet daily, but also as the basis of my artwork for both commercial and personal works.

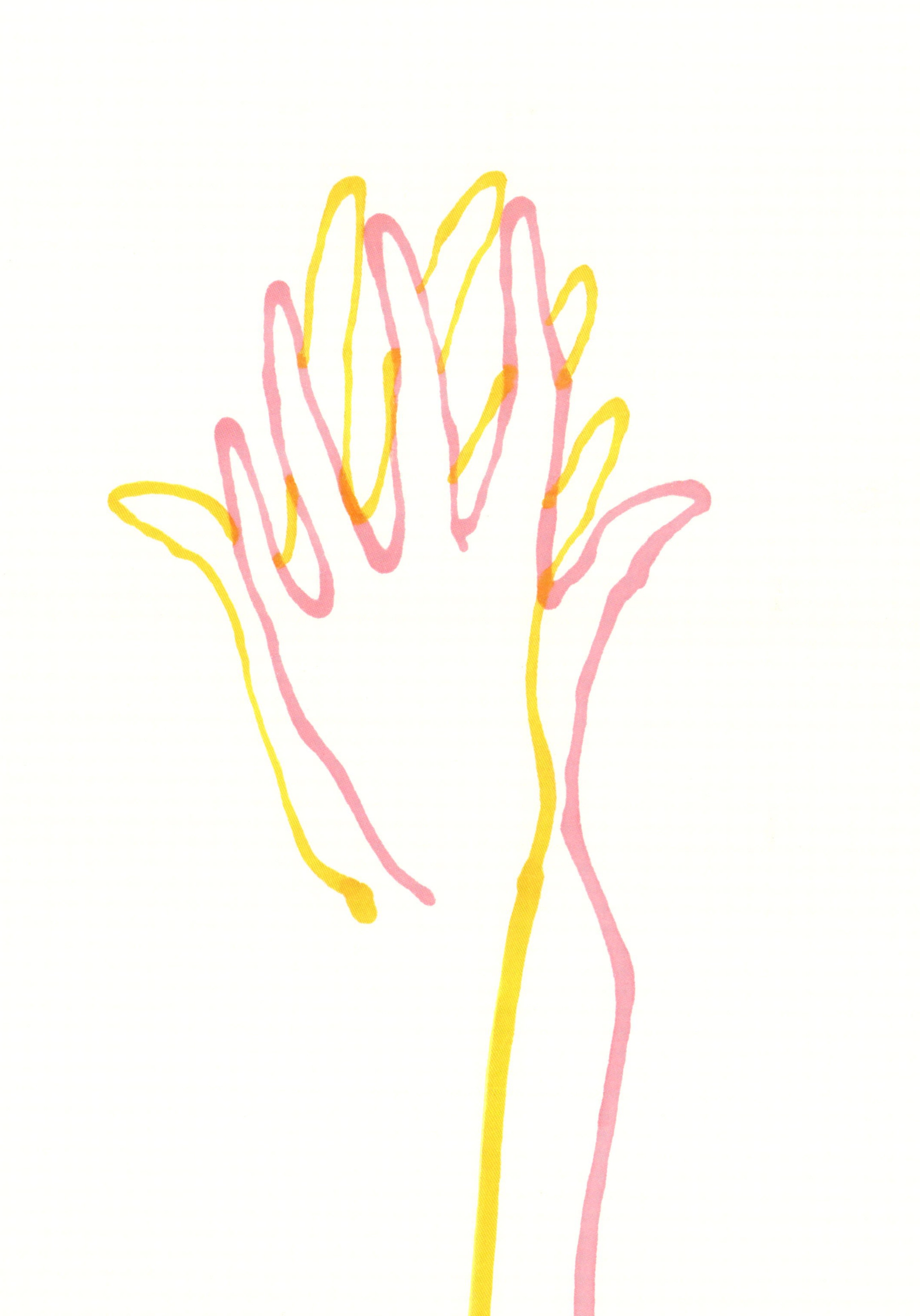

LEXICON

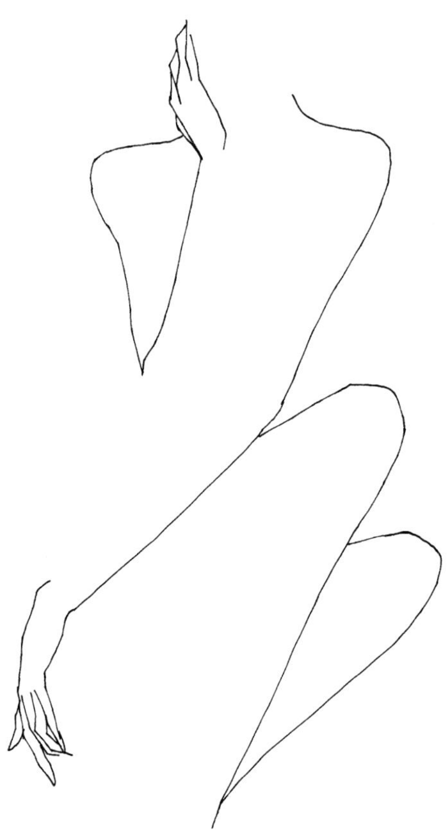

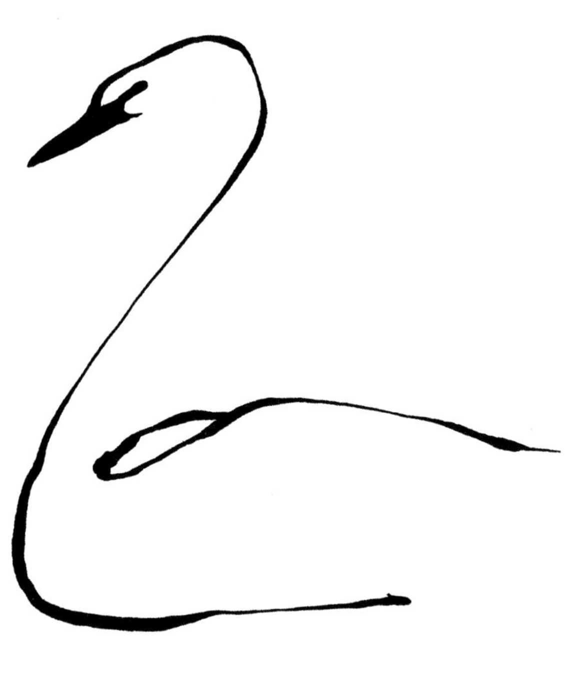

FINE LINE

Fine or thin lines will create a different effect compared with thick lines. They will soften a visual composition and are important in terms of rendering finer details. They can also provide artworks with more depth and three-dimensionality in terms of the background of an image. Typically, I use fine lines to focus on minute or delicate details: a collarbone, hands, facial features, an attitude, and so on. In today's digital world, they can also come in handy in expressing that a drawing was handmade because fine lines are often present in the "accidental" strokes that you can find, for example, when creating the curve of a knee or thigh. They really accentuate the human component of the drawing.

SMOOTH LINE

Smooth lines are, to me, much like a signature or a type of writing with lines. These lines are not harsh straight or angular lines. Rather, they are very natural and organic, allowing them to be used to create very legible images. Smooth lines are created by letting go and letting your hand move freely on the paper so that your pen or marker is almost dancing its way across the sheet.

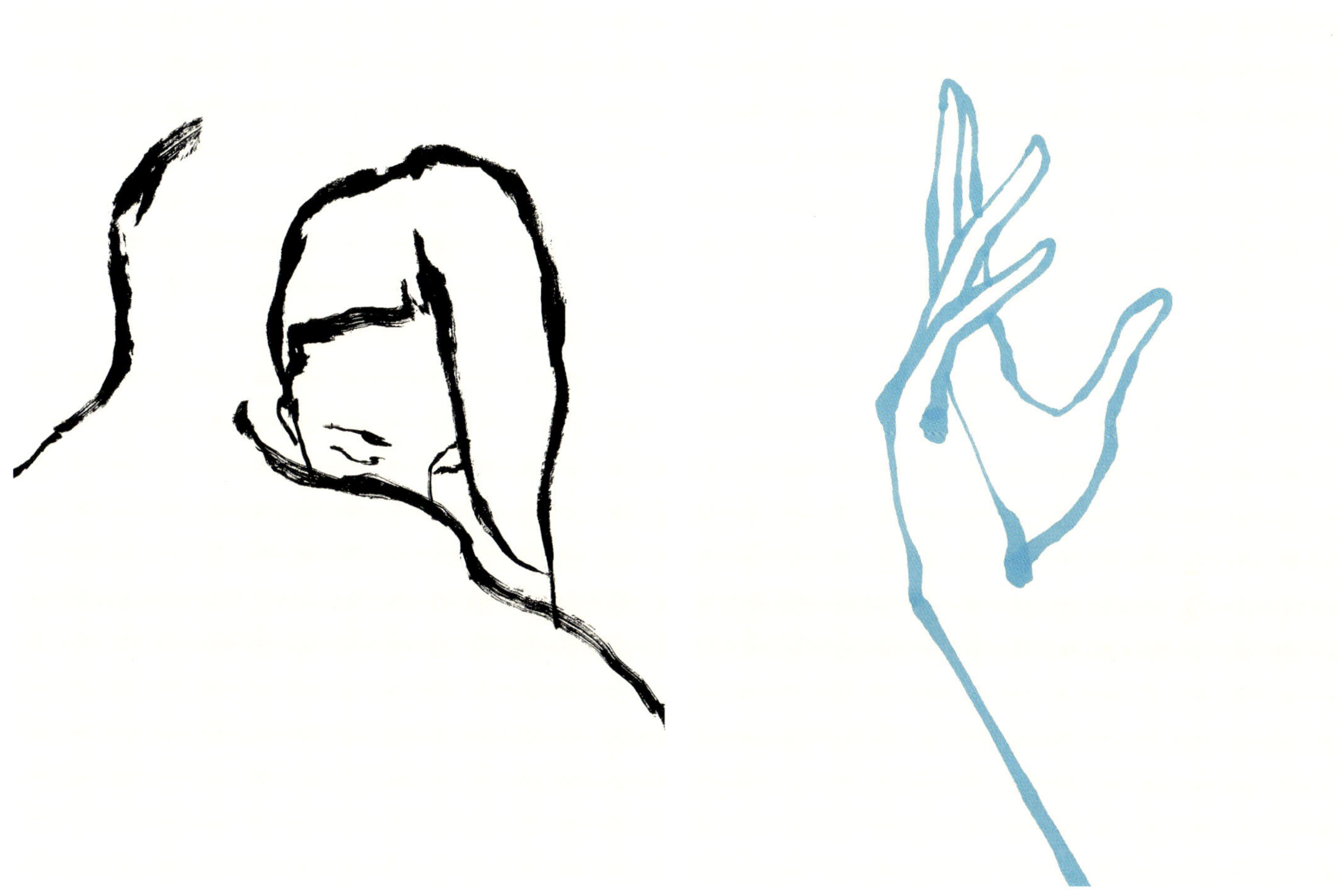

BRUSHED LINE

Brushed lines act as a sort of synthesis of a painting. A brushed line drawing is very far from a painting because it doesn't have multiple layers or the additional information or details you can find in a painted composition. Brushed lines prove to be very useful when trying to render textures; for example, your subject's hair, eyelashes, or even muscles.

COLORED LINE

Colored lines give a different dimension to a drawing. They are mostly used, in my personal work, to convey a vibrant emotion. Color is not always linked to realism in my work; however, colored lines can also be much more directly linked to the subject matter, such as using yellow for sunlight. Colored lines can also give dimension to your drawing or express a more imaginative or poetic vision.

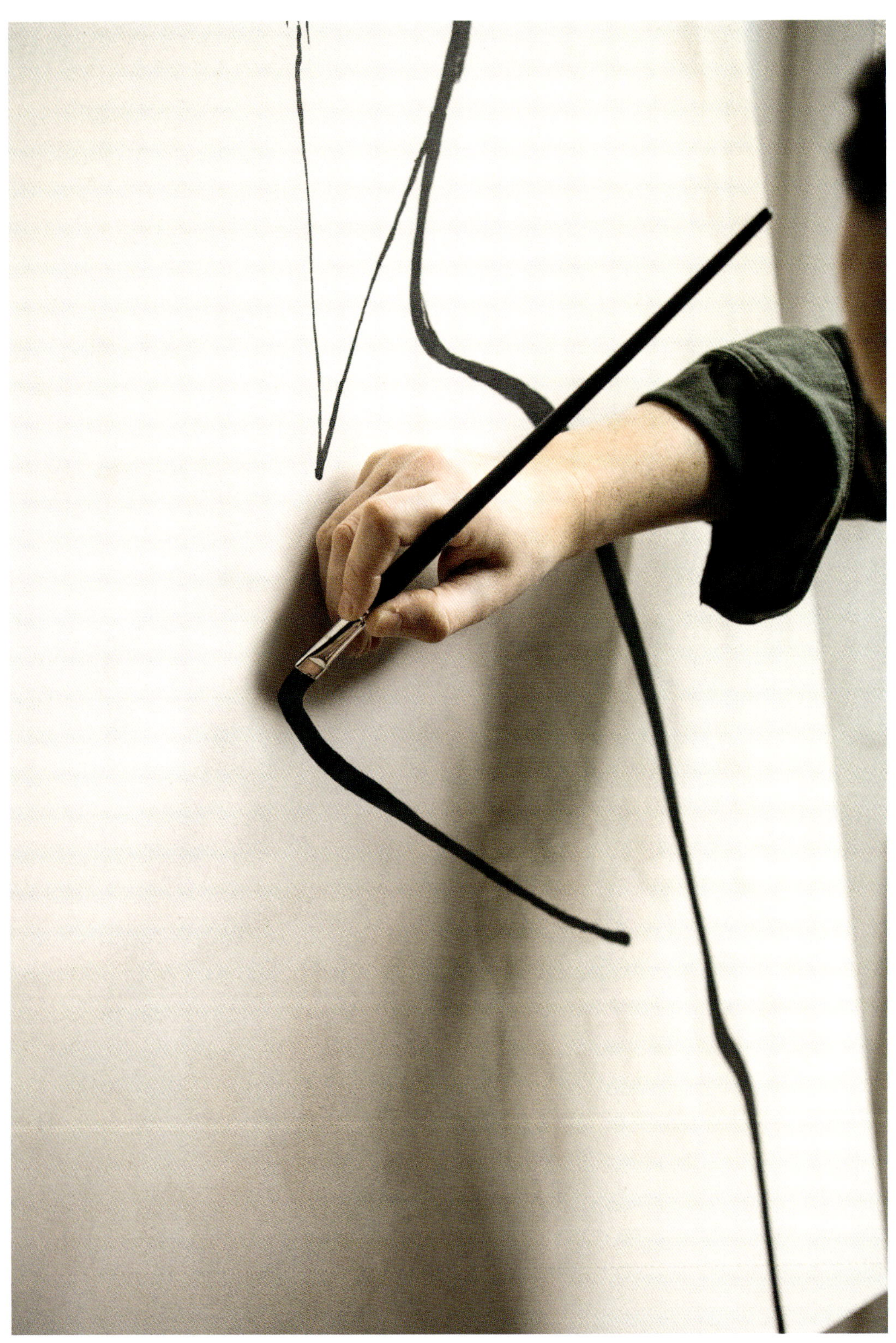

Frédéric Forest at work in his studio in Paris, France, 2022

ACQUIRED SKILLS

Line art as a practice and form of self-expression will not only allow you to explore the world around you differently, it will also help you gain a unique understanding of it. By practicing these lessons, you can learn to easily create impactful line art in either medium, be it traditional or digital. Once you have mastered line drawing, you will be able to not only express your creativity through it but also have the skills necessary to advance to other artistic methods and media as you pursue your artistic journey.

Line art embodies the foundations you will need to build any good work of art. We will touch base on many fundamental aspects of art such as anatomy, proportions, composition, perspective, light, edges, color, gestures, style, concepts, and communication. This basic overview will allow you to improve or perfect your current drawing skills, and along with the creative pauses, stimulate your creativity and imagination to create unique works of your own.

Along with the technical aspects of line art and its different forms, this book also aims to help you boost your creativity, develop confidence in your artistic vision, strengthen your ability to step back and critique your own work, and lastly, discern when the work you've made satisfies your artistic vision.

MATERIALS

PENS for MARK-MAKING

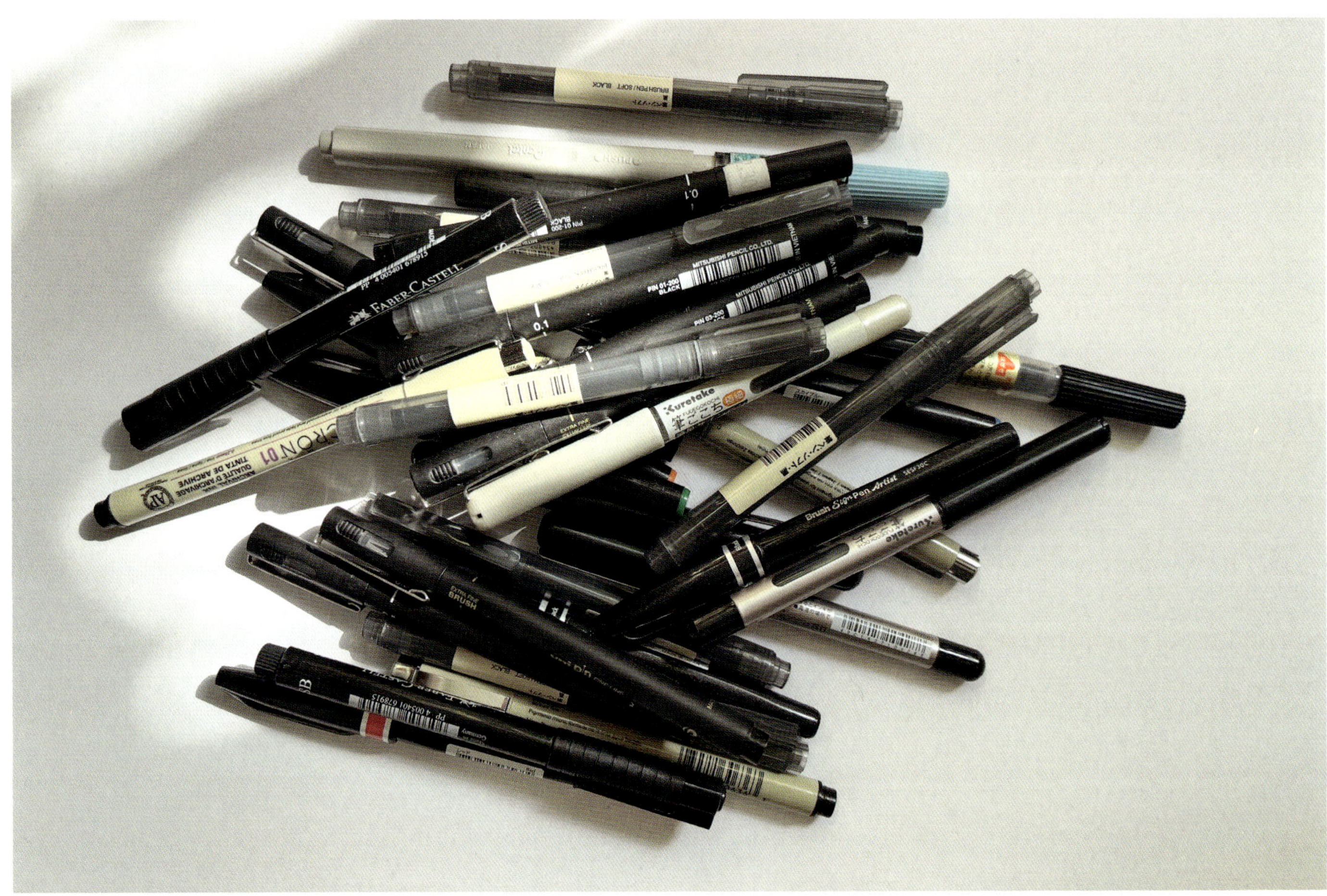

SIMPLE TOOLS

Here's what you will find in my pencil case. I use a lot of fairly classic or relatively common markers and pens that you can find almost anywhere. The following list of materials is not exhaustive, but it will allow you to have access to the basic tools needed to follow the lessons in this book.

I take these markers with me everywhere I go. They are not very expensive, and many of them are rechargeable. If you already have similar pens or markers that are more personal or special to you, use those! The main purpose of this book is above all to share with you my approach to line art, or rather lines in drawing, and the emotions they can create.

The list of materials is really quite simple. The best you can do is acquire such pens and markers from a store, local if possible. In this way, you will be able to manipulate and test them directly, and if you can't find them, you will surely discover other tools that are equivalent or that you prefer. It's also a great way to support your local economy!

IMPERFECT IS JUST PERFECT

The most important thing to note is that I don't erase. I never use an eraser. If I mess up or I do not like what I just drew, I start over until I am satisfied or finally realize that the pose, the lighting, or something was wrong with the chosen subject or what I had initially in mind.

I also do not use rulers. I find it is very important to accept any mistakes your hand gestures make and to keep the focus on what you are trying to express through your drawing. You will find that as you let go of this fear of messing up, you will gain more confidence in your line work and find that your sensitivity and strength will bloom. Your lines need to be your signature, something that cannot be easily copied. Even as you read and follow the steps in this book, do not forget to make your own lines and follow your own style.

TOOLS for FINE LINES

Pigma—Micron 01 to 05

There are many very nice fine-tip pens out there, but this series is definitely my ultimate favorite to work with. They are also easy to find all over the world. Since they cannot be recharged, I recommend purchasing five or ten of them at a time so that you don't run out while drawing.

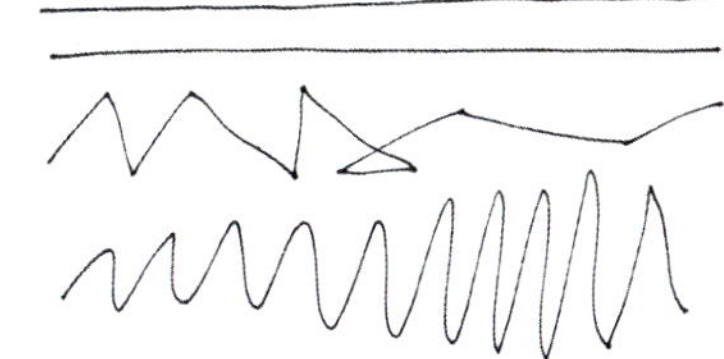

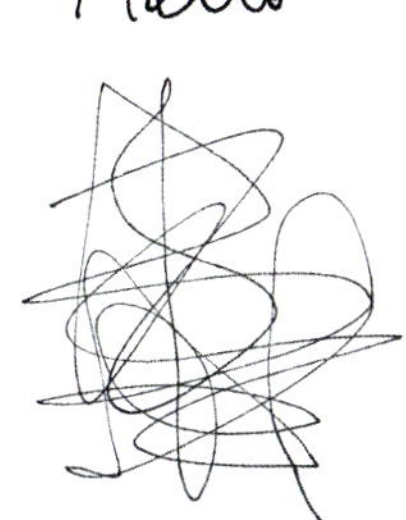

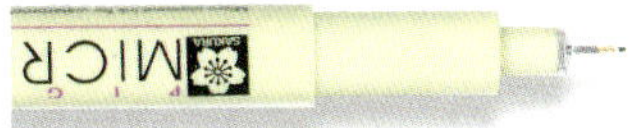

Uni—Fine Line 01 to 05

These fine-tip pens are admittedly not my favorite to work with; however, they are still good quality. They have a water-based fade-proof pigment ink and cannot be recharged, so I recommend purchasing a few ahead of time so that you do not run out of ink.

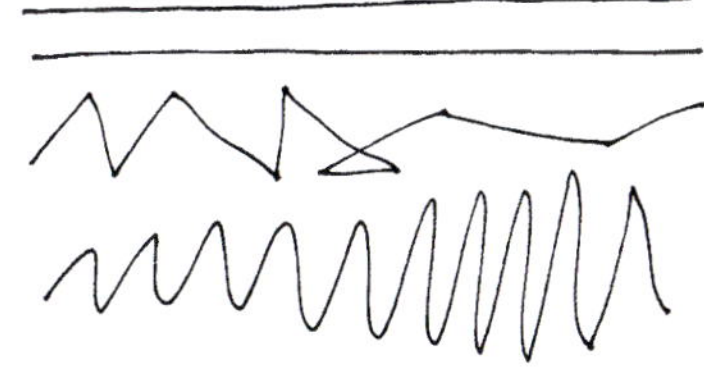

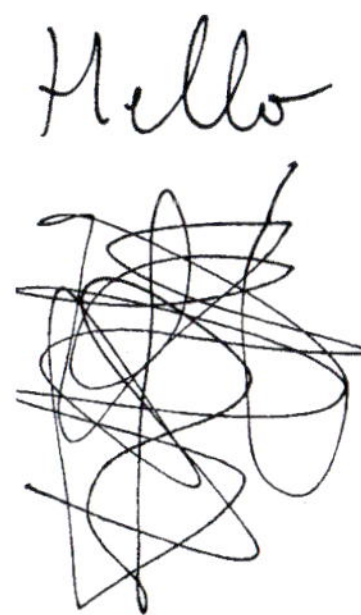

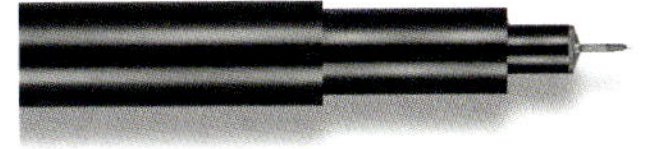

Kuretake—Fudegokochi Brush-Pen (Regular)

These markers are both flexible and dynamic. The tip allows you to create a nice curved line with varied thicknesses, ranging from very thin to thick, very smoothly. They are very sensitive. I discovered these markers during a trip to Japan. It is fairly easy to find them in stores now. Their only drawback is that the ink can take a long time to fully dry.

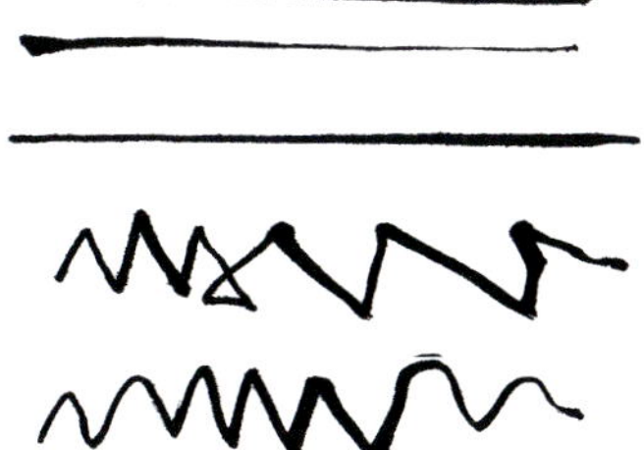

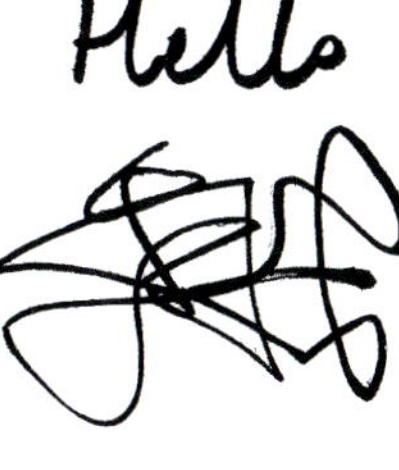

TOOLS for BRUSHED LINES

Uni—Extra-Fine Brush

This is an extremely fine brush-pen. You can achieve very fine lines as well as thicker ones, depending on the amount of pressure you apply on the tip of the brush. These brush-pens are not rechargeable, but they have water-based, fade-proof pigment ink. I use this pen for a wide variety of sketches.

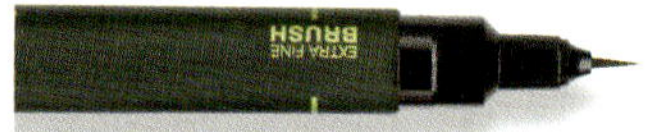

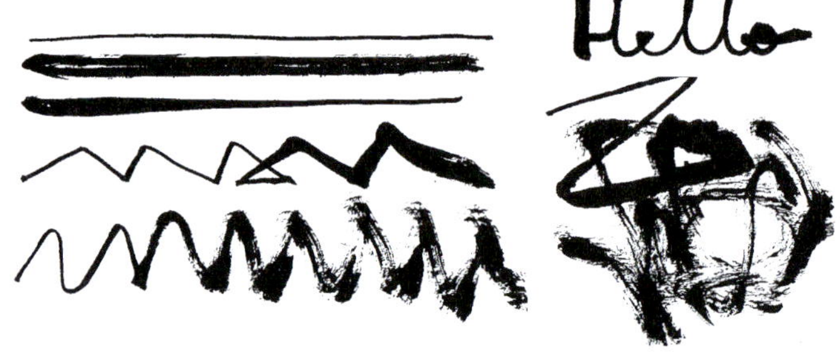

Pentel—Brush Sign Pen Artist

This pen has practically the same characteristics as the previous one. Its grip is a little more precise, and its bristles fan out a bit more when applying pressure on the tip. These brush-pens are really great when drawing landscapes or making architectural studies.

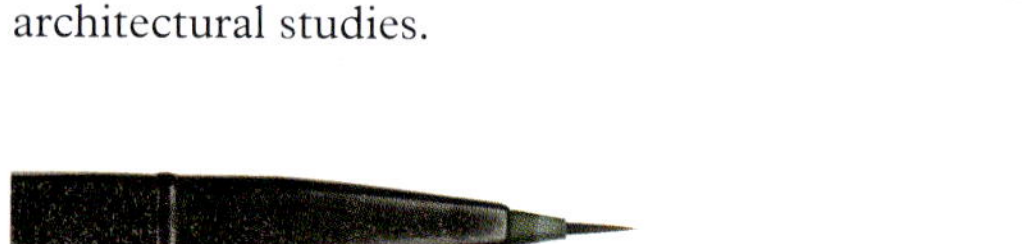

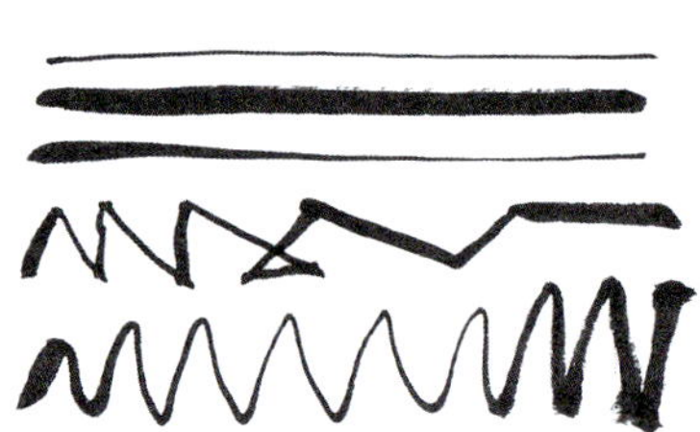

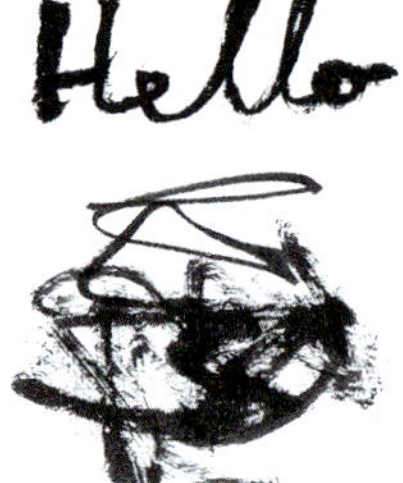

Pentel—Arts Brush

Definitely my favorite series. These pens offer many different kinds of brush tips, and they are easy to find. They are also rechargeable, which is very convenient and eco-friendly. The ink quality is excellent, and the charger is quite generous. I have five different brushes, but I always end up using the same two. Fun fact: I even use these brush-pens on canvas!

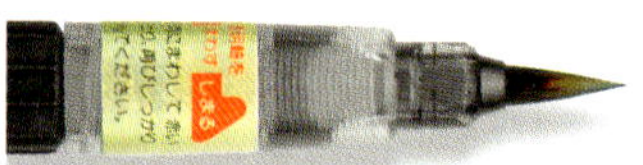

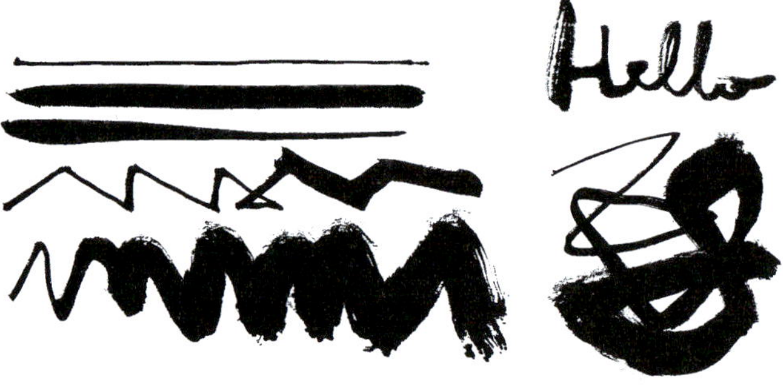

Muji—Brush-Pen

The quality of these brush-pens cannot be compared! They are unfortunately not rechargeable; however, once the ink runs out, they can be used as brushes by dipping them in ink bottles. They also offer nice, lighter marks once the ink starts to run out, so you can use them until the end!

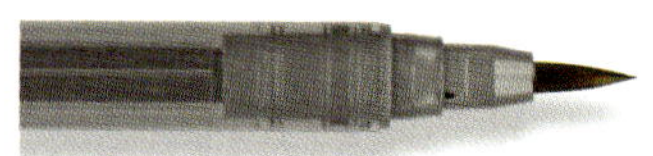

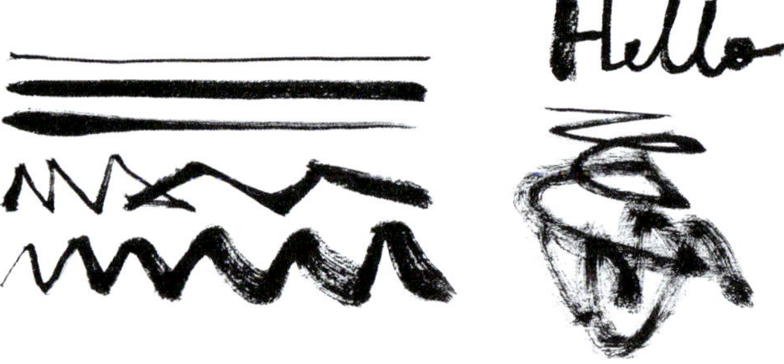

TOOLS for COLORED LINES

Pentel—Brush Sign Pen Artist

This collection of brush-pens is pretty amazing. Their colors are vibrant and darken in tone if you draw over your lines, which allows you to give them depth and variation. I use these for a lot of drawing studies, and I love mixing them with other, bolder colors for a unique result.

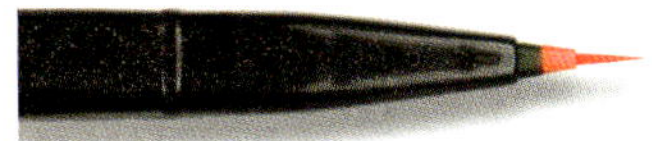

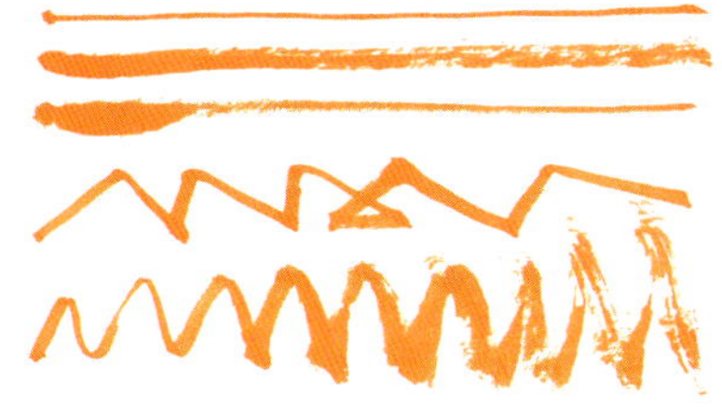

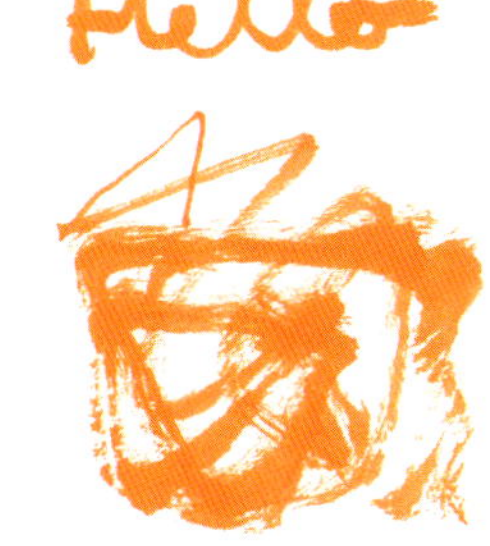

Graph'It—Brush-Pen

This is a strong brush-pen. You can achieve medium lines as well as thicker ones with rounded outlines. What I like to do is to let the ink dry and brush once more over the same lines. I even do this with multiple colors for a more original effect.

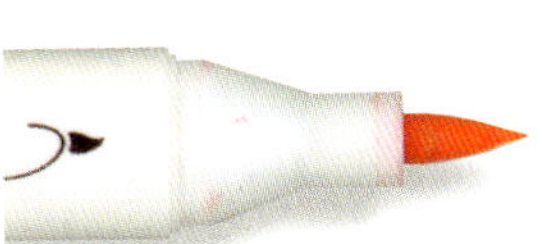

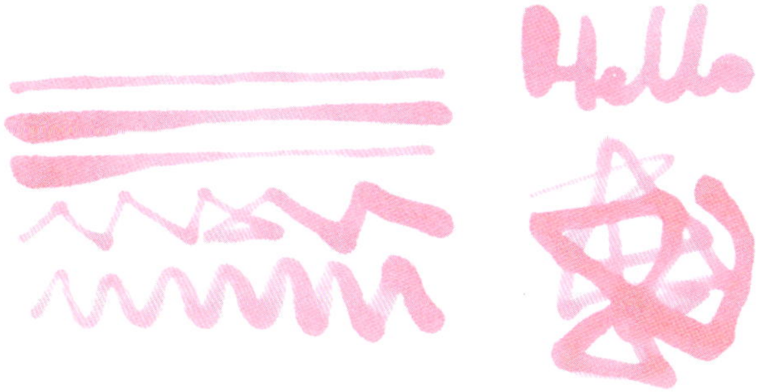

Winsor & Newton—Brush Marker

This is a strong brush-pen as well, but I like the quality of the tip better—it remains fine and dynamic longer. I can use them for handwriting and portrait or hands because they are quite precise.

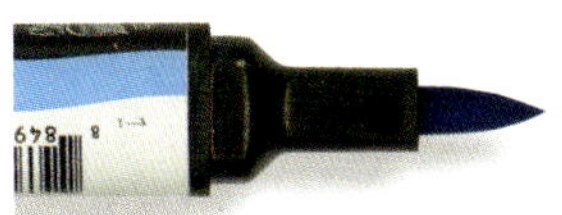

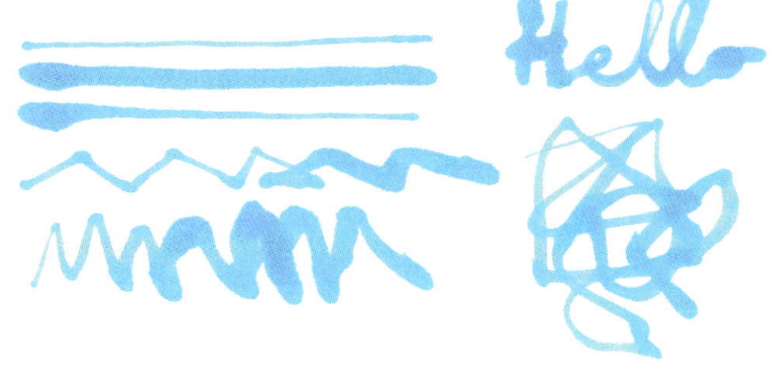

Winsor & Newton—Pro Marker

These pens have two types of brush tips, but I prefer to use the larger one because I find that its shape allows me to create medium-sized lines as well as larger ones. I love how the ink reacts when the pens are new and fully pigmented.

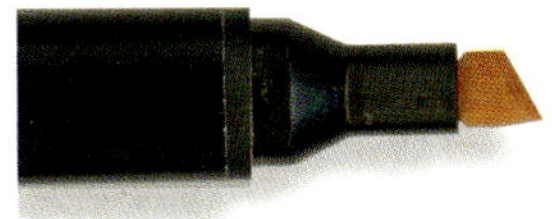

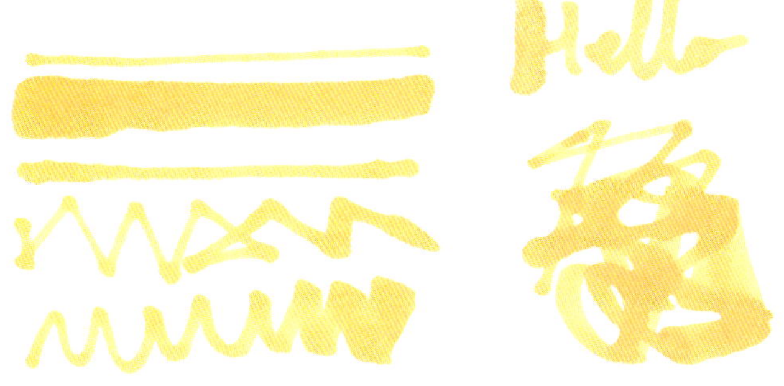

TYPES OF PAPER

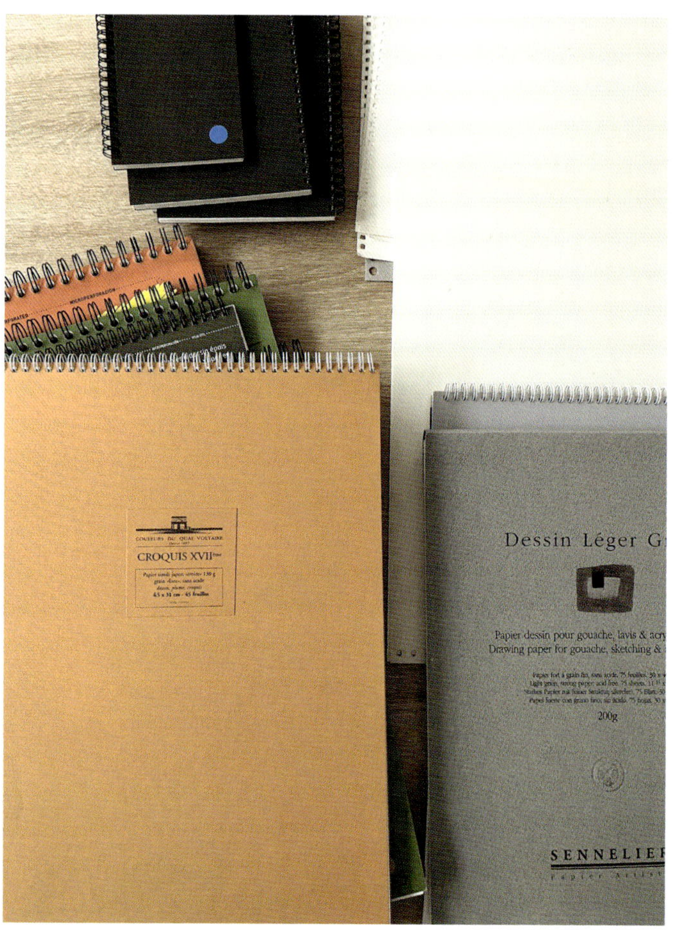

After spending lots of time testing out a wide variety of surfaces for my drawings, I have found that smoother surfaces and lighter papers work best for me and enable me to apply light layers of inks and pigments to get vibrant line drawings and complex hues. Keeping that in mind, I also steer clear of paper that is "too white" for multiple reasons. First of all, because my drawings are mainly done with black ink, I find that having a slightly off-white background gives dimension and color to the piece without having to add pigments. Second, it's important to keep in mind that your artworks should remain in good condition over a long time. Choosing acid-free paper is something you should strongly consider to keep your works from turning yellow or deteriorating over time, also affecting your art.

For my everyday sketching and work-related drawings, I use a wide variety of sketchbooks of all sizes and formats, like the ones pictured here from Muji or Canson. The paper is quite thin and smooth, which I like, and is adapted to the type of quick, steady sketches I want to make. I always carry a few of these sketchbooks with me because I never know when an opportunity to draw something interesting will arise! For final drawings and unique pieces, I prefer to use the elegant, grainy-textured Hahnemühle paper, which is also suitable for creating fine art digital prints.

The surfaces you will work on when creating art are just as valuable and important as the pens and inks you decide to employ. The correct tools will help you to complete each lesson presented in this book. As previously stated, the idea here is not to splurge on expensive and unnecessary items. I don't do so myself! In fact, you will be surprised to find that the materials I regularly use for sketching are quite basic. For final artworks, I will share with you my preferred types of paper as well for a long-lasting, textured, stunning result.

Paper is to me, at its core, a surface, which is how I think about it when making my selection. There is an endless amount of paper types, brands, textures, weights, and so on. In my humble opinion, choosing the right type of paper is a very individual experience. I personally like to draw in the same way that I ski or skate—gliding on a surface. In the same way that you would ski differently on snow versus concrete, I draw differently on smooth versus textured paper.

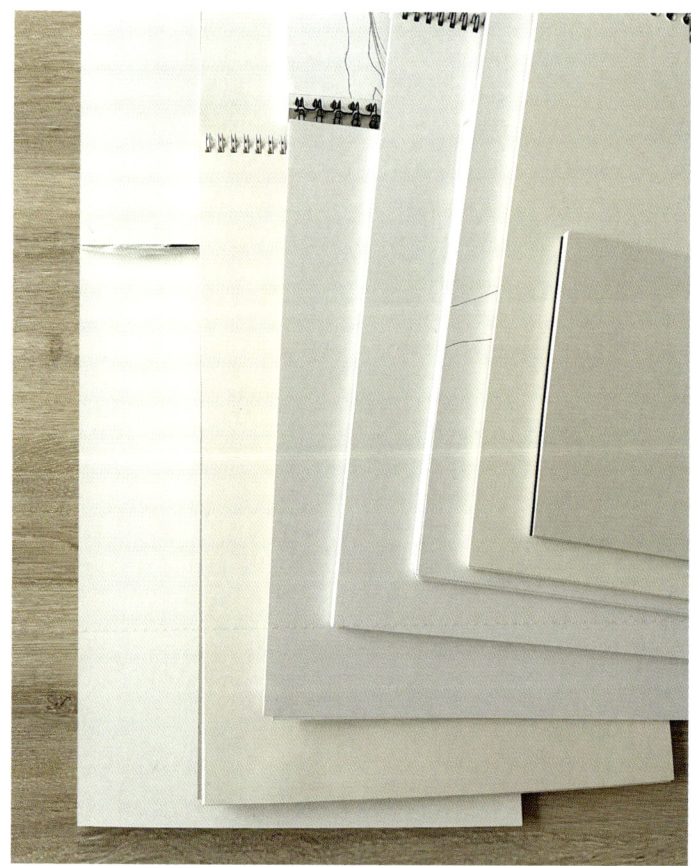

ADDITIONAL TOOLS

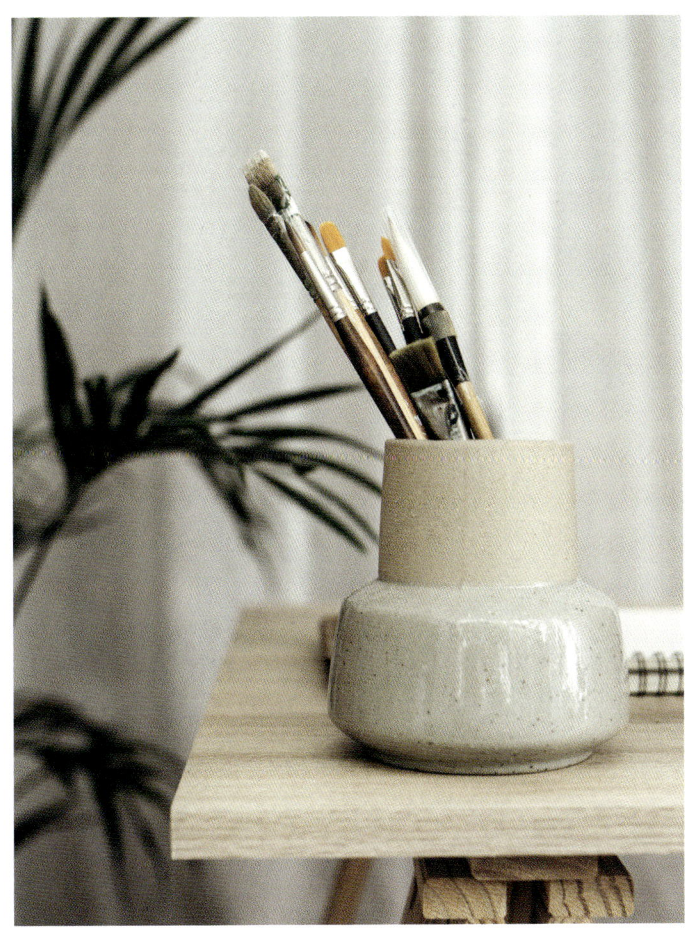

If you decide to use a sketch pad, I also recommend using some blotting paper to place under your drawings to keep the inks from seeping through and potentially ruining other sheets.

There are times when you may also want to mask certain parts of your drawing. This is a technique we will discuss in the sections on nature and architecture. To me, it is unnecessary to purchase expensive masking tapes and liquids when you can use simple sheets of paper or card stock you have lying around at home. No need for erasers or masking materials here—trust your creative instinct and perfect your line art drawing skills naturally with the basic, essential materials listed above!

The last tools you may want to have handy, but that are not necessary, are a camera or smartphone to either capture your own inspiration or photograph your process and final works, as we will see in the final section of the book.

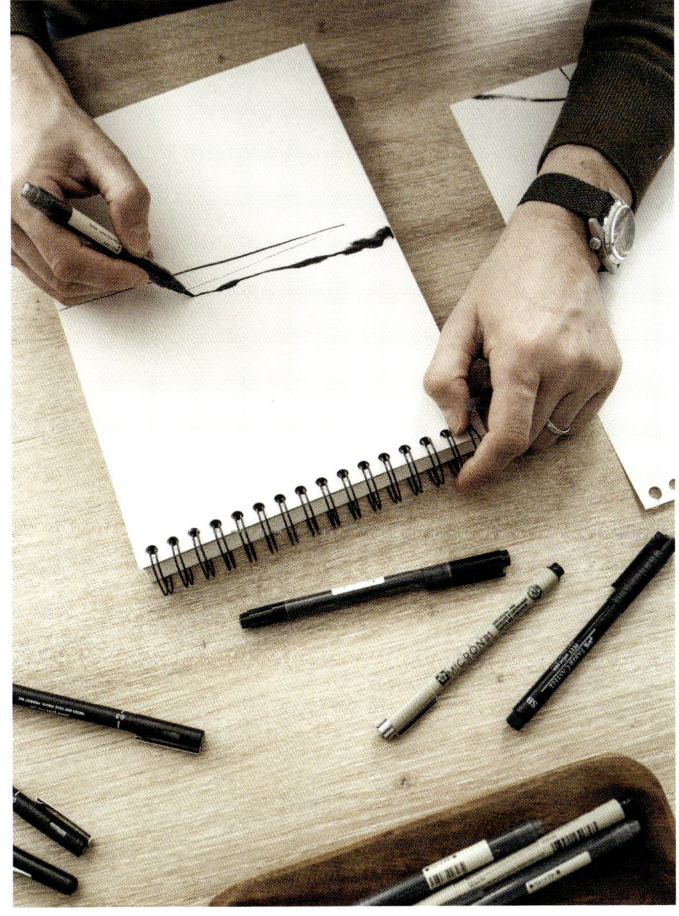

In this book, we will focus on using simple everyday papers and affordable ink pens, but there are other materials that can be helpful in mastering line art techniques over time. Line art, as we will see, can also translate to paintings, so you may also want to experiment with canvas surfaces and simple brushes later on, applying the concepts and skills you will have learned from the lessons in this book.

Different brushes, like different pen tips, will provide a broad range of effects. My advice would be to stay away from very expensive brushes and instead pick out simple ones that you can have fun experimenting with and watch what happens when you apply pressure to the bristles of the brush as you create your drawings, how the brush reacts to more or less pigment, and so forth.

To experiment with any materials, I also recommend having a few sheets of paper on hand to test your inks, pens, markers, and so on. throughout your practice sessions. These sheets can also serve as preliminary warm-up sketches or as ways to experiment with line movements.

GETTING
STARTED

SETTING UP YOUR WORKSPACE

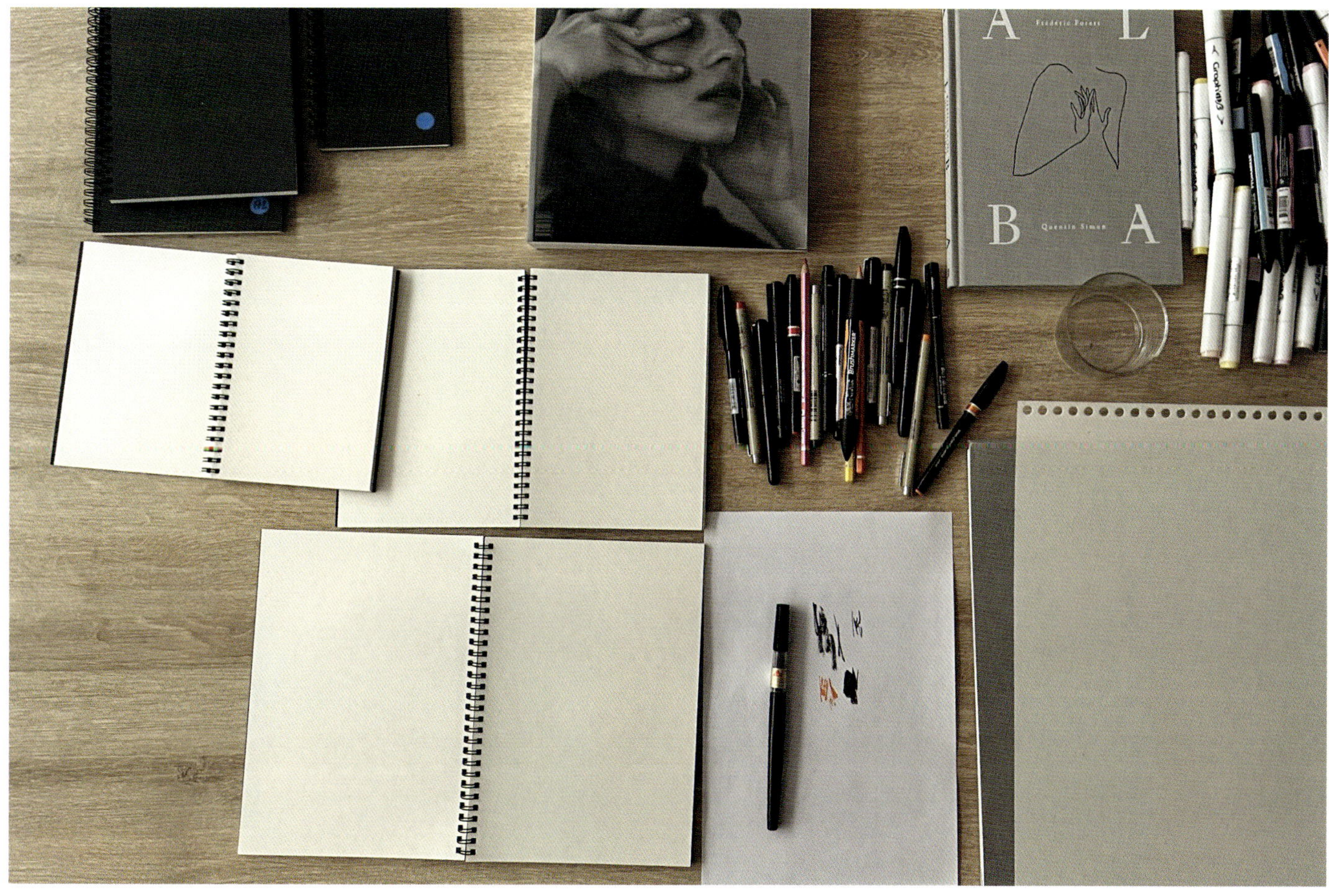

Your workspace should be set up so that it enables you to focus on creating your best work without taking away from your productivity or distracting you from the task at hand. My workspace is my "happy place," so I make sure that I have everything I may need nearby and in this way I can stay focused on what I'm making instead of looking for materials, searching for forgotten tools, or getting distracted by unnecessary items.

My workspace, no matter where I am drawing (at the studio, at home, or on the move) looks like this. When wondering about what you may need to set up your own space, think of the tool box you have in your garage, and include everything you may need to perform a task. In my case, I take out a few sketchbooks of varying shapes and sizes, some blotting paper and test sheets, a selection of pens and brushes I intend to use, and a second selection of pens and brushes I may end up needing—you never know where your drawing may take you!

Make sure everything is organized and easily accessible according to your specific way of creating. Much as each office of everyone on a work team looks different, everyone's art space will be set up in a different way, reflecting each individual's personality and methodology. Do you prefer silence or music playing in the background? Do you want to follow the book's images or apply the lessons to your own sources of inspiration? What makes you feel comfortable and focused? Ask yourself these questions as you prepare your very own workspace and set yourself up for success!

CHOOSING YOUR SUBJECT

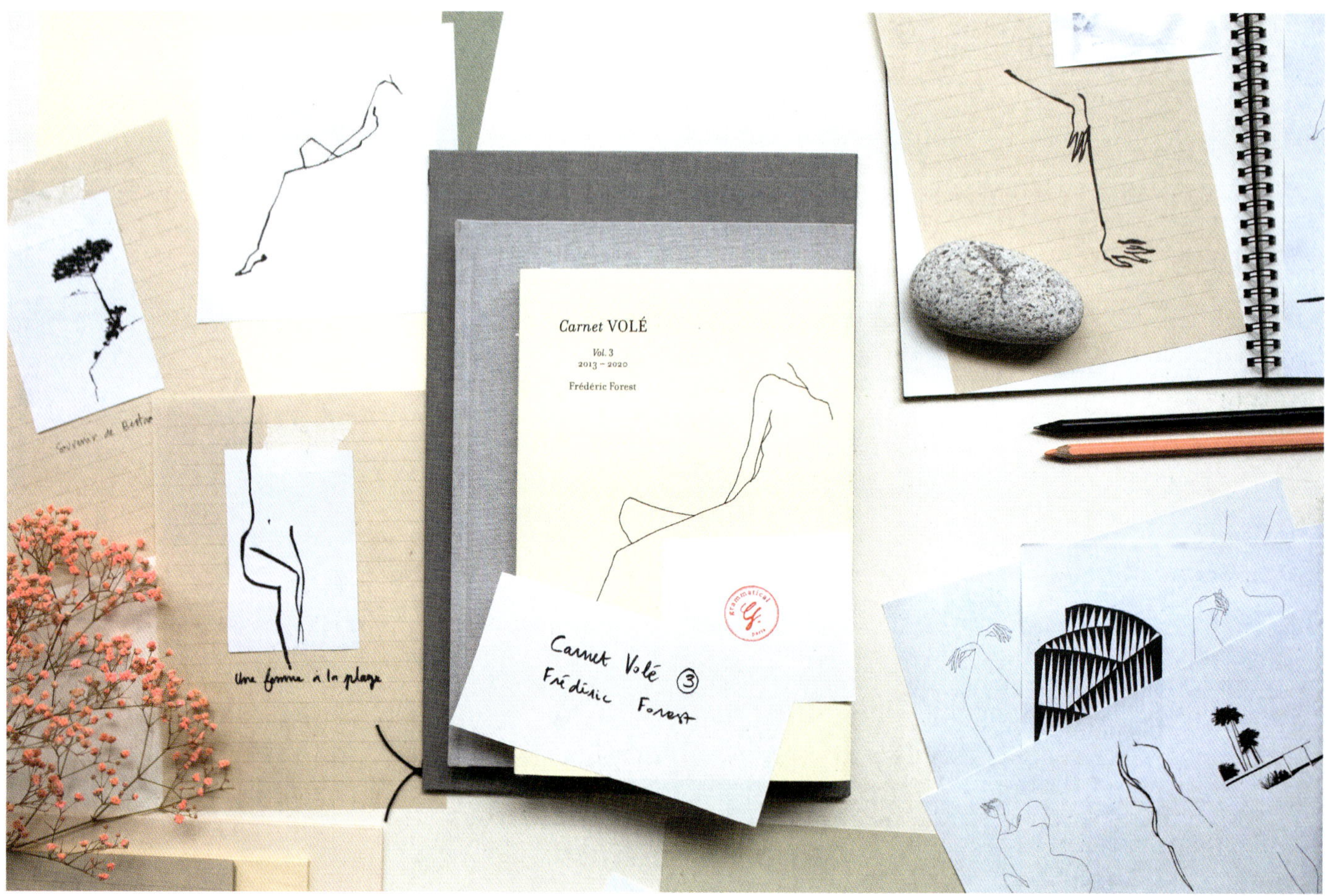

There are multiple ways to seek out inspiration in today's society. I personally glean a lot of my subjects from everyday life during my morning commute, walking in the streets, people-watching at a café, sitting at the park, shopping, and traveling.

Inspiration is everywhere!

Have you found a particularly satisfying landscape, an interesting posture, or a unique object? Take a quick photo with your phone and save it to an album for later. In this way you'll constitute your very own collection of inspiration to go back to anytime.

A good idea is also to create a mood board of content that you find interesting (images, artworks, quotes, colors, and places) and either keep them safely stored on your phone and computer to have them with you at all times or print out the collages to keep them connected to your workspace.

I also like to turn to books and magazines, which provide an excellent source of inspiration through images of course, but also a text that can resonate in a specific way or a story that can stimulate your own imagination. In the same way, museums and galleries also provide amazing visual inspiration.

INSPIRATION at the MUSEUM

I strongly believe that growing as an artist resides in actually "doing" the activity daily: drawing, painting, and sculpting from direct observation or life. However, looking at and studying great art that inspires us also plays a huge role in our maturing and evolving as an artist. Surrounding ourselves with great art will always find its way "through" us, and into our own work. Here are a few examples of works I've made during museum visits that clearly resonate with Auguste Rodin's famous sculptures and yet are my very own.

The idea of finding inspiration at a museum or gallery exhibition is to let yourself feel the works you see instead of trying to replicate what you see. My interpretations are rarely done on site. They are usually done once I leave and sit down in a park or café to sketch. The result is my very own modern interpretation of certain romantic poses and poetic ideas.

Hope you enjoyed visiting the Rodin Museum with me. Now, surround yourself with great art and go visit your own local museum or travel to one you've been wanting to visit to find your own inspiration!

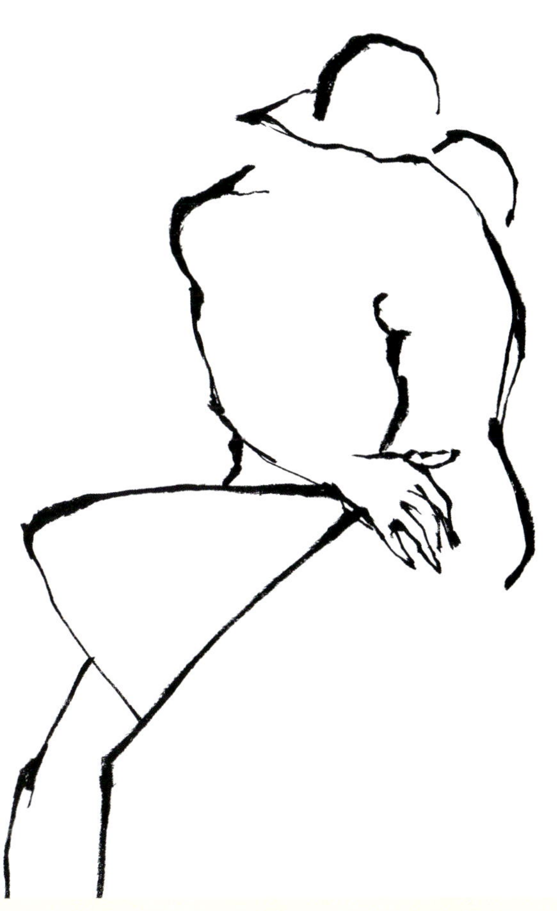

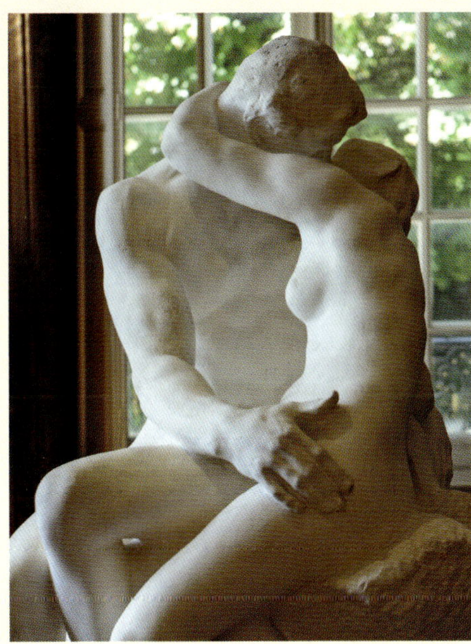

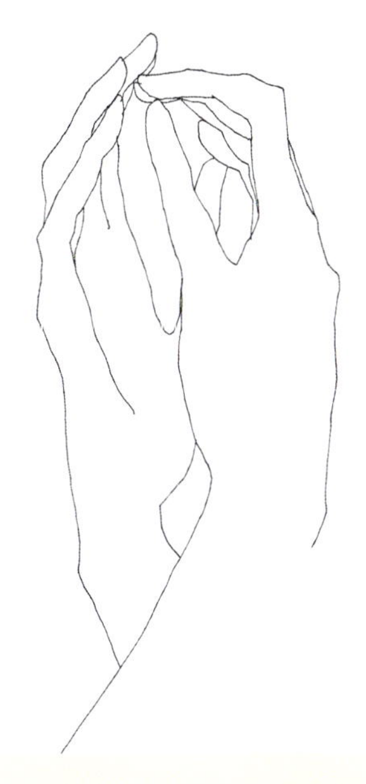

INSPIRATION on the STREETS

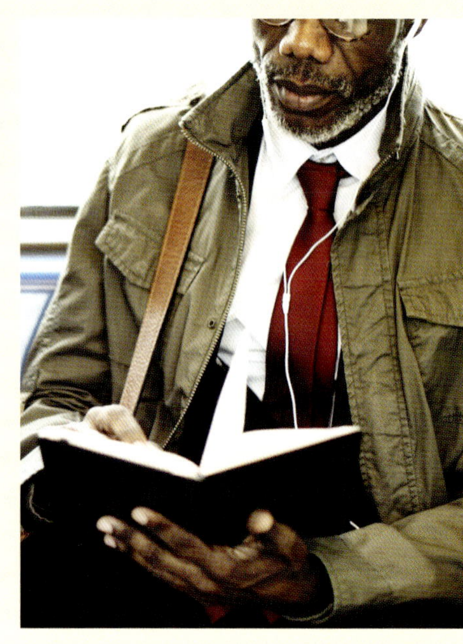

Another great source of inspiration that has the benefit of being free: the world around us! Nowadays we are so very much solicited with images and videos during our days that we sometimes forget that the best source of inspiration is right in front of us. On your morning commute, take the time to look at the people sitting around you on the subway: the pose of the girl reading quietly, the couple embracing, the students laughing in a group, the classiness of the old man with his hat and cane in hand. All these people have stories and lives of their own: What do you think they are doing? Where are they going? Make up your own stories and sketch ideas, shapes, silhouettes, or details that stand out to you in the moment.

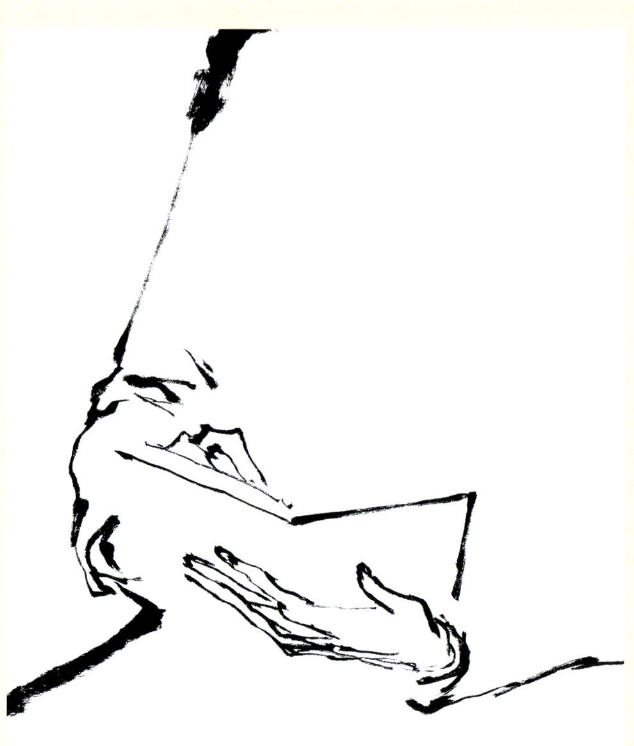

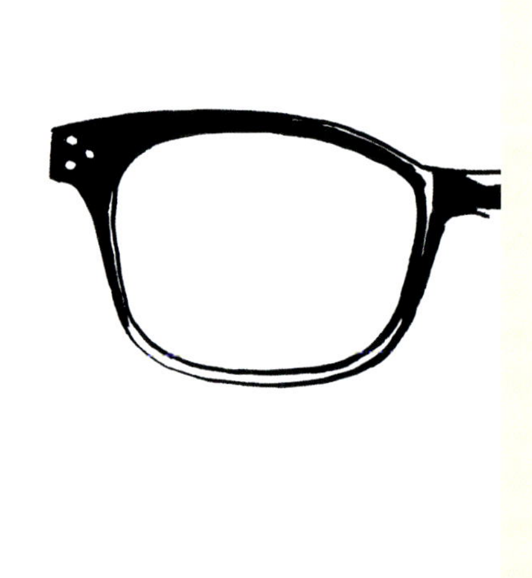

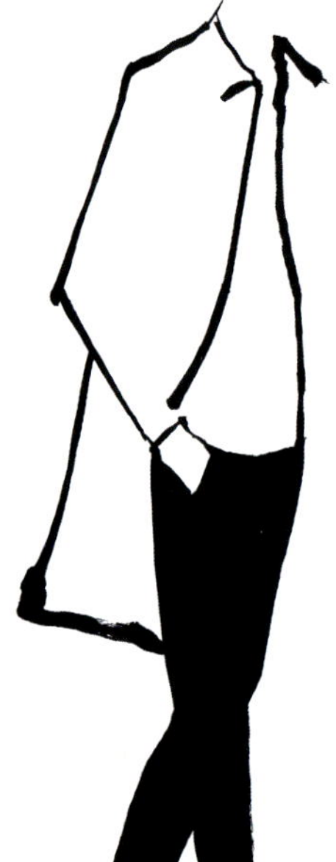

INSPIRATION from FEELINGS

A POEM

There are many other great ways to trigger emotion and inspire yourself as an artist: Go to the cinema, read books, go to the opera or the theater. I'm going to focus on a short poem I really enjoy, "L'amoureuse" by Paul Éluard, written in 1926. I read it out loud to myself after having read it quietly in my studio. Then, I let the words carry me to draw whatever comes to mind first. In this case the poem brings back a vivid memory of my wife sitting in front of me on one of our first dates.

A SONG

Let's begin with a song. Choose one that you want, isolate yourself so that you hear only the song playing, and let your hand dance freely on the paper. What does this song make you feel and who does it make you think of? Was it a souvenir, something you're looking forward to? Here I've chosen a lovely song and allowed myself to drift back to a summer afternoon in Provence.

"L'AMOUREUSE"

by Paul Éluard, 1926

"HEART OF GOLD"

by Neil Young, from *Harvest*, 1972

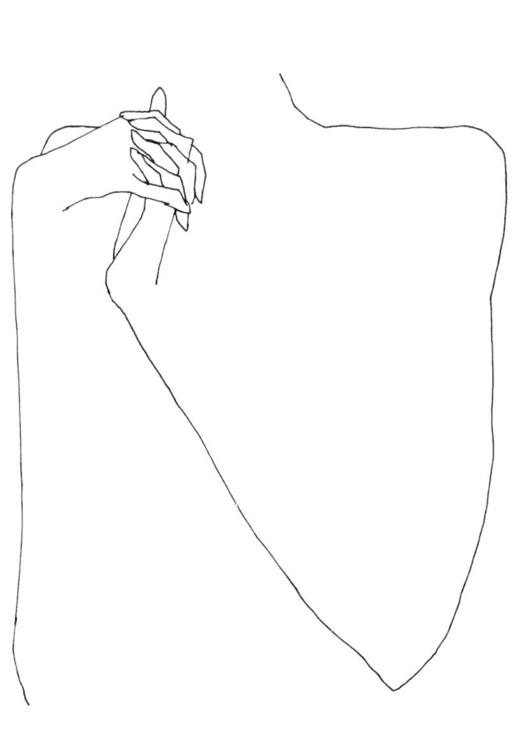

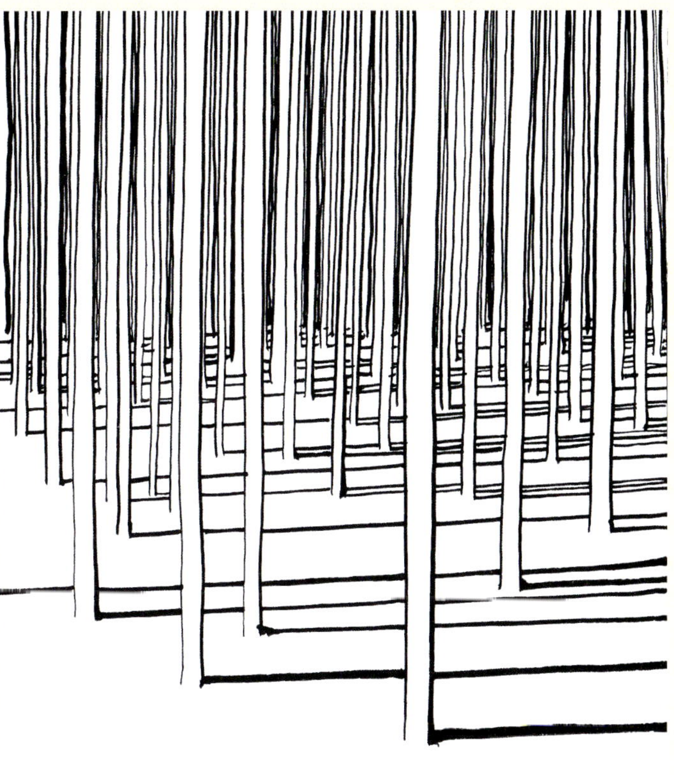

INSPIRATION from Your IMAGINATION

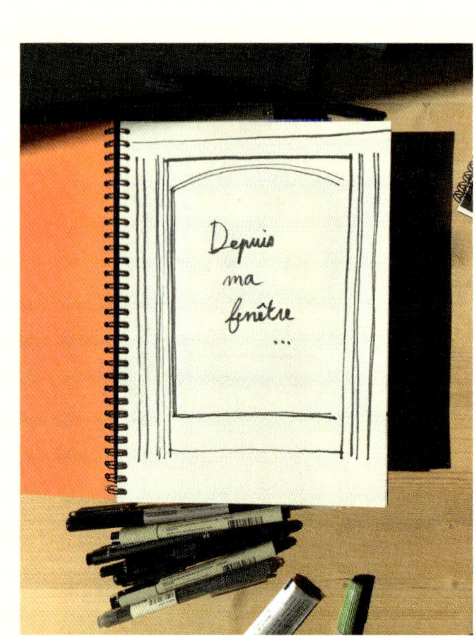

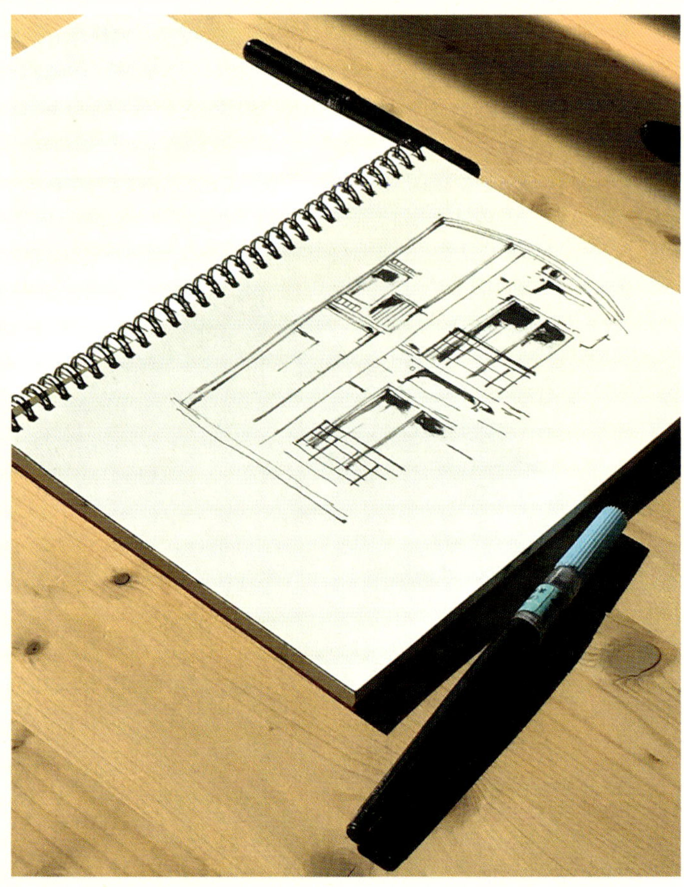

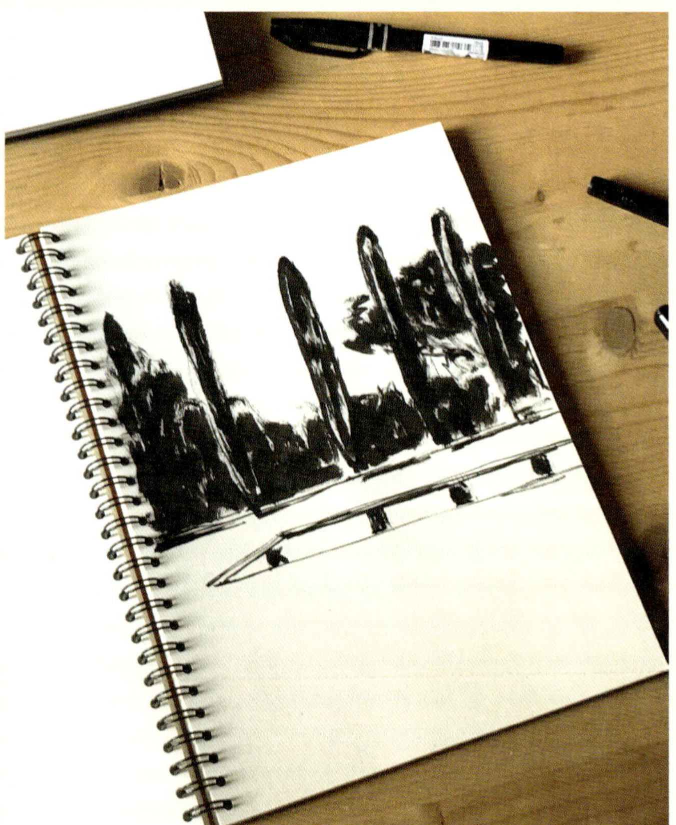

The most difficult yet satisfying way to be inspired is through your very own imagination! Whether you enjoyed creating scenarios in your head as a child or not, your imagination as an adult only grows and needs to be cultivated. Recently, with quarantine I learned to escape the confines of my own home to "travel" to the sea, "visit" a museum, enjoy a hypothetical moment with strangers, family, or friends. Whatever you want to envision or make happen can be done. Here are a few drawings that I made from the comfort of my own home when I could not leave except for emergencies. I spent hours imagining what could be happening outside and what I could see from my window.

WHERE TO PRACTICE

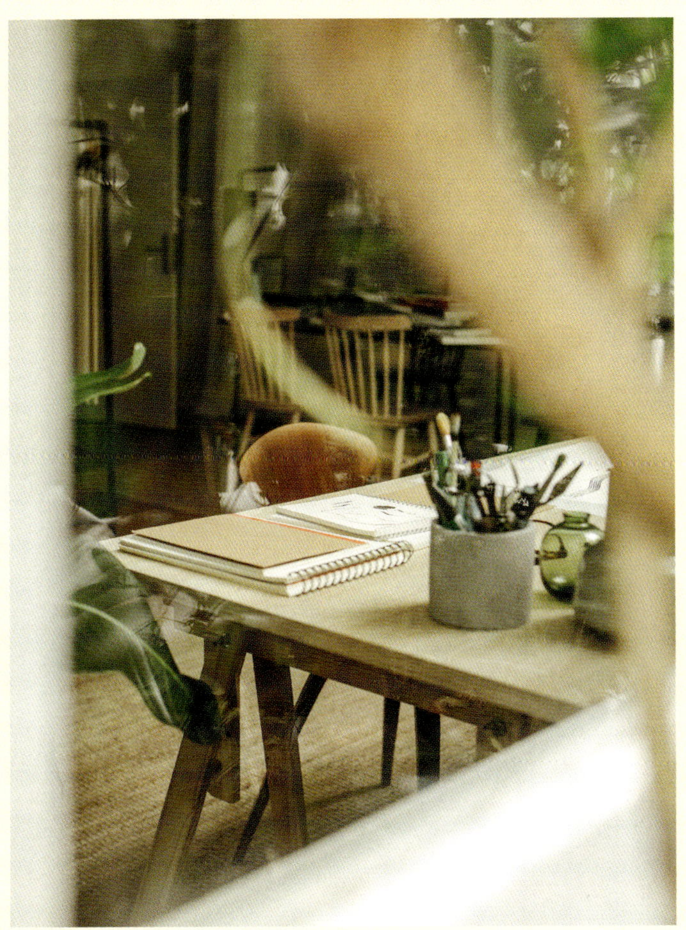

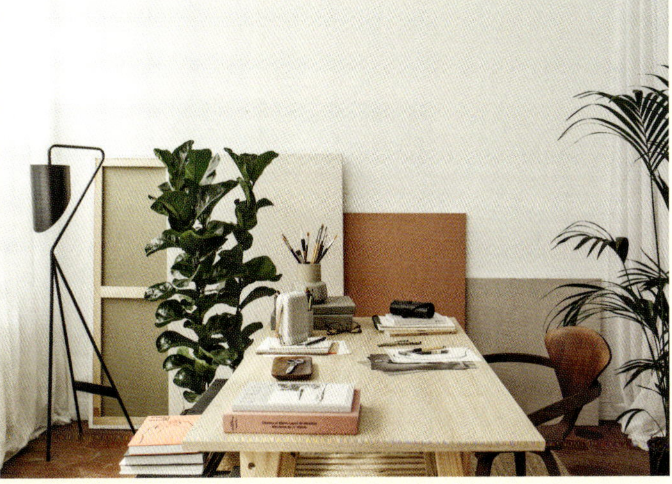

The space is also very natural and the daylight always hits perfectly inside, meaning that most of the time I work in natural sunlight, which is very important to me also.

The studio is shared with my wife Clémentine, who is also a ceramist and creates pieces on site. I also use this space to store and ship out my works, limited-edition prints, and books. I love that so many different things take place in this small space!

AT THE STUDIO

The fact that I have an art studio space is quite recent. I'm very fortunate to have this special spot, nestled in one of Paris' historical neighborhoods, Montparnasse. It is located in the Chemin du Montparnasse, a bucolic alley located in the fifteenth district of Paris.

A vestige of the great history of Montparnasse, the Chemin has seen the biggest names on the artistic scene. In 1908, the painter Marie Vassilieff opened the Russian Academy there, attended by Erik Satie, Henri Matisse, Amedeo Modigliani, Ossip Zadkine, and Chaïm Soutine. The Chemin du Montparnasse continues to welcome many artists, fine arts students, avant-garde actors, publishers, photographers, filmmakers, galleries, and the Musée du Montparnasse, transformed into the Villa Vassilieff in 2016.

The history of this space is very important to me and makes me really think about what I am creating within these walls that have already seen so much! With this in mind, I have really envisioned this space as an open space where artists, collectors, or anyone really who is interested can stop by, see my works, and discuss.

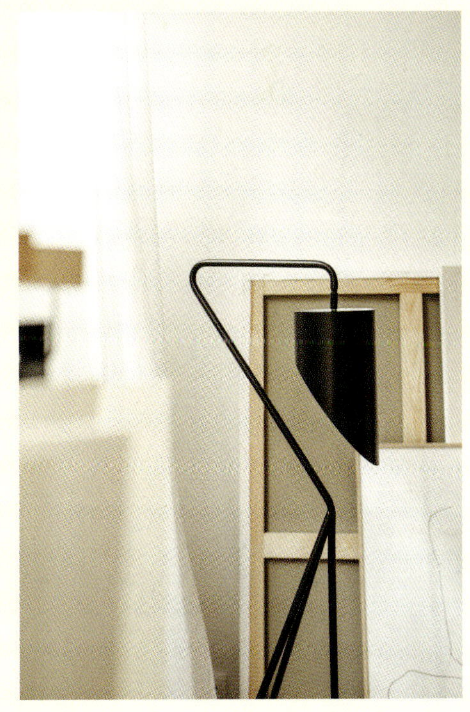

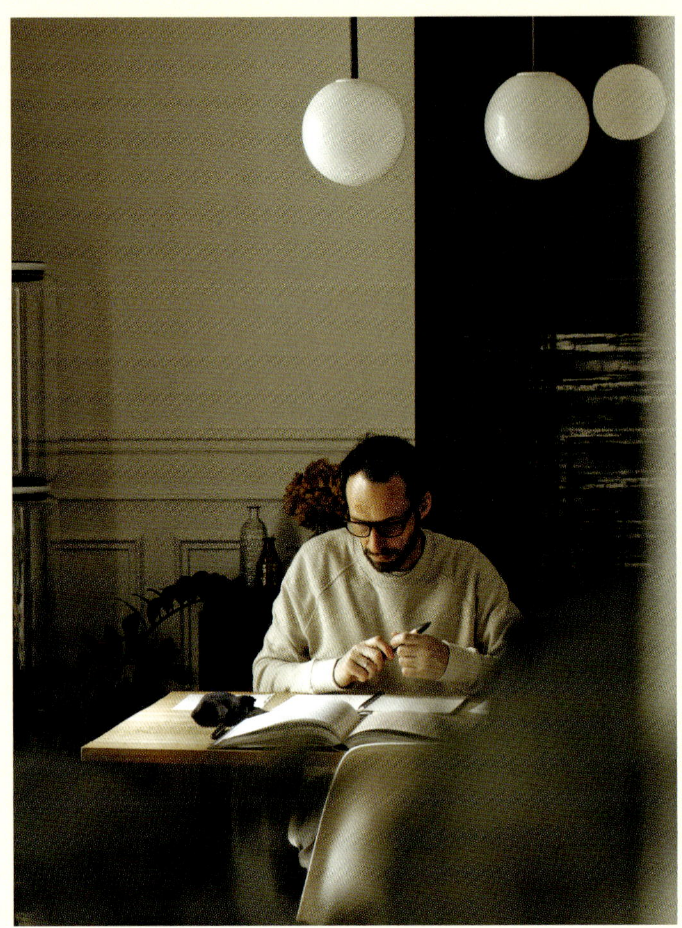

AT HOME

When I draw at home, the vibes are very different. I'm looking for an intimate moment of quiet practice, by myself. I can draw in the morning before going to the studio or meetings, or at night when my wife and daughter are asleep. I mostly draw in black and white because these moments are dark, so I focus on black ink sketches, mostly of fairly small things. I really enjoy the idea of being alone with my drawings in the comfort of my own home. It reminds me of the time I spent drawing in my room when I was a child.

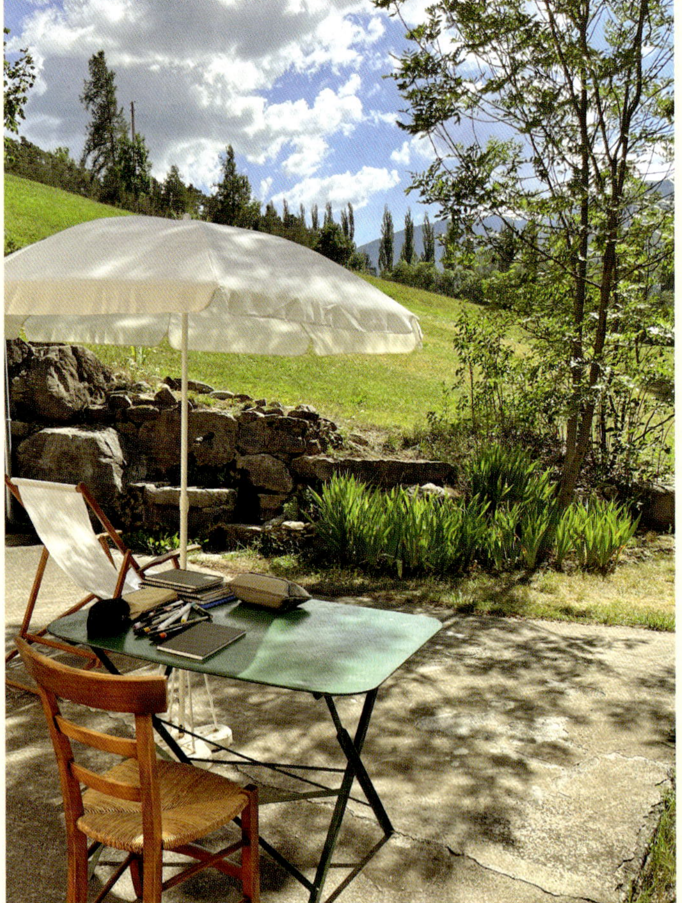

ON VACATION

Yes! I draw on vacation because I draw all the time and hope I never stop doing so. It's not a chore to me, and on vacation I can enjoy practicing outdoors in nature like I did last summer in Provence. My workspace is pictured here, and one of the things I enjoy the most in these moments is the way the sunlight dances on the paper, creating the most delicate shadows and shapes.

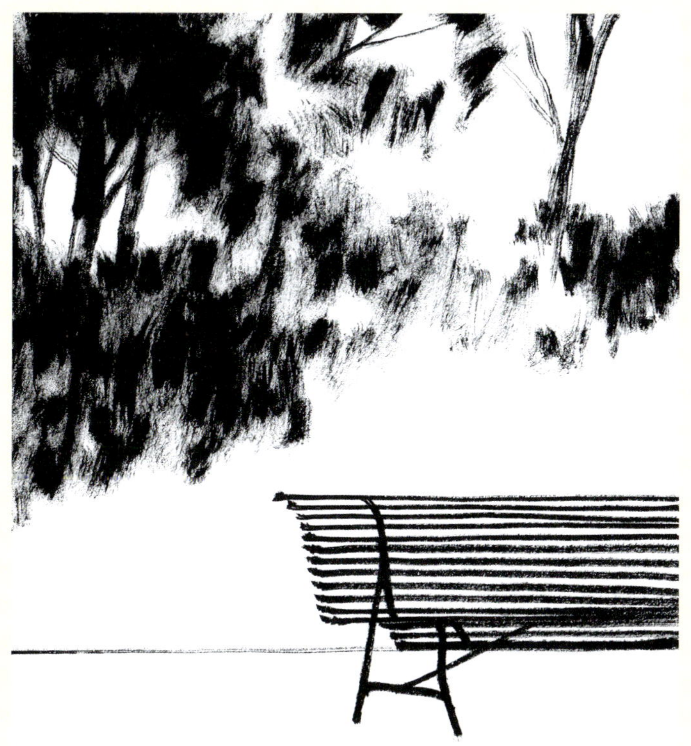

IN A PARK

I really enjoy sitting on a bench in a park and taking the time to draw. Living and working in Paris, parks have this magical quality of mixing nature and city life. When I'm there, I feel transported elsewhere while still hearing the hustle and bustle of the city surrounding me, children's laughter, and conversations, mixed in with birds chirping. I'll go to the park after visiting an exhibition or as a break in my day to sit and watch what's going on around me and make small sketches from these scenes of either the people passing by or the nature surrounding me. In Paris, my favorite parks and gardens are the Jardin du Luxembourg, the Tuileries Garden, and the Montsouris Park.

AT A MUSEUM

When I go to the museum, I always have a sketchbook and pens with me, but I keep it light so that I can find a small space to draw what I feel or see without bothering anyone around me. I can draw what I see, how I feel, the people around me, or details of the furniture I like in the spaces. I particularly enjoy the Rodin Museum for its authenticity but also because I can sit outside as well, which is quite nice. Because there can sometimes be too many people in the exhibitions or too much noise to concentrate, I can also just take quick photos with my phone of what I am inspired by and revisit those drawings at a later time.

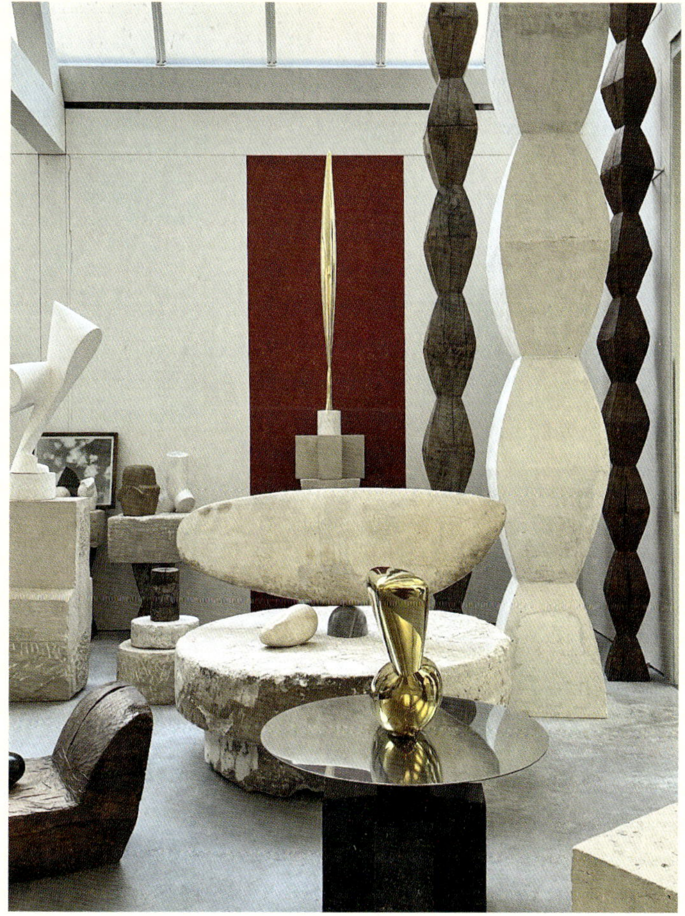

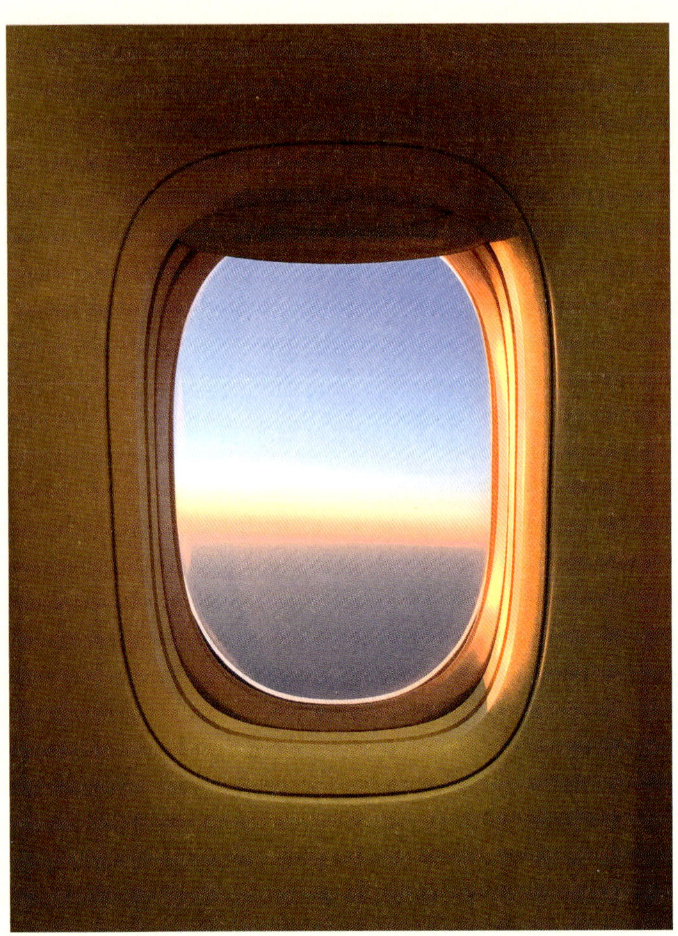

ON THE ROAD

Clearly, this is the place that's the least convenient for multiple reasons: There are many people, you are on the move, there is constant noise, and the space is often quite small. That being said, it's a good time to jot down any thoughts or ideas I may have or to do research by experimenting techniques and making test drawings. In motion, nothing can be perfect, so I ignore that and focus on trying new things. I used to find this difficult to do because people sitting around me would stare or ask questions, but in today's world most people don't even notice anymore, look at their phones, or simply do not engage in conversation!

IN A CAFÉ

It may sound a bit cliché, but this is a great place to practice. I usually do this when I'm waiting for someone or picking up my daughter from her after-school activities. There is something I like about the small tables, the smell of coffee and crêpes, the brouhaha of everyone's chatter, and the short amount of time I'm on site that makes this exercise quite nice!

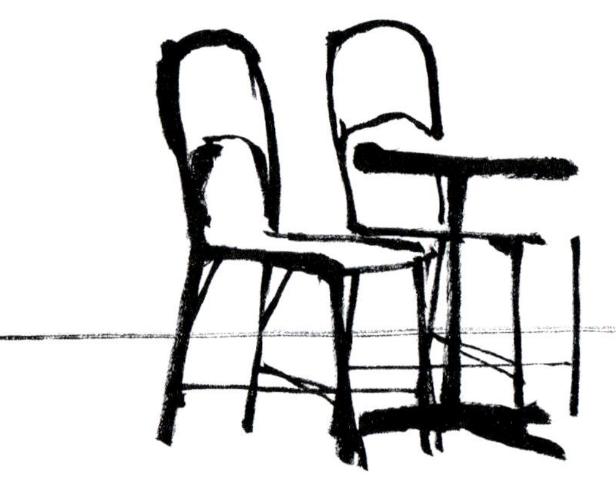

DRAWING LESSONS

A WOMAN'S SILHOUETTE

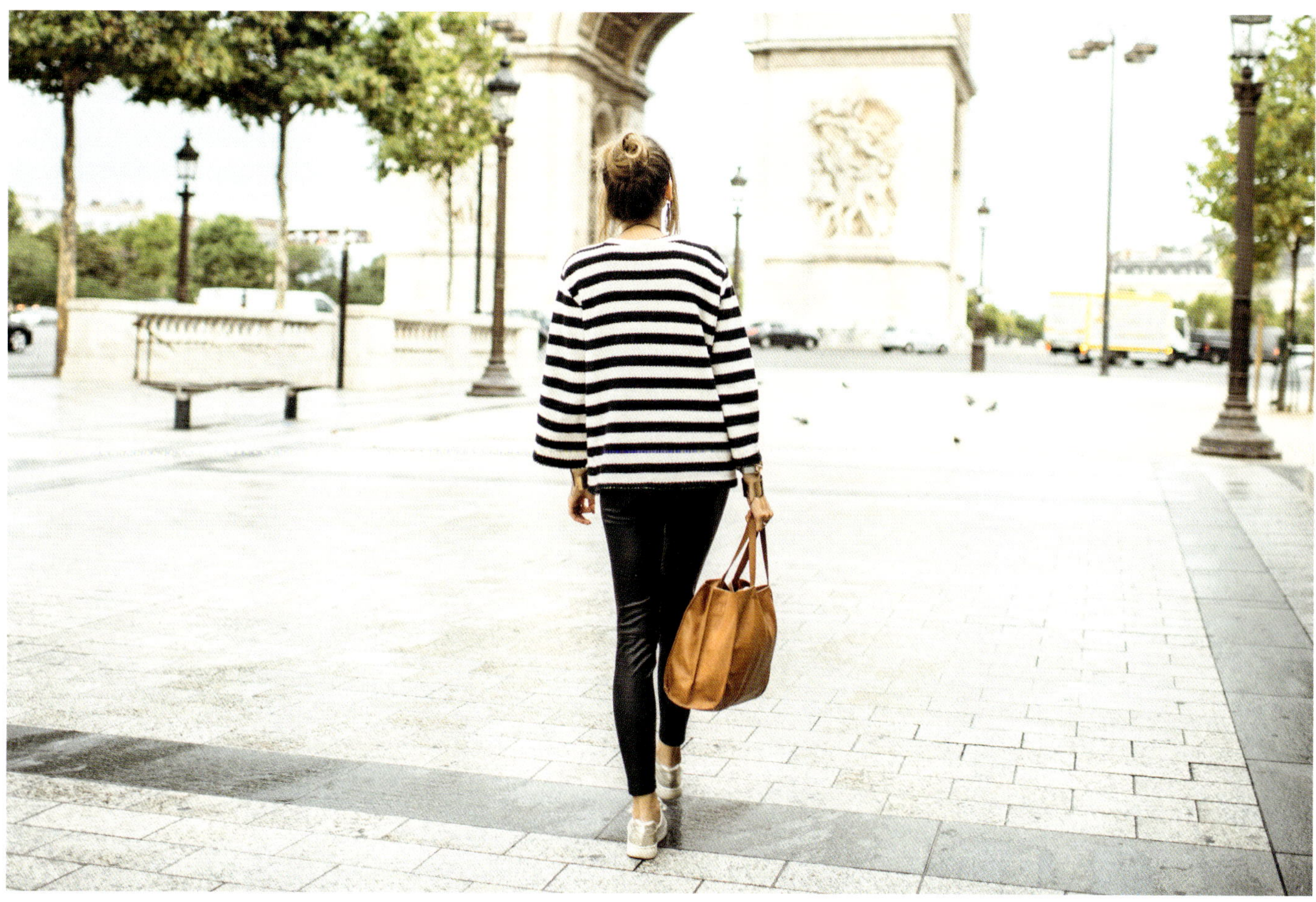

THE IDEA

Drawing silhouettes forces you to retain and focus on a single subtle movement or attitude that can say a lot about the person being portrayed. A silhouette is a shape that grabs your attention. This particular photo retained mine, because it was taken in a place that I know (Place de l'Étoile, at the top of the Champs-Élysées in Paris), but I have never seen this person.

We are therefore looking through someone else's lens, but with our perception. We don't know if the subject is going somewhere or just leaving, but it doesn't seem to be the topic. To me, this is clearly a street fashion shot. To draw a silhouette well, you have to imagine this person as if you knew them, you knew what they were doing or thinking, or it were you. I would even say that you have to imagine yourself wearing their clothes, feeling their weight and the textures of the materials on your own skin.

WHAT I WANT TO EXPRESS

INTERPRETATION 1

I'll start with a thin line first. This will capture the right shape of the silhouette and retain important details.

INTERPRETATION 2

The first interpretation will serve as my base, and I will use a thicker brush to obtain something completely different in both construction and result.

STEPS

1—I start my line at the subject's hair-line, "combing" her hair, falling on the shoulder, and going down to the sleeve of her sweater.

2—I first draw her left hand and then trace her right hand using the first hand as my base model. It is not necessary to draw all the fingers because her purse will be placed in her right hand later.

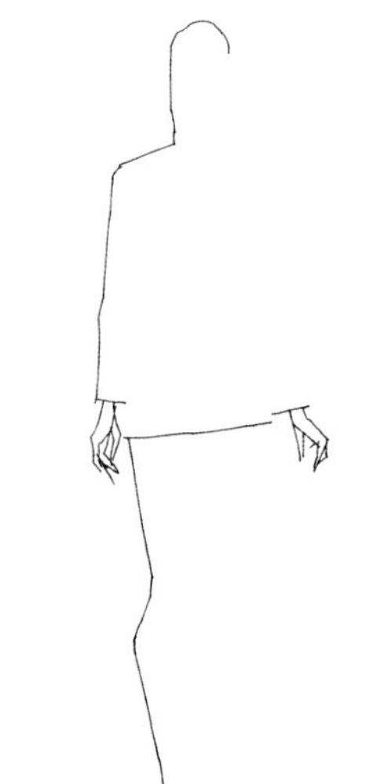

1

2

3—Now you have to draw the bottom of the sweater. It may not seem like much, but the sweater alone creates the movement of this woman's gait and gives structure to the drawing's composition.

4—I then focus on her leggings by creating a line that comes from her sweater and falls down to her shoe, allowing to show the shape of her leg. In the photograph, the model is walking, so I use the same line that outlines her left leg to show this shape and keep the line open at the bottom to hint at her feet/shoes.

3

4

5—I add a second line to place the second leg, the one in the background. I could stop there, but her right hand's position indicates that an element is missing.

6—I therefore add the simple shape of the bag while giving it a certain dynamic to show movement, and the outline of the foot to finish the silhouette and place my figure on an imaginary floor, grounding my drawing and giving the silhouette more presence.

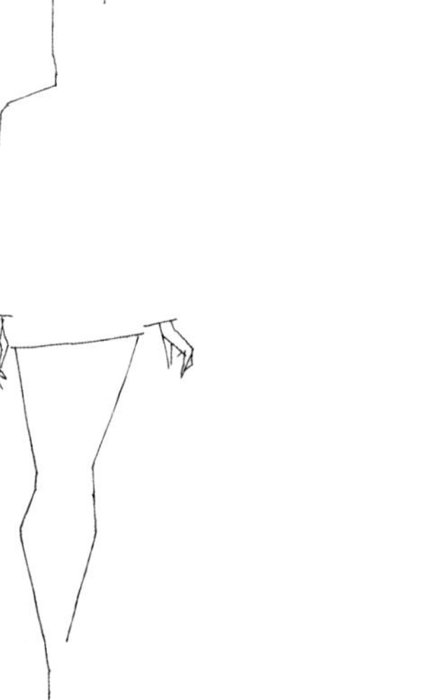

5

6

STEPS

1—This time, I start with the left hand and work my way up her arm. I then mark her shoulder with a slightly thicker line and hint at the beginning of her neck.

2—I switch to the other shoulder and finish by drawing her other hand.

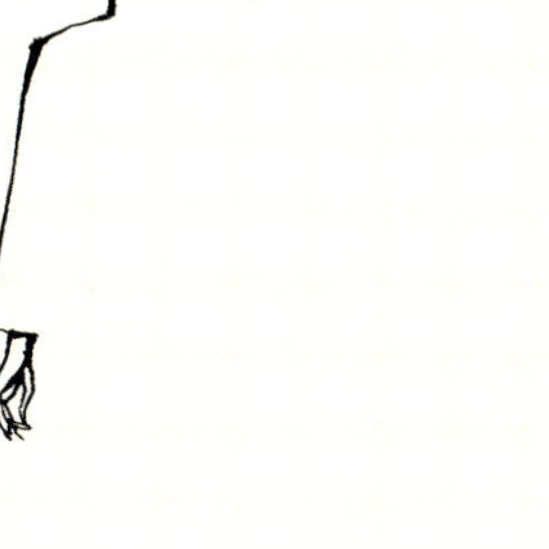

1

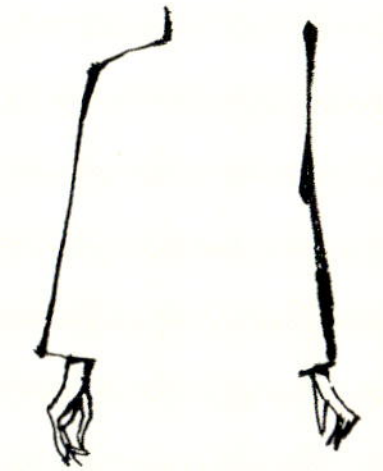

2

3—Then, I draw the bottom of her sweater like I did in my first interpretation, but this time marking the beginning of the line more strongly, allowing it to act as a shadow. This will indicate the movement of the garment and also the body's position.

4—My line starts from the neck and continues upward to draw the outline of her head and outline her ears.

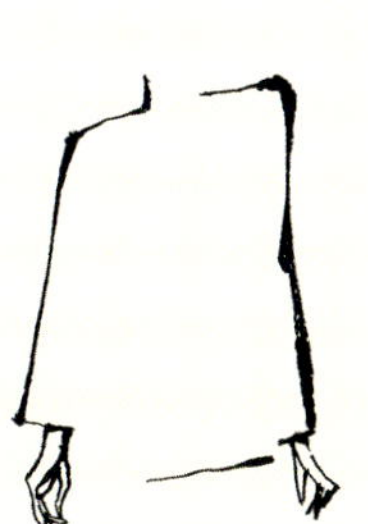

3

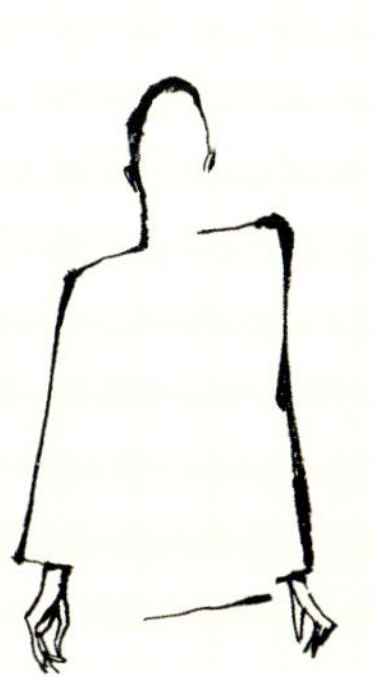

4

5—The tilt of the subject's head as well as the edge of her right shoulder indicate a reach and that the bag should be drawn in stride.

6—Once I draw the head and the bag, I can suggest the movement of the legs by simply drawing a few lines.

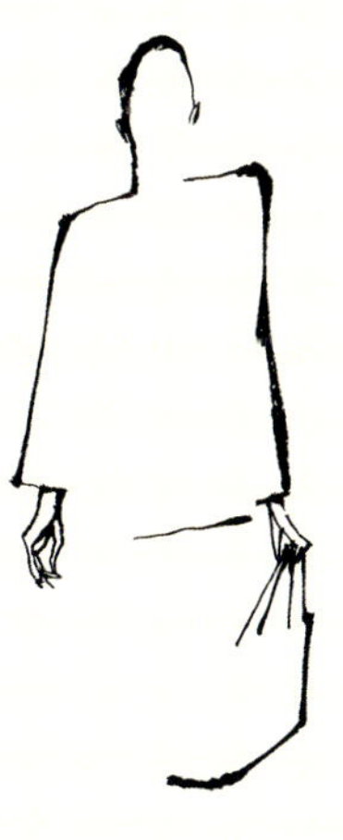

5

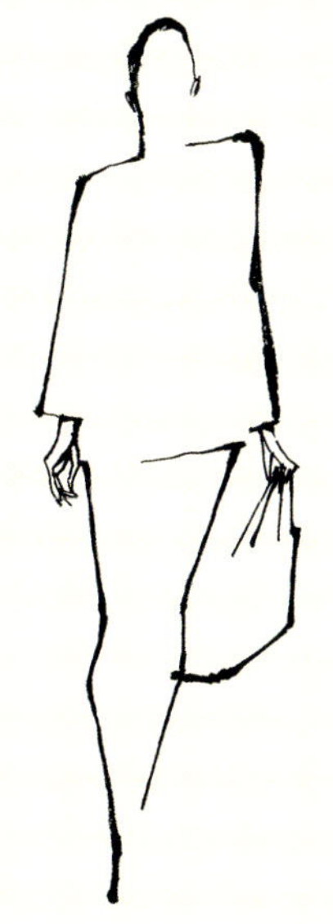

6

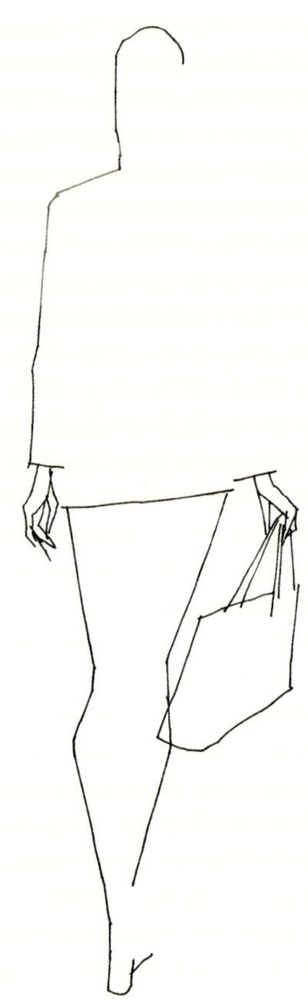

Interpretation 1

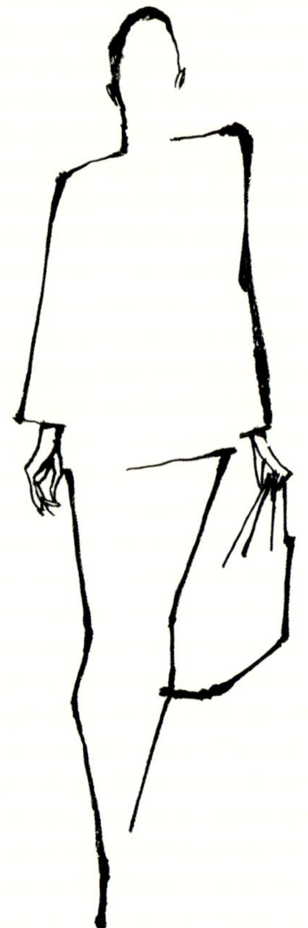

Interpretation 2

Interpretation 3

By adding and shading in the hair and the pants of the silhouette in black, it is no longer necessary to outline or fill in the rest of the silhouette's features or clothes. The eye fills these in automatically and allows us to maintain a minimalistic drawing.

Interpretation 4

By creating a cropped detail of this same scene and pose, you will find that the drawing tells a completely different story.

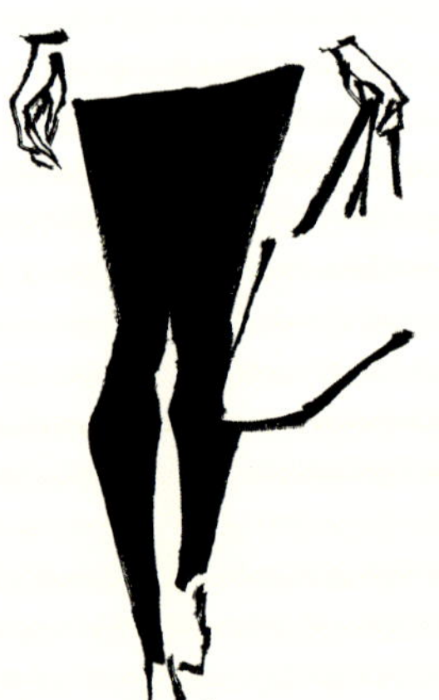

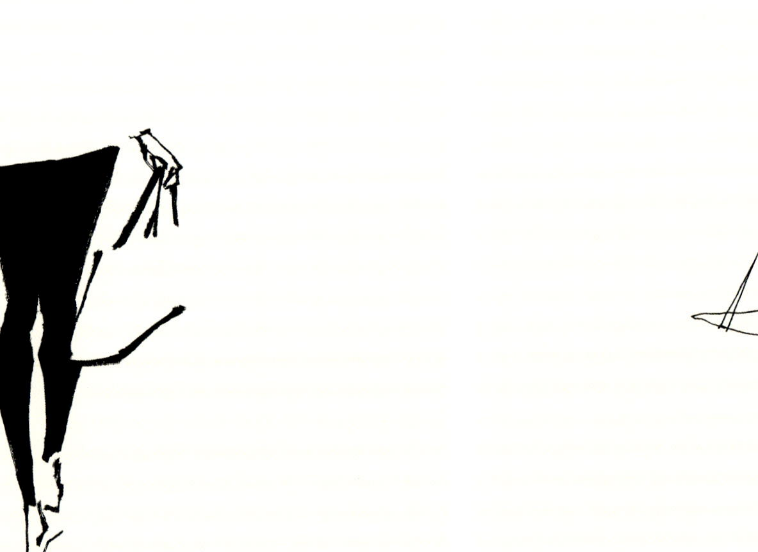

THINKING OUTSIDE THE BOX

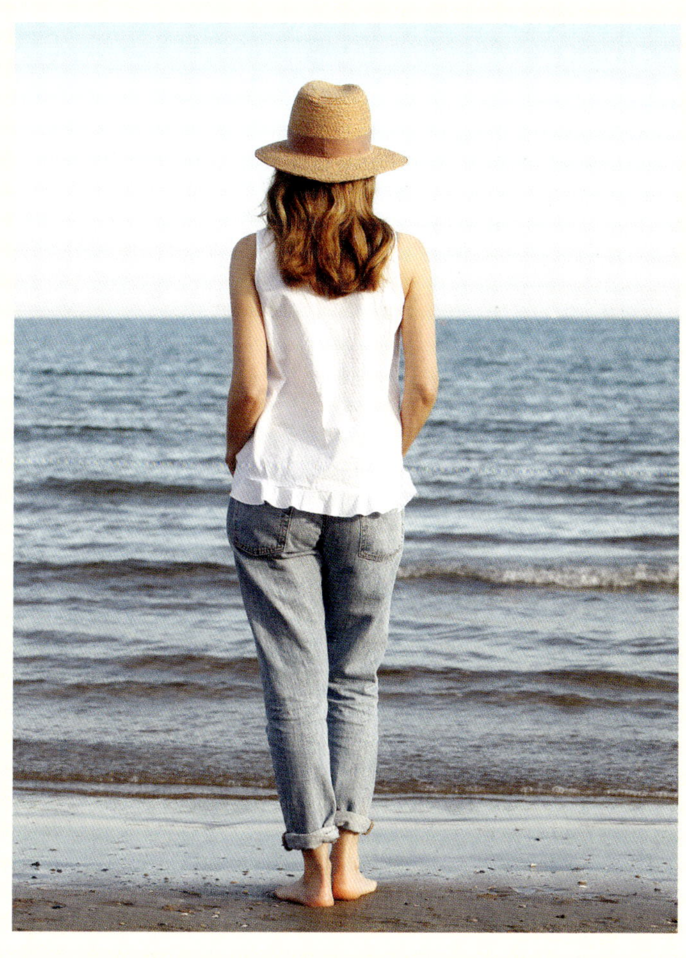

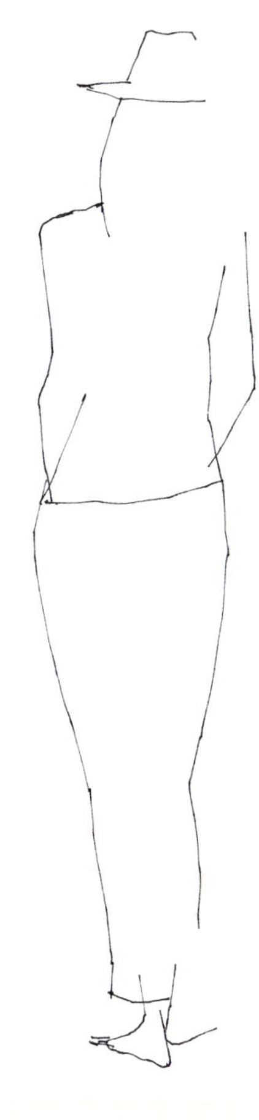

THE IDEA

If you're reading an art instruction book, you are surely already a creative mind that is used to thinking outside the box. To me, drawing is anything but stiff and academic. It is a freeing activity that allows me to do anything I want without limits.

Let's look at how we can do that in our everyday lives using practical examples.

WHAT I WANT TO EXPRESS

In this first example, I will show you how I draw different things from the same photograph of a clothed woman whose back is to us. Everything is therefore coming from my own imagination: her clothing, her pose, and her attitude.

A recurring question I receive from people who inquire about my art is if I draw from live models and how I manage to draw so many. To most people's surprise, I do not draw from live models posing in a studio. In fact, I've very rarely done so.

It's not something I find stimulating because there is little to nothing left to the imagination. What I prefer is finding my subject (from a book, magazine, photograph, or in the streets) and letting my imagination do the rest. Let's take this silhouette of a woman and fully imagine and create what we want to draw, using only the reference image for details.

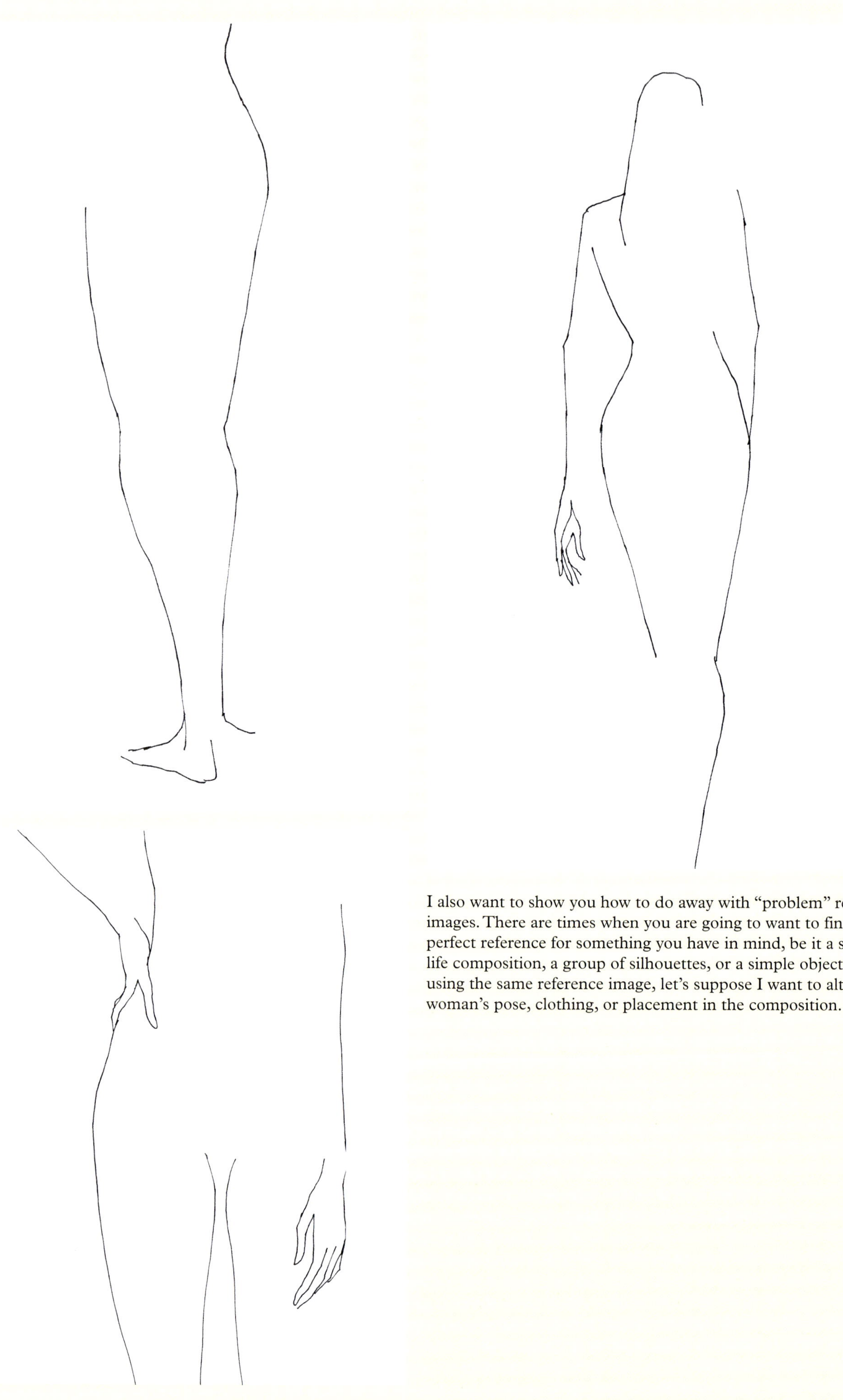

I also want to show you how to do away with "problem" reference images. There are times when you are going to want to find the perfect reference for something you have in mind, be it a still life composition, a group of silhouettes, or a simple object. Still using the same reference image, let's suppose I want to alter the woman's pose, clothing, or placement in the composition.

WOMEN

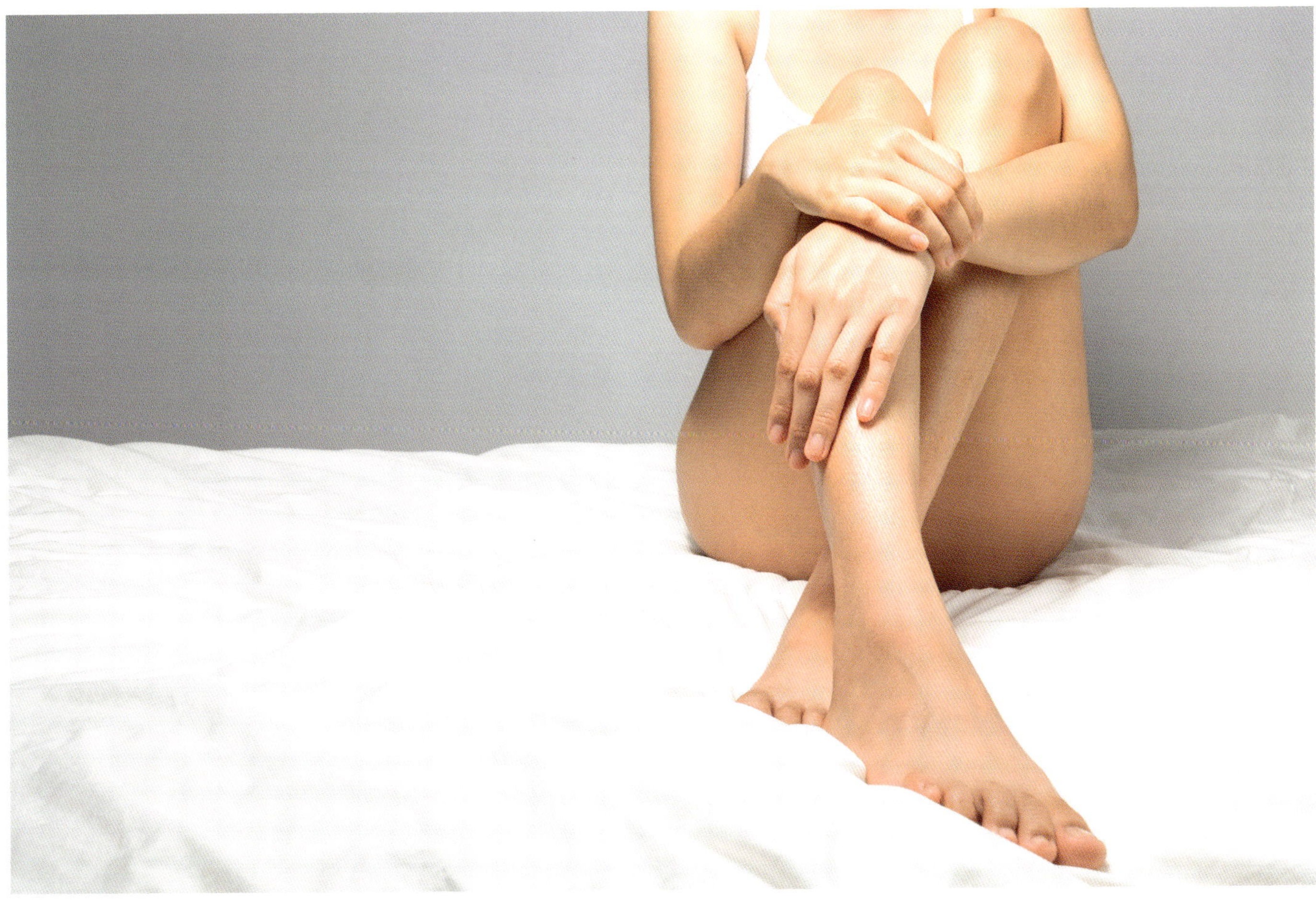

THE IDEA

This pose symbolizes rest or expectation. It expresses a kind of
serenity. The hands gently hold each other and embrace the legs.
There is a certain calm and self-confidence radiating from this
image, and that is what we are going to express through drawing.

WHAT I WANT TO EXPRESS

INTERPRETATION 1

I will try to capture the whole pose and sketch the upper part of
the body that we do not see in the photo. A fine line seems to be
the most suitable here.

INTERPRETATION 2

I will focus on the hands and spend less time on the rest of the
pose to let the imagination do the rest.

STEPS

1—I begin with the top hand. Because it is at the center of the pose and I like its movement. My line starts from the top, then I draw the outline of the pinky finger. I then proceed to draw the rest of the fingers, and I finish with the forearm.

2—The drawing of the second hand begins with the pinky finger because it starts from the end of the fingers of the hand above. I then place the thumb and the index finger and add the rest of the fingers. Now I need to draw the forearm.

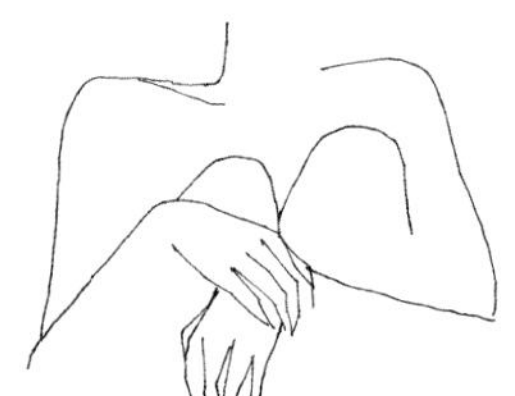

1

2

3—Immediately after, I place the upper arms and the shoulders. I make the collarbone appear on the right to energize the pose and initiate the line of the neck that we do not see in the photo.

4—I draw the top of the two knees and center them in the middle.

3

4

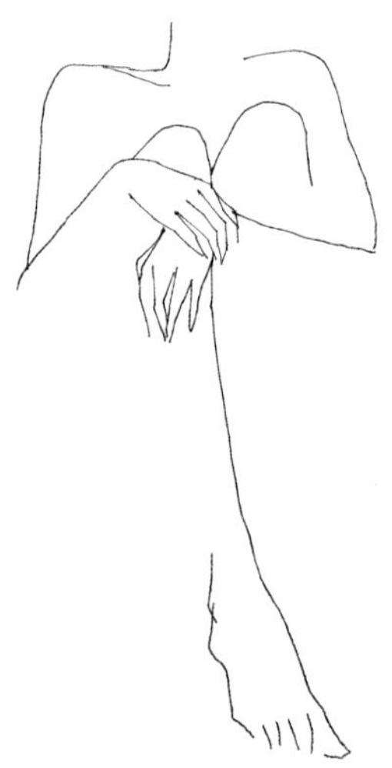

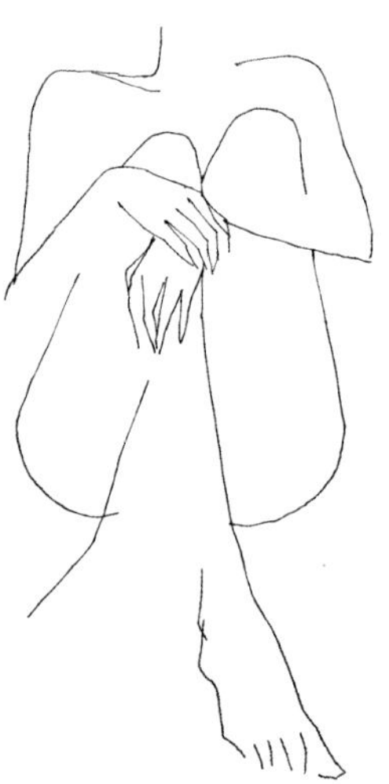

5—I draw the line of the front leg going down, from the tibia to the foot's big toe. Then I outline the foot, starting with the heel and the arch, and end with the small toe. Next, I outline the toes, one by one, pointing them downward to express a stretched leg.

6—At this point, I can draw the other leg without drawing a foot. I don't know if it's necessary yet. I then add the thighs, starting at the top and ending with her behind. Finally, the second foot does not seem useful to draw.

5

6

STEPS

1—Similarly to the previous interpretation, I start with the top hand, but I draw it larger and linger a little more on the movement of the fingers. I finish with the forearm.

2—I also start the second hand with the pinky finger, then move to the thumb. The rest of the fingers are more detailed than the previous interpretation, and I show the thumb more effectively.

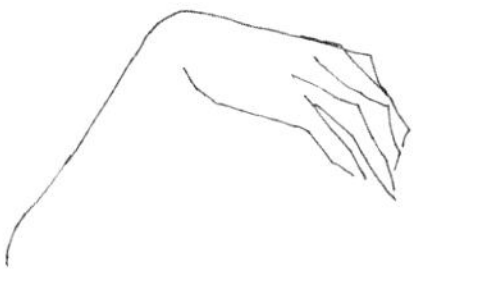

1

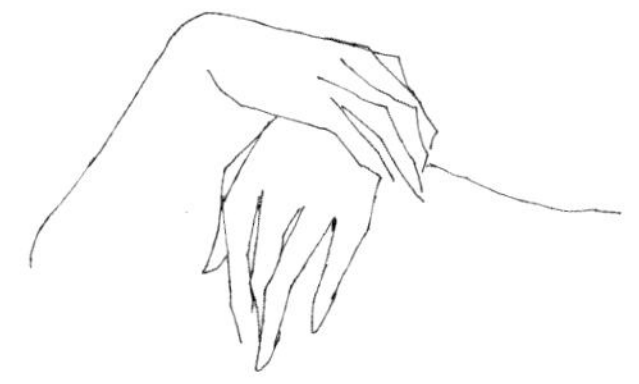

2

3—This time, I'm going to energize her right shoulder a little more and ensure that the collarbone appears.

4—I add the upper left arm starting from her elbow and going up. Immediately afterward, I draw the left knee.

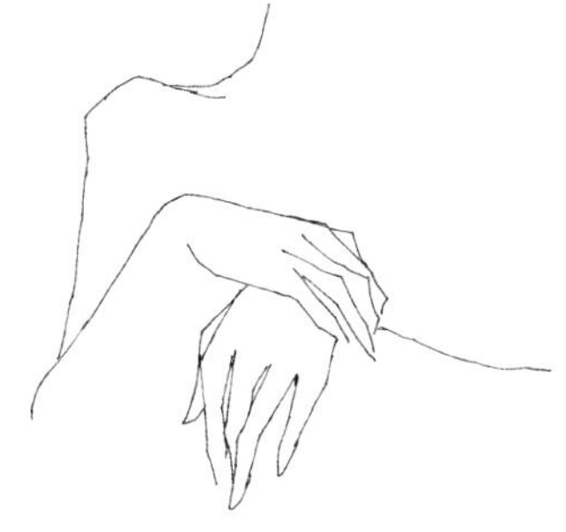

3

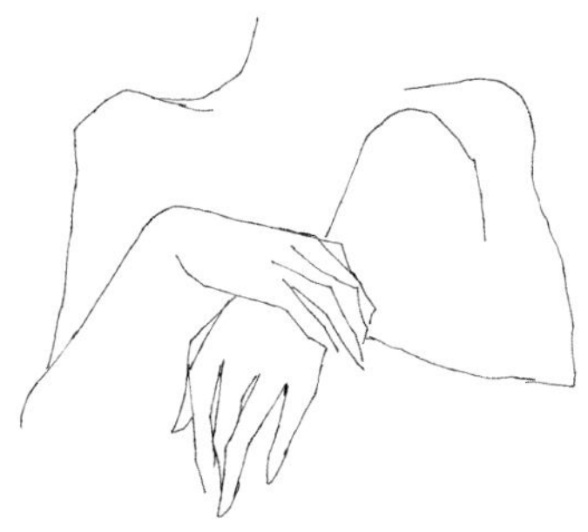

4

5—I draw the right knee and end it by making it fall toward the center, on her hand. Then, my line can begin again and go down to the beginning of the foot. I'll stop there for now. I will see later if this line should be reworked or added to.

6—I then draw the left thigh as well as her behind, which will go to the tibia of the leg. This seems incomplete to me, so I draw the beginning of the other leg, which goes down. The pose now seems sufficient to me.

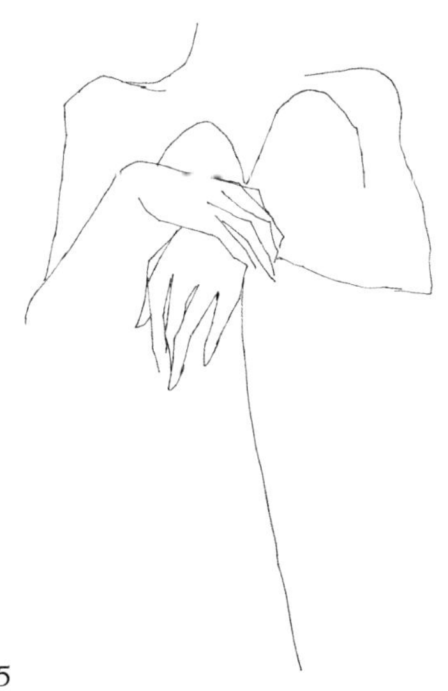

5

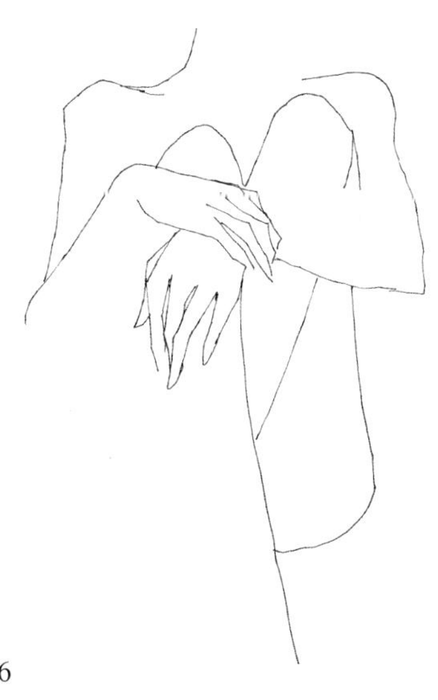

6

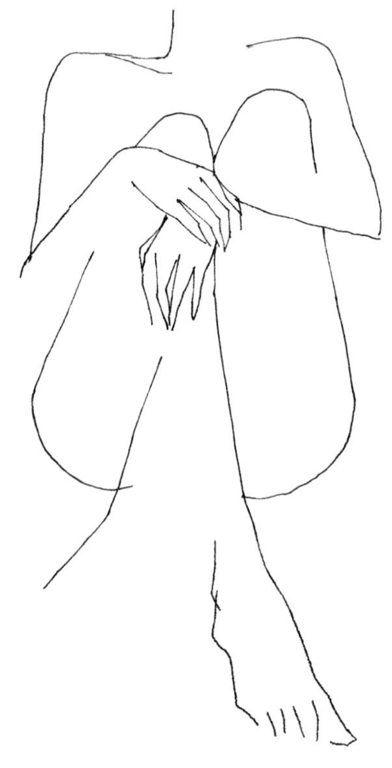

Interpretation 1

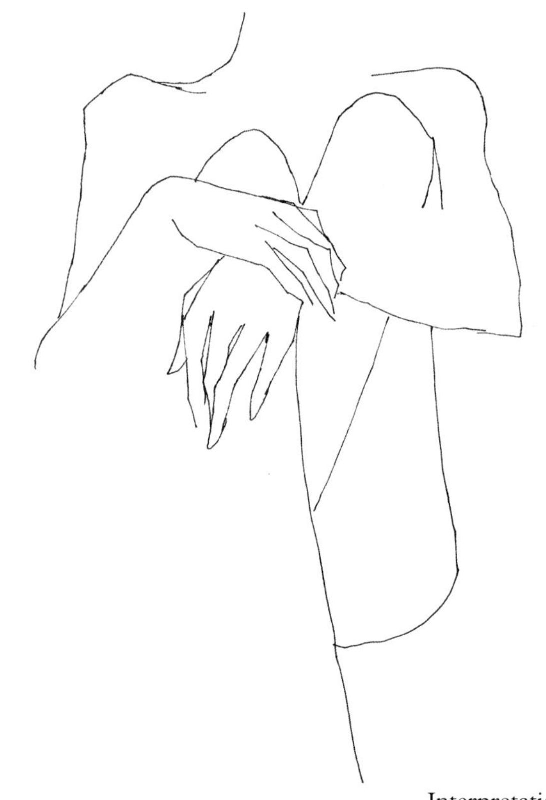

Interpretation 2

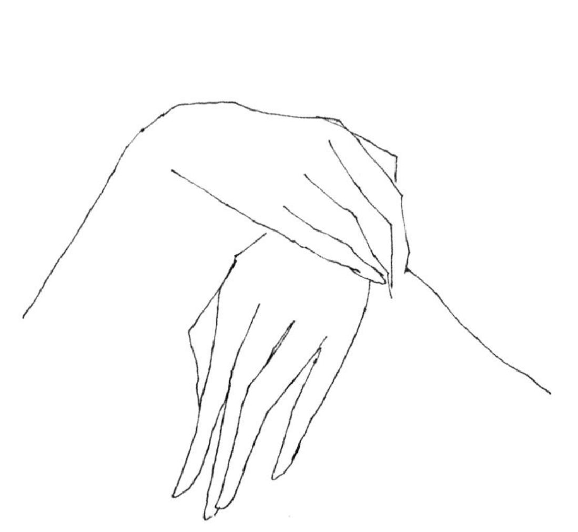

Interpretation 3

*I was going to make an improvement of
interpretation 2, but finally decided to stop and
focus on the hands and what they express.*

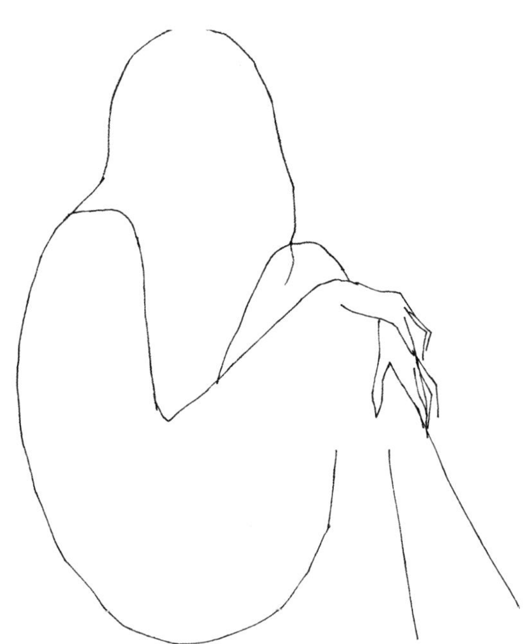

Interpretation 4

*I made a quick test of the same pose, imagined
from a different angle. As you can see, it gives off
a completely different vibe and tells another story.*

SAME POSE, DIFFERENT SHAPES

The intention of this re-creation is to show that a single pose can adapt to a variety of body shapes. Only certain parts like the placement of the head and the hands can remain similar.

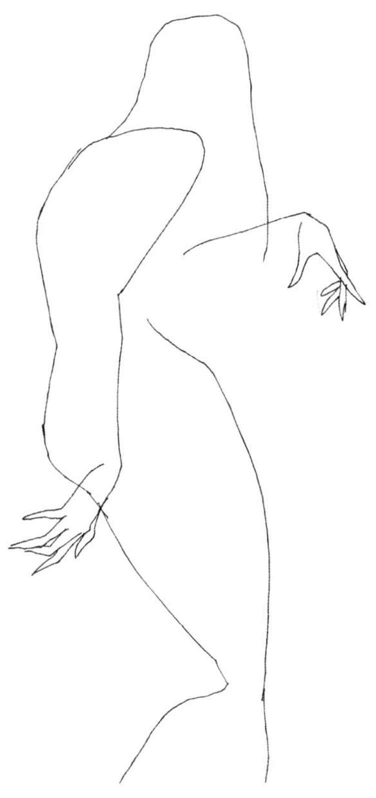

BODY SHAPE 1

Here is the original version, the first silhouette. The movement suggests the woman is dancing and possibly turning. The placement of the hands pleased me, much more than the silhouette. It almost seemed as if this person's identity as a dancer was being fully expressed in the hand gesture. Furthermore, the right hand was smaller but the expression was stronger, which is why I chose to use a more open line on it.

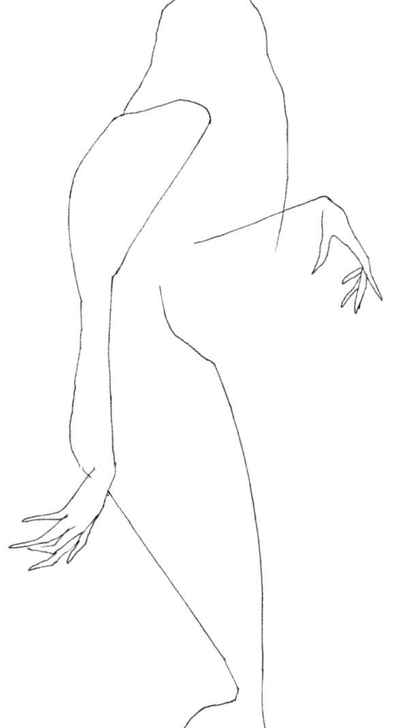

BODY SHAPE 2

Keeping the same pose, I imagined a leaner woman, almost like the famous painter Egon Schiele would. The joints are more prominent, the fingers slightly thinner, the behind less prominent, unlike the shoulders and hips.

BODY SHAPE 3

Still using the first silhouette as my basis, I tried to give it a
rounder shape while remaining as natural as possible. The
idea is to always remain delicate and to apply this sensitivity
to a softer, rounder body. I slightly rounded the fingers, but
it was not completely necessary. The most important thing
is to still portray the same movement.

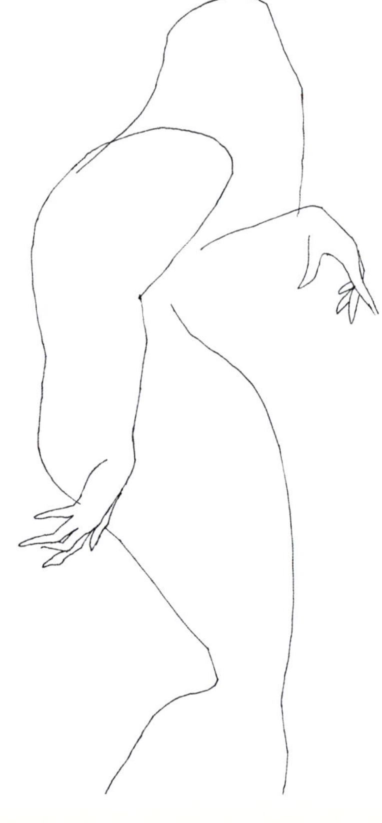

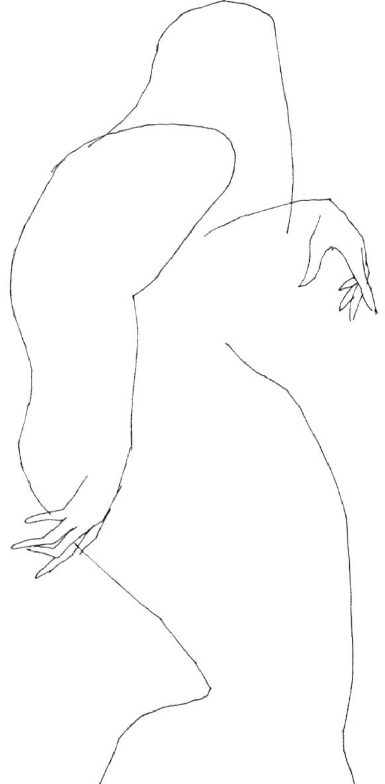

BODY SHAPE 4

I continue this approach by attempting to portray a more voluptuous body. For this pose, I applied the roundness of the shoulders to her back. Once I had drawn the back, the behind, and the
left leg, I had to place the line of her right leg further. It is above
all this element that signifies a difference in silhouette. The rest is
essentially the same. It is not for ease but to show that the size of
a body does not prevent its beauty nor its elegance, that it is first
of all a woman before the image of a body, and that I appreciate
all these silhouettes, their intermediaries, and those that cannot
be represented here in this book because there can only be so
many pages!

BODY SHAPE 1

For this first silhouette, I deliberately focused on the
contours of her legs, hips, stomach, and the beginning
of her chest. It is her belly button that will indicate the
placement and position of this body. With this series,
I chose a slightly thicker and more dynamic brush to
show the possibilities of interpretations despite a
reduced amount of brushstrokes.

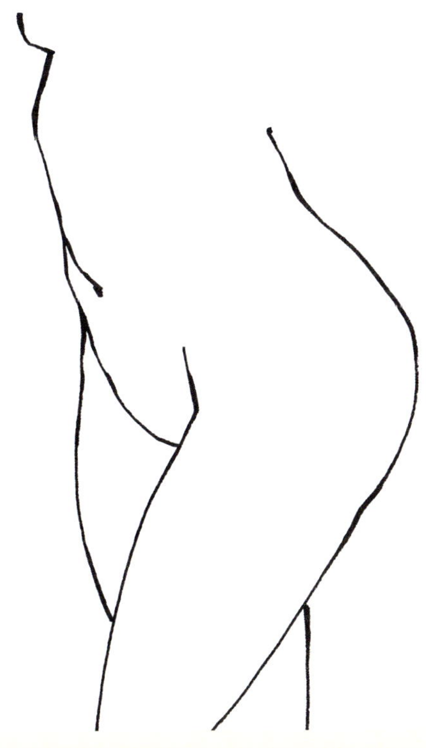

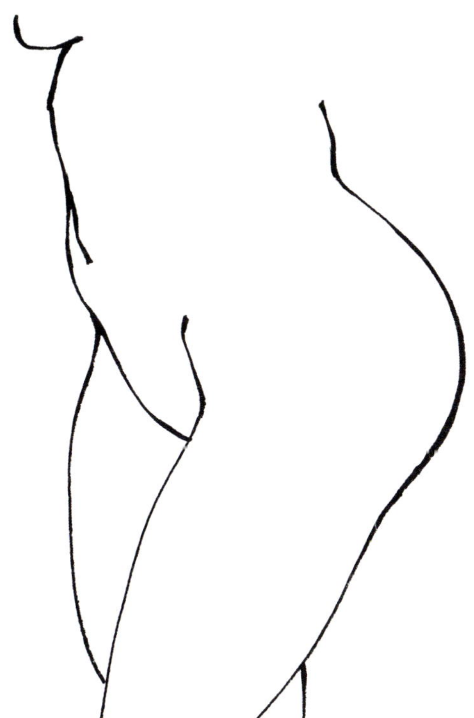

BODY SHAPE 2

This time around, I focused on giving more volume to the overall
shape. The line is intended to be wavier, and the choice of brush
lends itself to this exercise. By slightly spacing out the lines, I
already obtain a variation of the silhouette. Then, all I have to do
is simply add or modify a few aspects of the body, such as the
birth of her back or the shape of her stomach, to obtain
something more voluptuous.

BODY SHAPE 3

If you want to refine the silhouette, it is better to start with the stomach area and the front part of the body. The curves of the hips, behind, and leg will be more instinctive to place. Afterward, it's up to you to draw the shapes you want from the model you have in front of you or if you want it to reflect you. Moreover, it is not necessarily a naked body. The model I used to draw the first silhouette wore leggings. I only drew the shape of her body without placing the belt or the bottom of her bra. This allows the model to be more relaxed and the pose to be more natural as well.

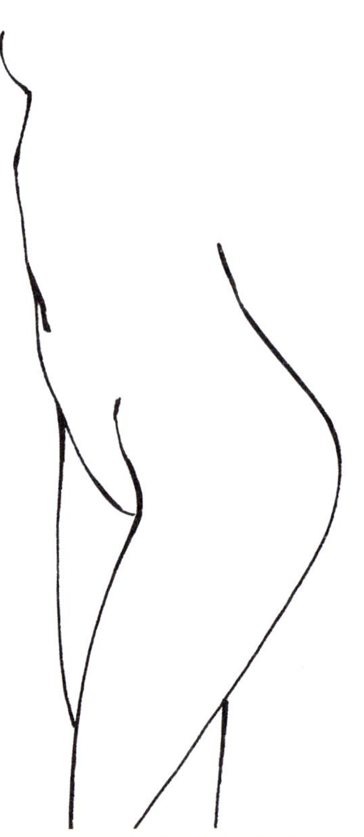

BODY SHAPE 4

If you want to slim down this silhouette even more, it is better to sculpt it, be more prominent, and do not hesitate to add more angles in your lines. You have to significantly strengthen your line or be faster in your mark-making to boost the end result.

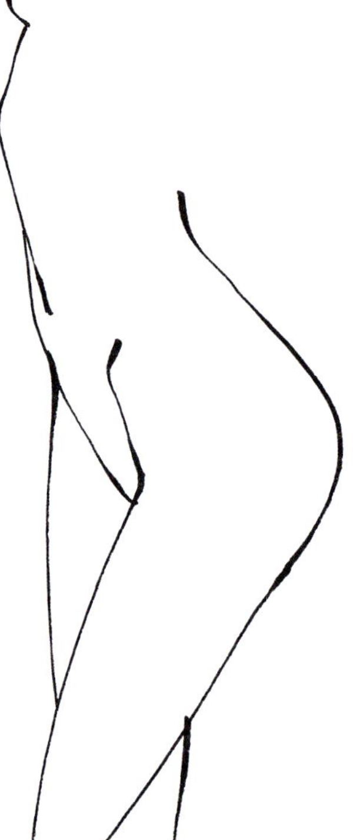

A WOMAN'S PORTRAIT

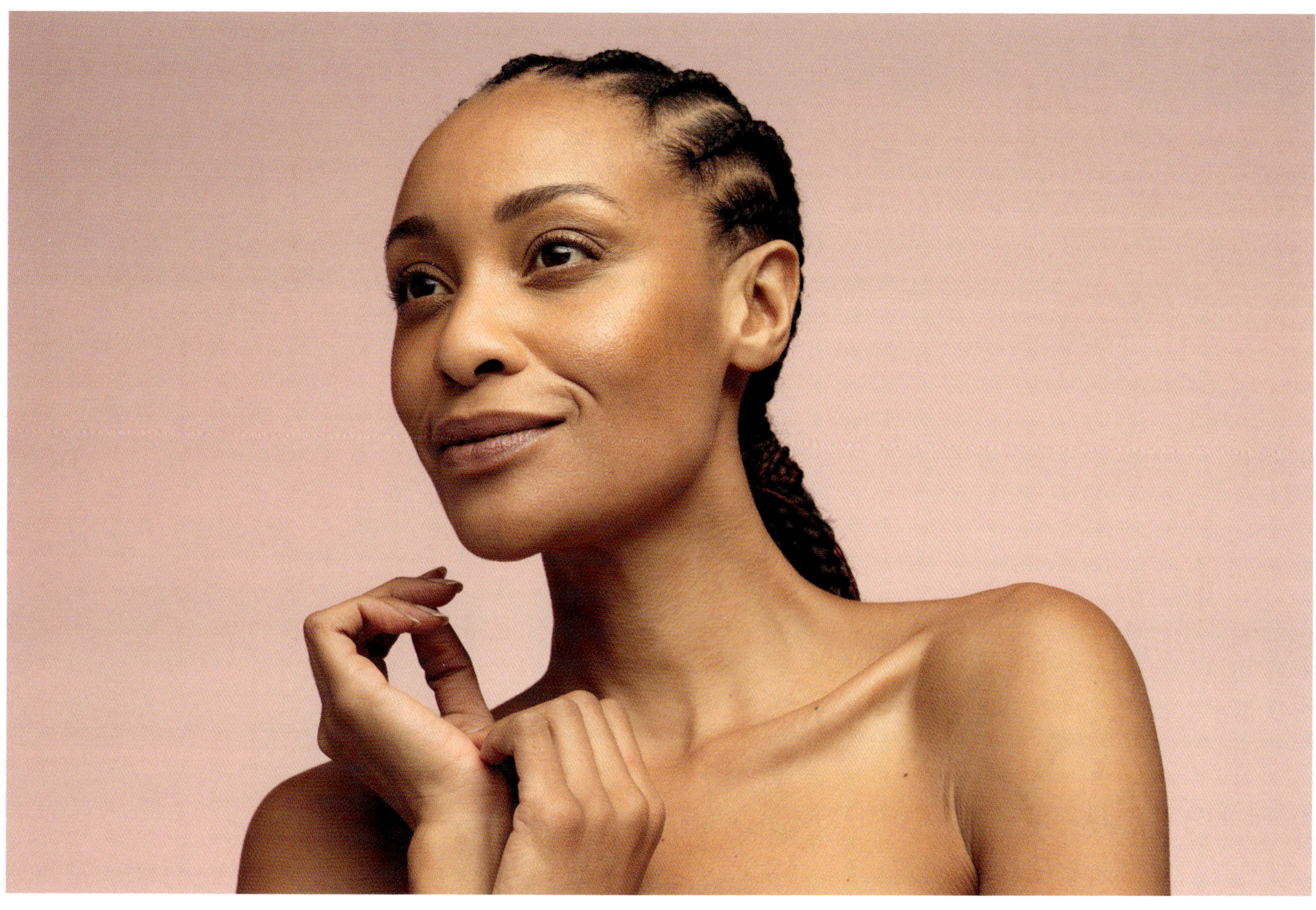

THE IDEA

The portrait is a subtle and delicate art. It is all about finding the right balance between the personality of the person being portrayed, their characteristic traits, and those this person will recognize in themselves. It is obviously even more difficult when using just a few lines.

WHAT I WANT TO EXPRESS

INTERPRETATION 1

I will to choose a fine and flexible brush-pen that will allow me to be precise with the details and more flexible with other aspects of the portrait, such as the subject's hair.

INTERPRETATION 2

I want to be a bit bold and use an unexpected color. I will experiment with placing shadows. I will use a brush-pen that can be both very sharp and intense for the shadowed areas.

STEPS

1—I start with the most important trait, the woman's gaze. I advise you to think about the space that the rest of the drawing and the portrait will take up so that you can place the eyes accordingly. I begin with the contour of the eye and add the eyelashes, then draw in the eyeball and the eyelid and end with the eyebrow.

2—If the eye I have drawn suits me, I then proceed to placing the nose, or at least suggest its presence, because I don't know yet if the details I'm drawing will be sufficient for a full portrait in the end. I realize that it is important to go back to the eye and shade the beginning of the eyelid, then I go back to the eye by shading in the lower section of her eye to add depth and dimension.

3—As I did for the nose, the mouth must be sketched. Note its position, shape, and size. I start with the top outline, then the center, and finally add a line below to suggest her lower lip. The subject's face slowly begins to take shape.

4—For the contour of the face, I place a point that marks the second eye's position. Then, I let my line run down the cheek to the chin and around the mouth. I go back from where I started and work my way up, stopping at the eyebrow as if marking it lightly, then quickly sketching the forehead.

1

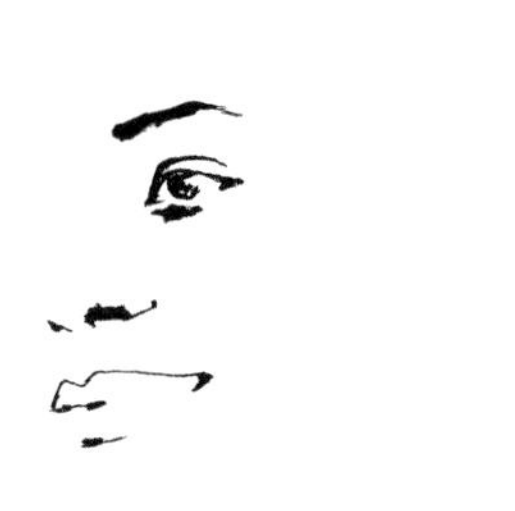

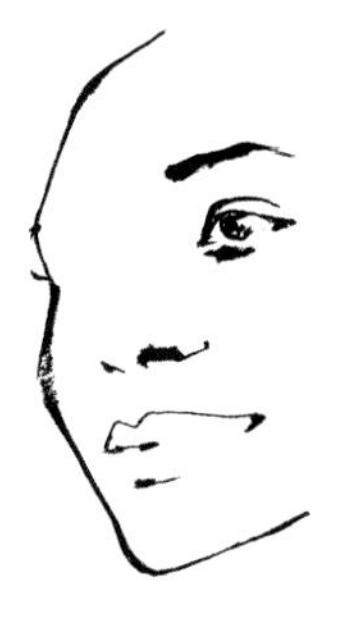

2

3

4

5—I continue my line to suggest the hair. This time, however, I press down harder on my pen's tip to thicken the line and signify the volume of her hair, stopping at her shoulder. The portrait could potentially be made up of only these lines. It seems sufficient to me.

6—I try to push the drawing a bit further by adding her neck. The end of the broad line of hair tells me where I need to turn to subtly hint at her shoulder, mark her collarbone, and pursue the line down to add her arm.

This last feature was useful in placing the subject's portrait onto the body, and since the format of the paper corresponds, it makes for a nice composition.

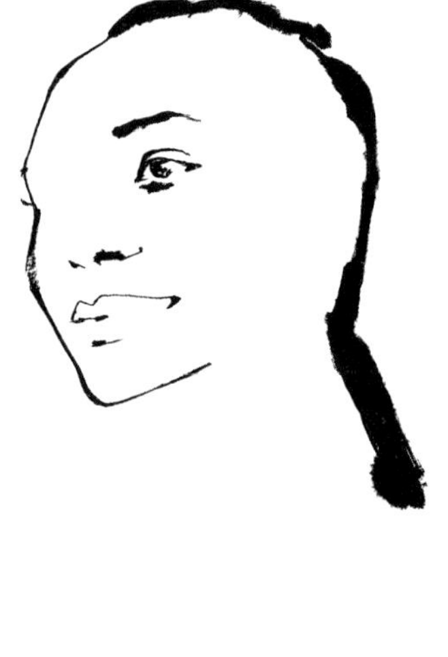

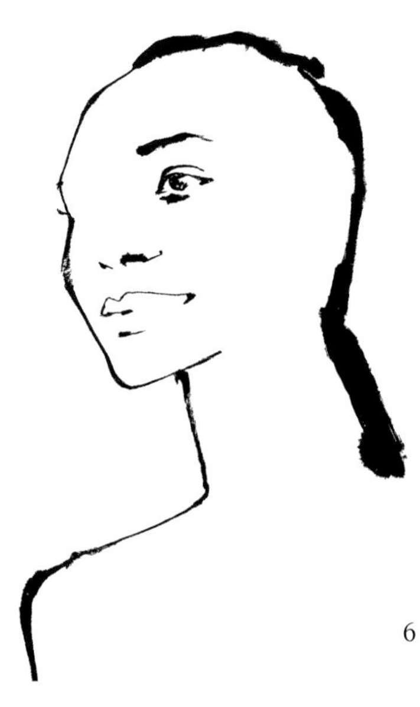

5

6

STEPS

1—Like I did with the first interpretation, I begin this second portrait by drawing the subject's gaze.

2—I continue by sketching her second eye, but I choose to not fill in the pupil because the focus of the portrait this time around will be on the other half of her face. The eyebrow line allows me to place her nose using shadows. I outline her mouth next and add a thick line to mark its volume.

3—I don't know yet if I'm going to outline her face entirely. I start by sketching her hair instead by starting at the top of her forehead, waving the line slightly to signify her hairstyle type and stretching a wider line over her braid. It almost feels like I'm the one doing her hair! I then add the outline of her ear.

4—The drawing is starting to please me, but I try to mark her gaze and add shadows around her eye and the lines of her hairstyle. A shadow under her mouth seems important to me to balance everything out. One line is enough.

5—I like the shadows on her cheek. I use a thicker stroke from her forehead to her chin. This is another way to mark the volume of her face and let my gaze imagine the rest. At the end, I thicken the line of her braid to balance the overall composition. This could be the final drawing.

6—I push the drawing a bit further by adding her neck and marking the shadow of her jawbone. I then add the line from her collarbone to below her neck. The portrait now seems defined and structured.

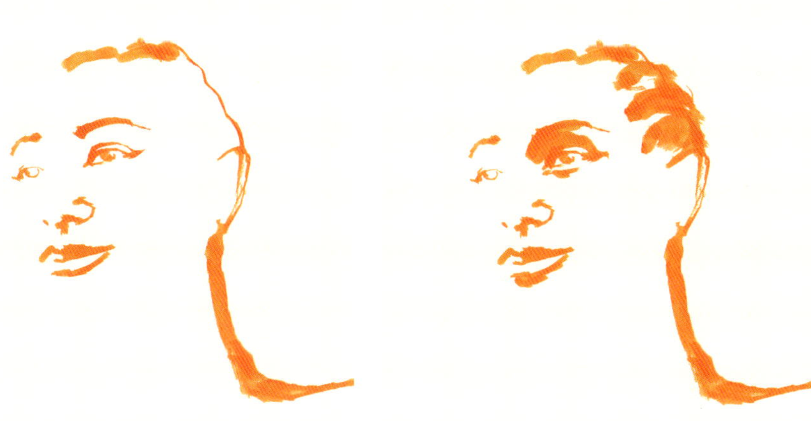

1

2

3

4

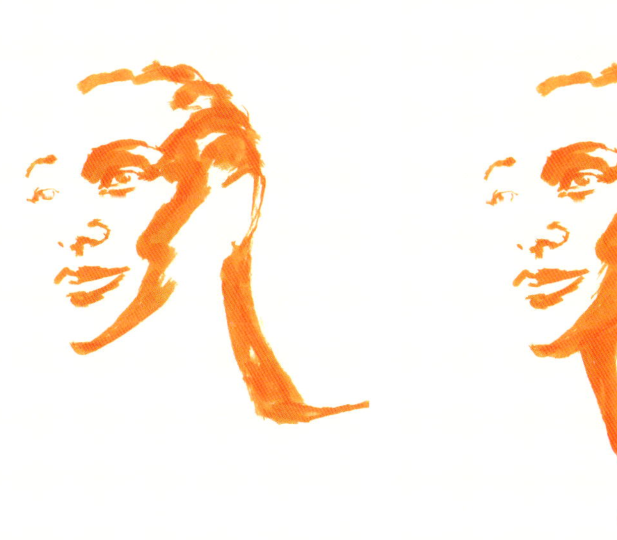

5

6

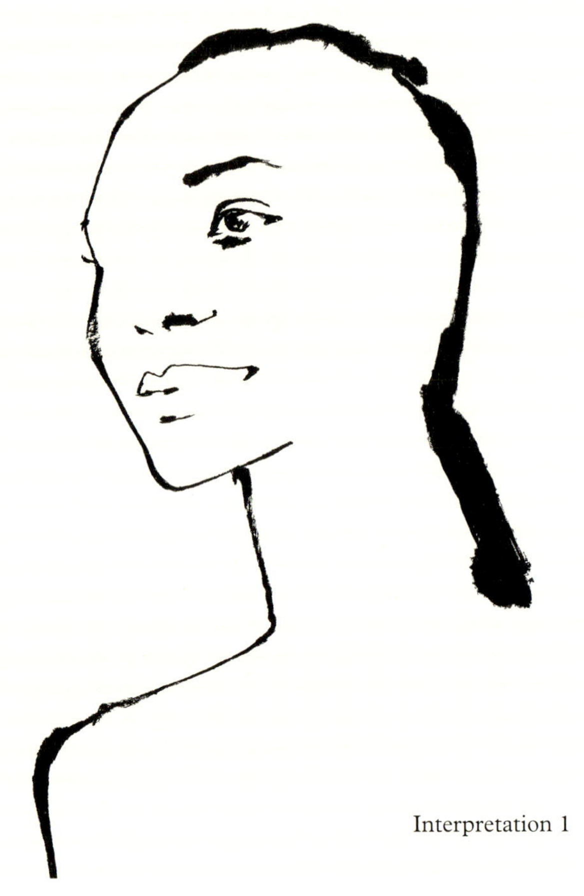

Interpretation 1

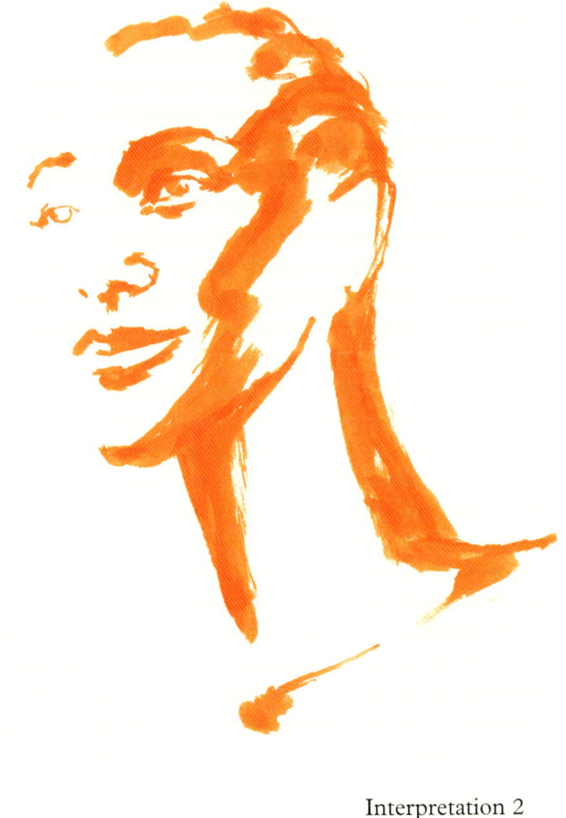

Interpretation 2

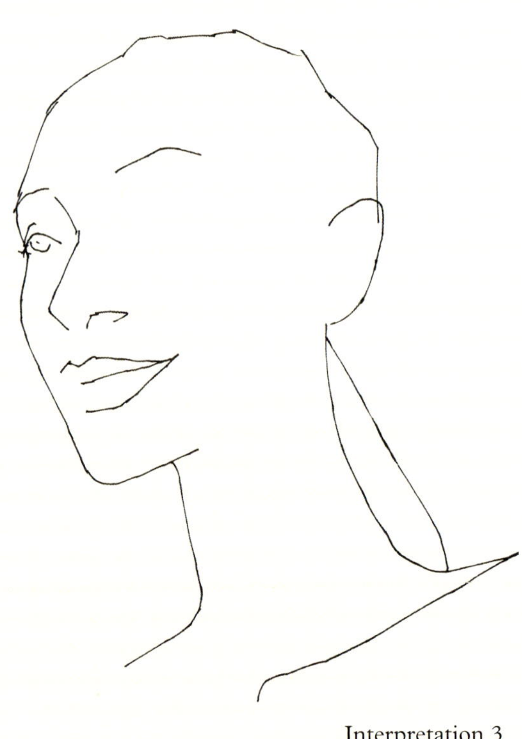

Interpretation 3

*Using a thin line, I focused on her nose and
her eye that hugs the contour of her face.*

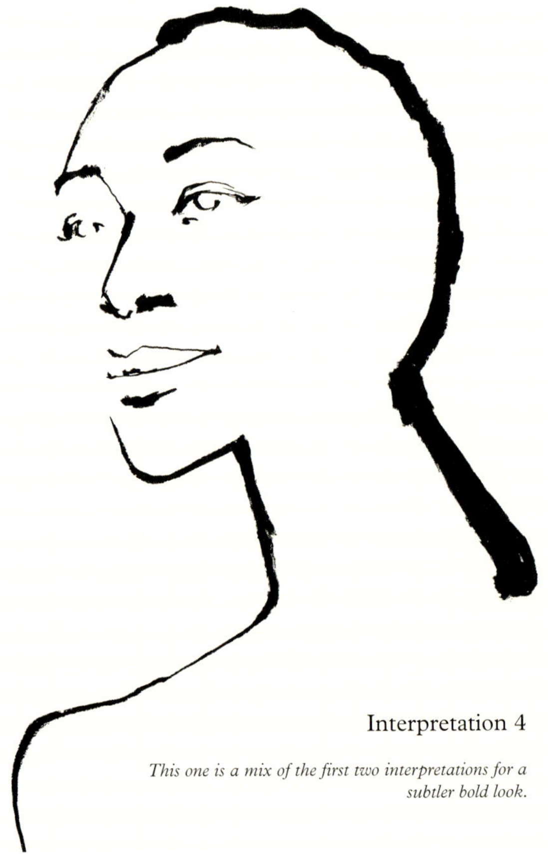

Interpretation 4

*This one is a mix of the first two interpretations for a
subtler bold look.*

A MAN'S SILHOUETTE

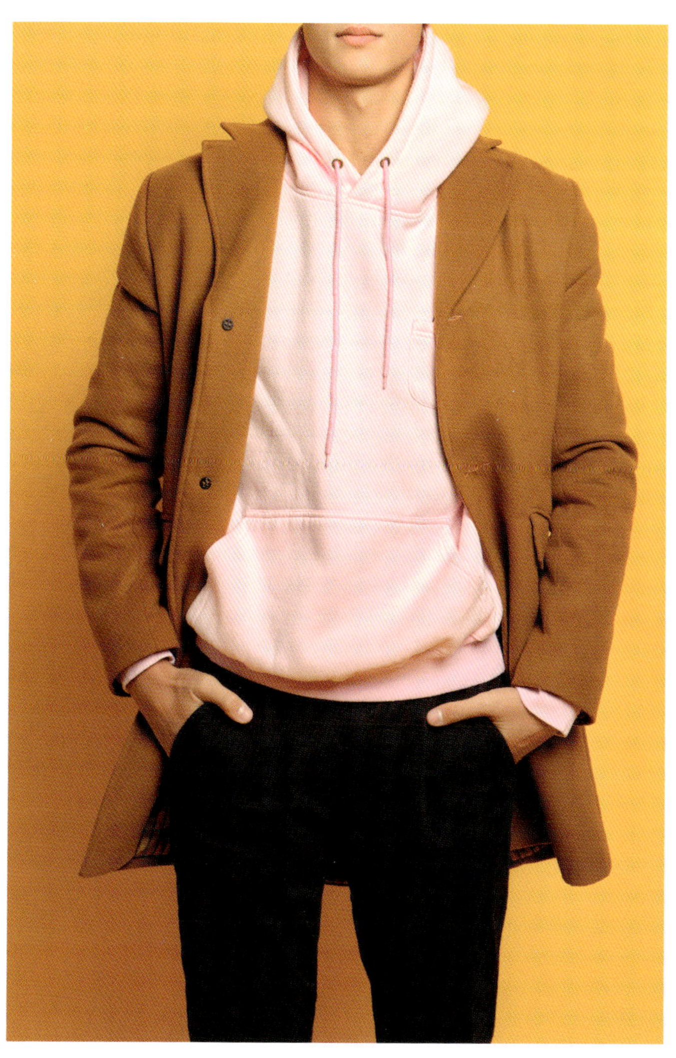

THE IDEA

This silhouette is halfway between a natural pose and an attitude that we regularly see in fashion magazines. The idea will be to capture this attitude as well as the look.

The three colors that we see in the image (the pink of his sweatshirt, the orange-brown of his coat, and the black of his pants) will be a great opportunity to try mixing different types of lines and brush-pens.

WHAT I WANT TO EXPRESS

INTERPRETATION 1

I will start with three different types of brush-pens. With these different tools, I can render the movement of the clothes and the bodily details in their place.

INTERPRETATION 2

I will create a black ink version as well to focus on the overall shape of the silhouette and the important lines that make up this pose.

STEPS

1—I start with the sweatshirt because it is the central element of the pose. I begin by placing the center of the hood by making a *V* shape, then a *W*. Then, I continue to run the line down along the line of the coat until it reaches the level of the model's belt.

2—I mark the bottom of the sweatshirt with two lines and then place two other lines to make the pockets.

3—I switch colors and pick the orange brush-pen that is similar in style as the pink I started with. I mark the outer outline of his coat up to his sleeve, only hinting at the wrist. I extend the line lower, placing the bottom of the coat. I end up deciding to draw once more over the vertical pink line of the opening of the coat to define it a bit more.

4—I draw the other side starting from the shoulder, around his arm to his hand, then add a simple line at the bottom of the coat.

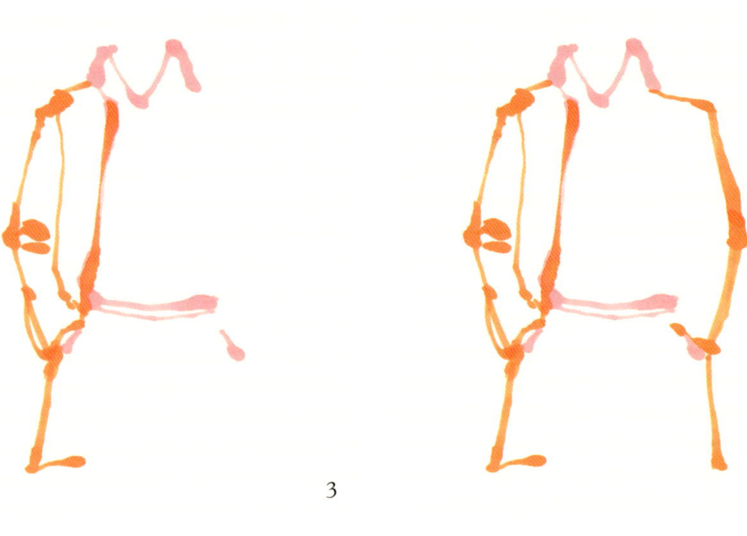

5—The base I've created with just these two colors is now enough for me to draw the model's face. It is incomplete in the picture, but we can imagine the features. I start with his neck, going up to his ear. Then I outline the hair. It seems a bit too abstract to me still, so I add his chin. I could stop here.

6—I try to continue with the black ink by sketching his thumbs sticking out of his pockets. I then proceed to add a frank, stiff line to illustrate the pants and their solid, grounded position.

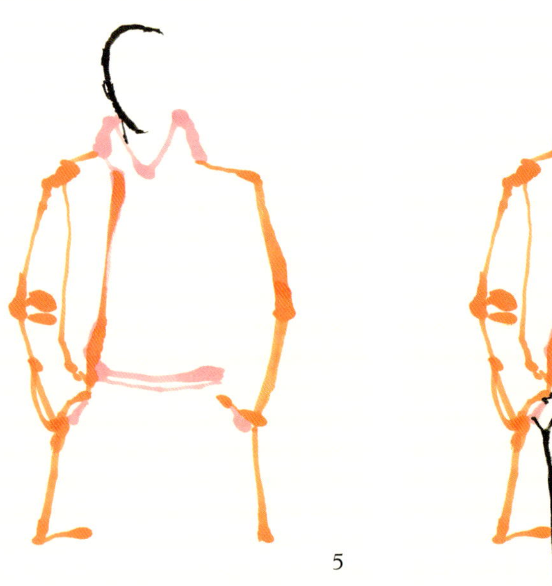

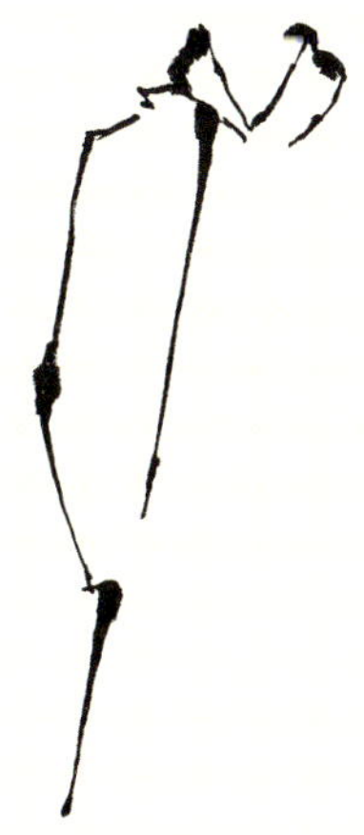
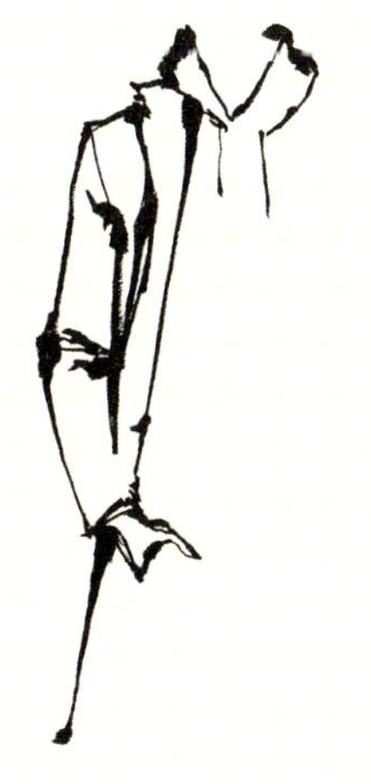

STEPS

1—I use the same starting point, the hood. I then proceed to outline his shoulder, then going down to his hand. I start from his collar to mark the opening of the coat, stopping before I get to his hand. I follow this line from the sleeve to the bottom of the coat.

2—I draw the detail of the hand and the thumb. I add the lines and folds of his coat and the cords of the hoodie.

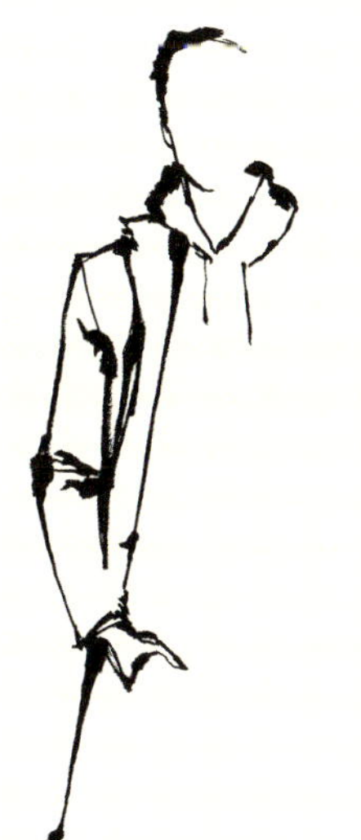
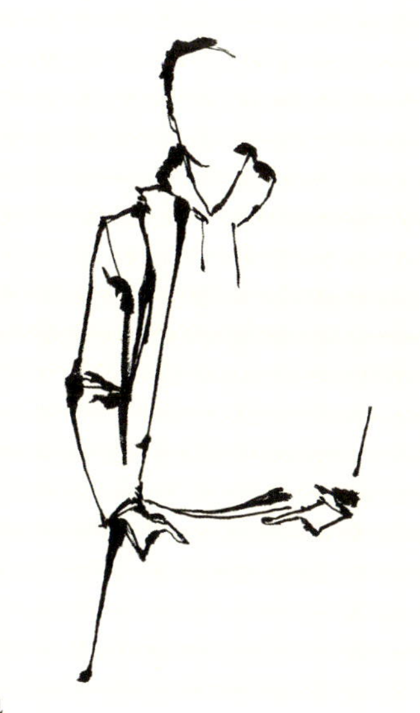

3—It then seems important for me to position the face.

4—I draw the bottom of the sweatshirt. This places the second hand and the beginning of the other sleeve.

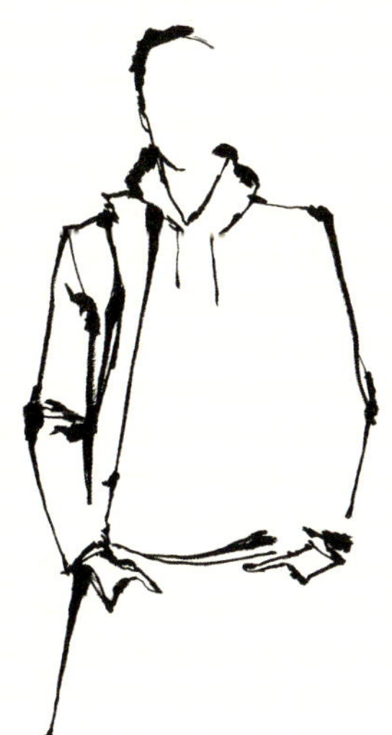
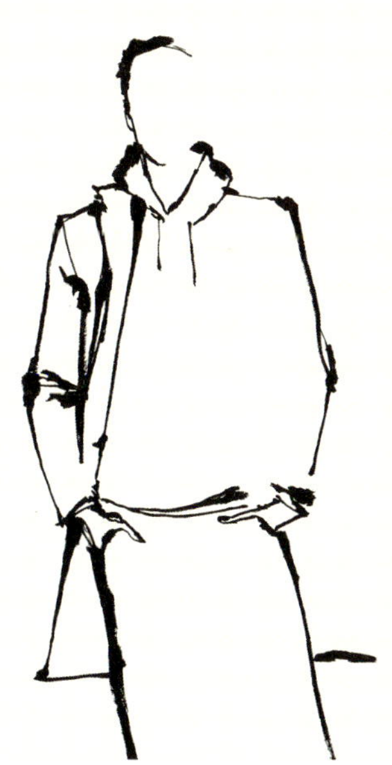

5—I switch to the other shoulder and run the line down to the sleeve.

6—I mark the line of the pants on the left with a thicker stroke to ground the silhouette. A second finer line places the second leg. There is then only a little left to add for the bottom of the coat.

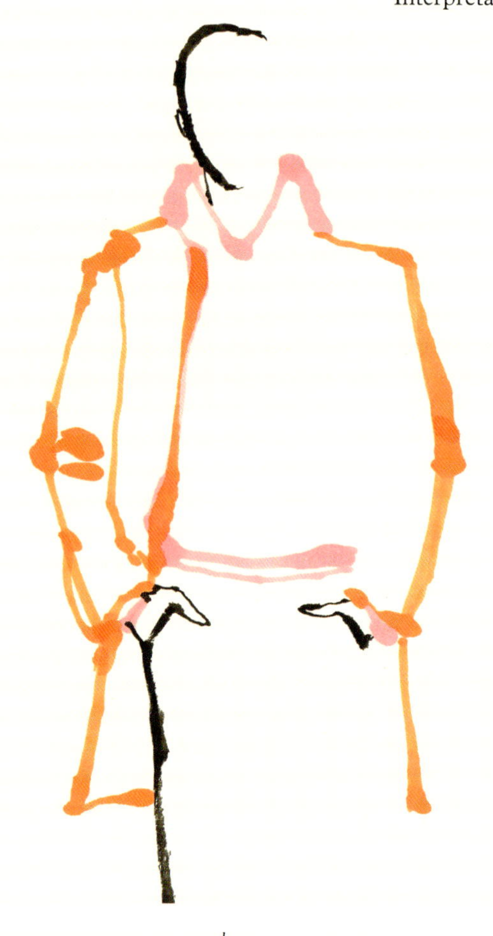

Interpretation 1

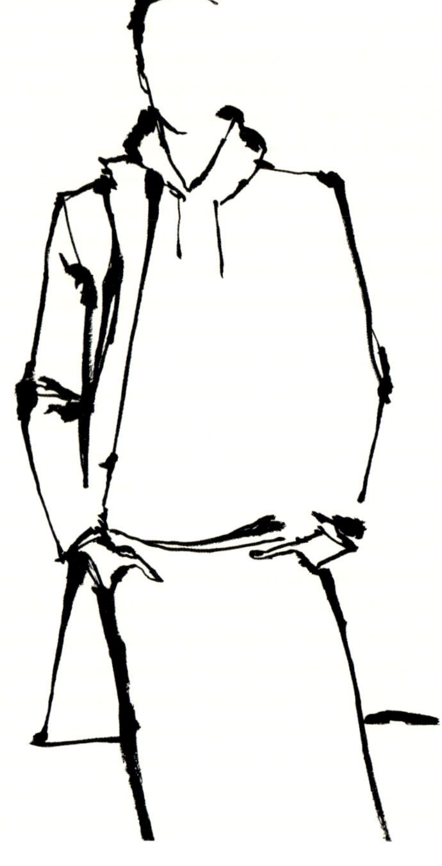

Interpretation 2

Interpretation 3

Here, I felt that using a finer line was more interesting on a close-up of the silhouette.

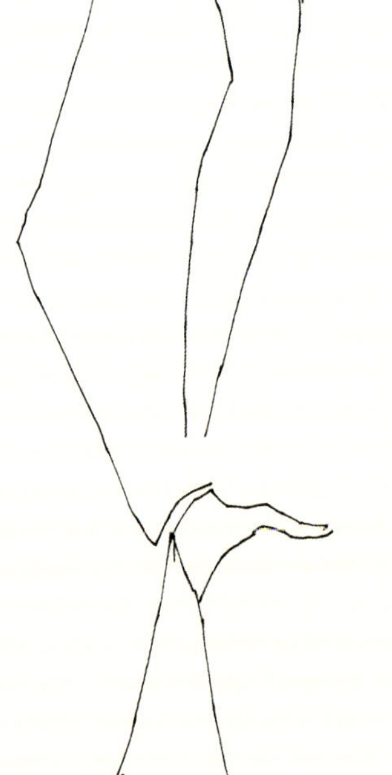

Interpretation 4

This is a faster sketch I made with a colored brush-pen with a more brushed feel. The head has a fuller outline. I also varied the types of lines I used to illustrate the other details.

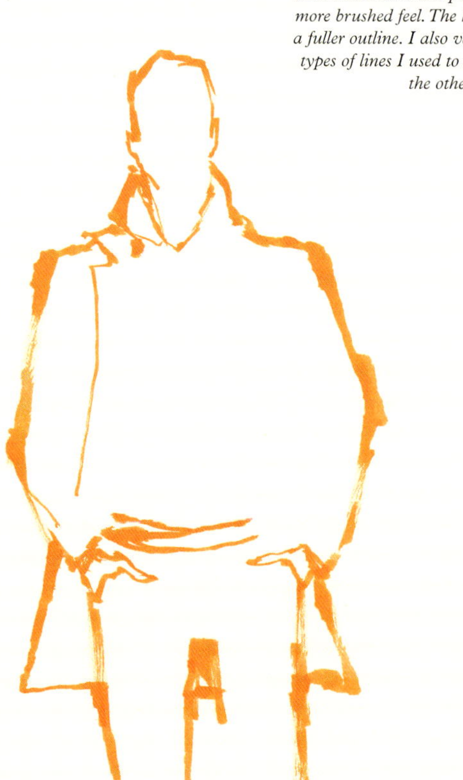

MEN

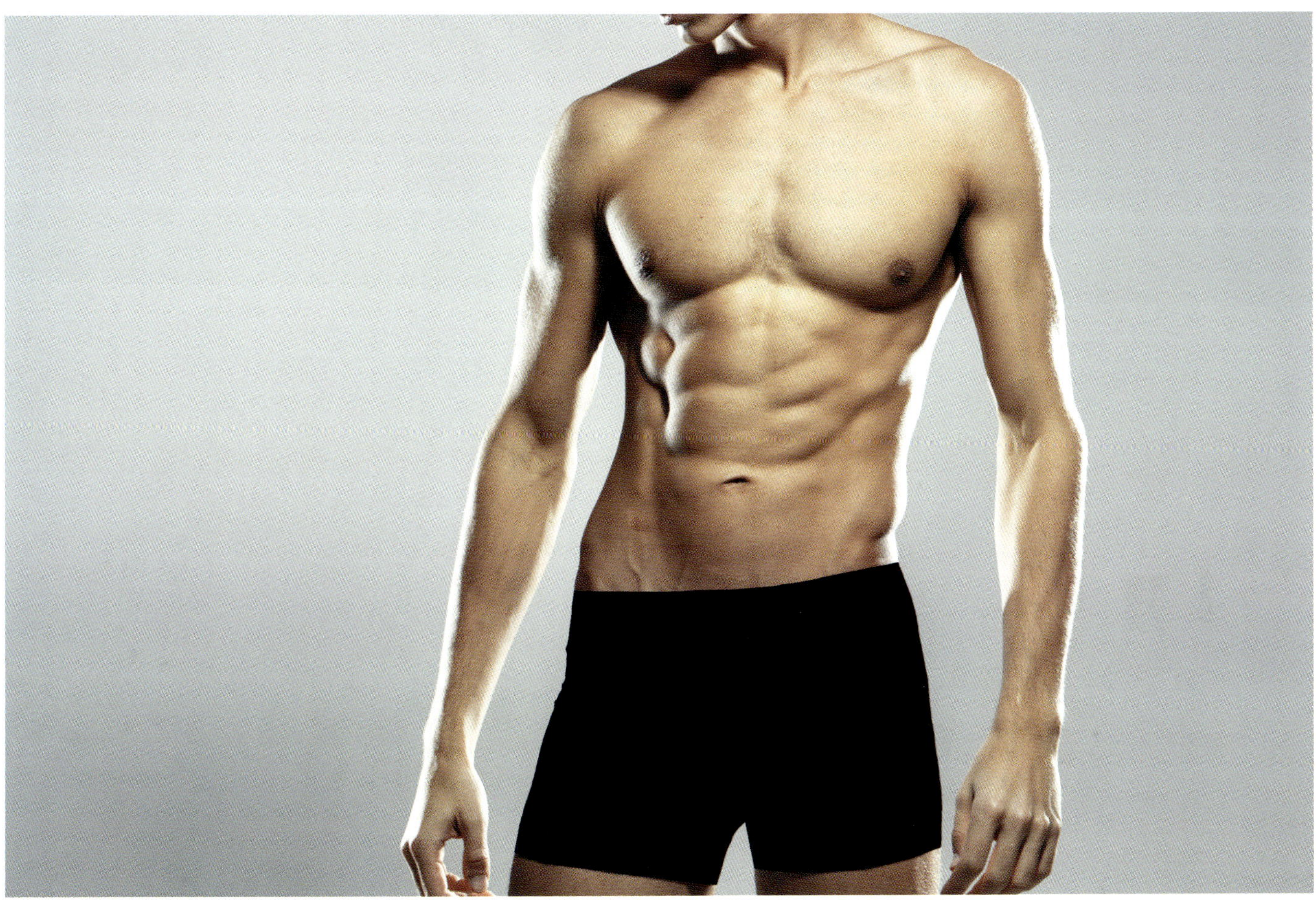

THE IDEA

This pose appears to be simple. Luckily, the side light noticeably sculpts the torso and arms. The body is already sculpted for us!

WHAT I WANT TO EXPRESS

INTERPRETATION 1

I will take advantage of the lines that contrast this male body. A black and very flexible brush-pen is ideal.

INTERPRETATION 2

If I use a fine line, the contours and other lines that will take the spotlight.

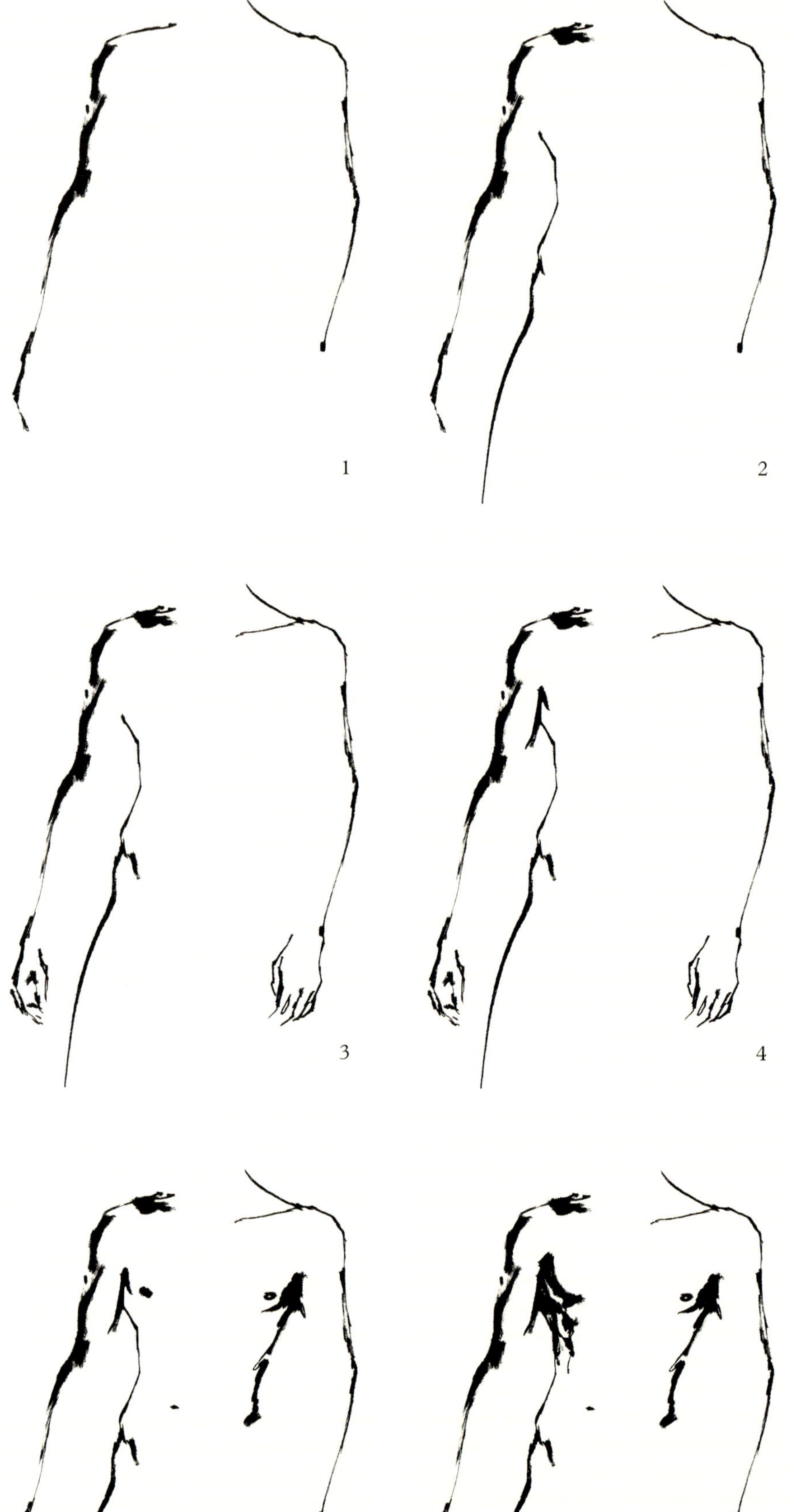

1

2

3

4

5

6

STEPS

1—I begin this drawing a bit differently than the rest by imagining I am in the position of the spotlight. I try to envision where the light would hit first. I begin with the shoulder, outline his biceps, stop at his elbow, and continue up to the first hand, without drawing the fingers just yet. I start another line from the neck and flip to the trapeze before quickly drawing the outer outline of the right arm.

2—Before drawing the hands in more detail, I sketch the outline of his chest, marking his hip in the light and ending with the thigh. I add a thicker line above his shoulder on the left to signify the collarbone.

3—I can now take care of the hands and be more precise about their sizes and details. I start by continuing the line on the left by drawing his index finger and thumb. I can then more easily draw the other fingers and their movements. For the right hand, I begin by drawing the pinky finger and then the thumb. The rest of the fingers will also then be easier to place and sketch. I draw the line of his collarbone. The drawing could potentially be done.

4—I decide that I would like to mark his torso a little bit more, so I start with the biceps and the beginning of his pectoral. This will help indicate the correct place-ment of his torso.

5—I then draw the other side of his chest and mark his other pectoral. Once I draw that, I sketch his two nipples and his navel.

6—A second line on the left side will reveal the light that is shining on his chest and give the silhouette a virile attitude.

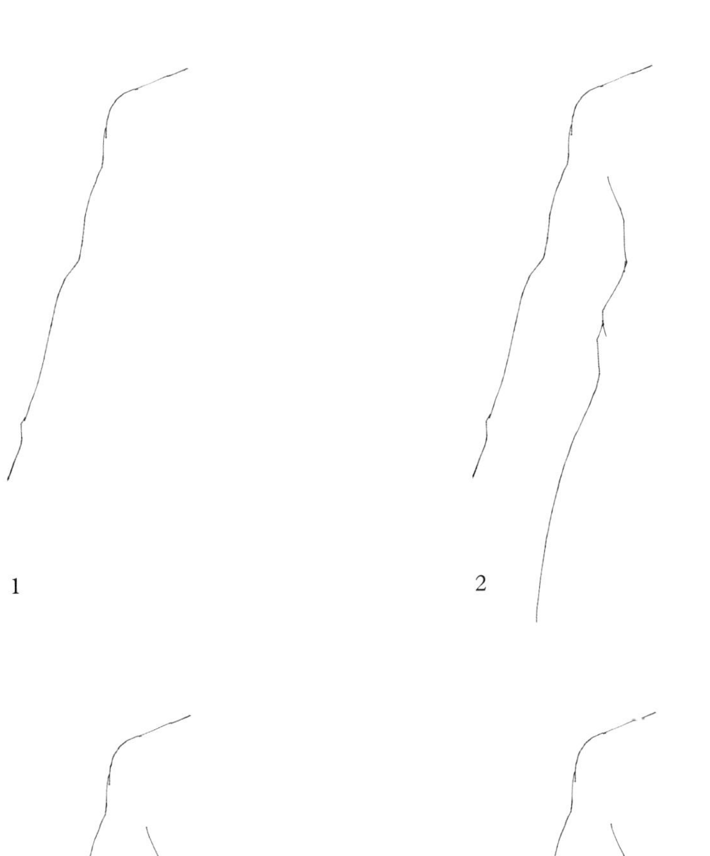

STEPS

1—I am right-handed, and I begin with the left part of the photo, starting my line with the shoulder and going down the arm to the wrist.

2—I then place the torso and hip before continuing on to the hip.

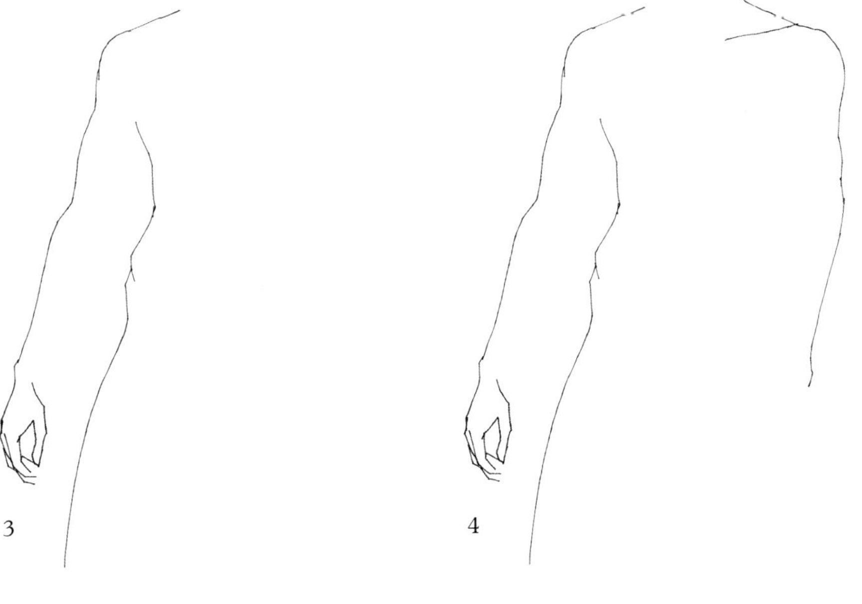

3—The hip placement allows me to move forward and draw the hand. I start with the index finger and then draw the thumb. From there, I still need to draw the fingers that are less visible, one after the other.

4—I then draw the outer outline of the other arm. I add a line to mark the model's collarbone.

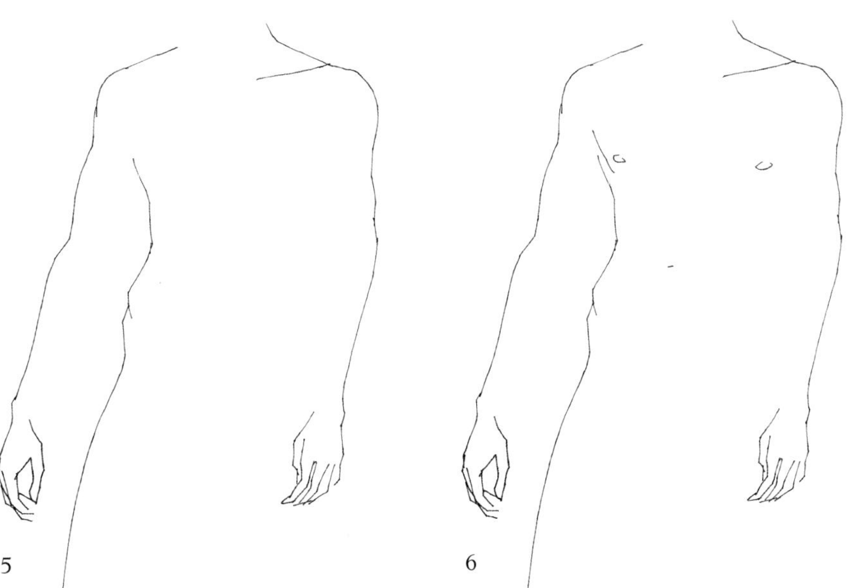

5—This is when the other hand should be drawn. Like I did previously, I first sketch the pinky finger and the thumb. The other fingers must be drawn in stride.

6—Now I am only missing a few small details: the beginning of the pectoral, two unclosed ovals to illustrate his nipples, and a short line for the navel.

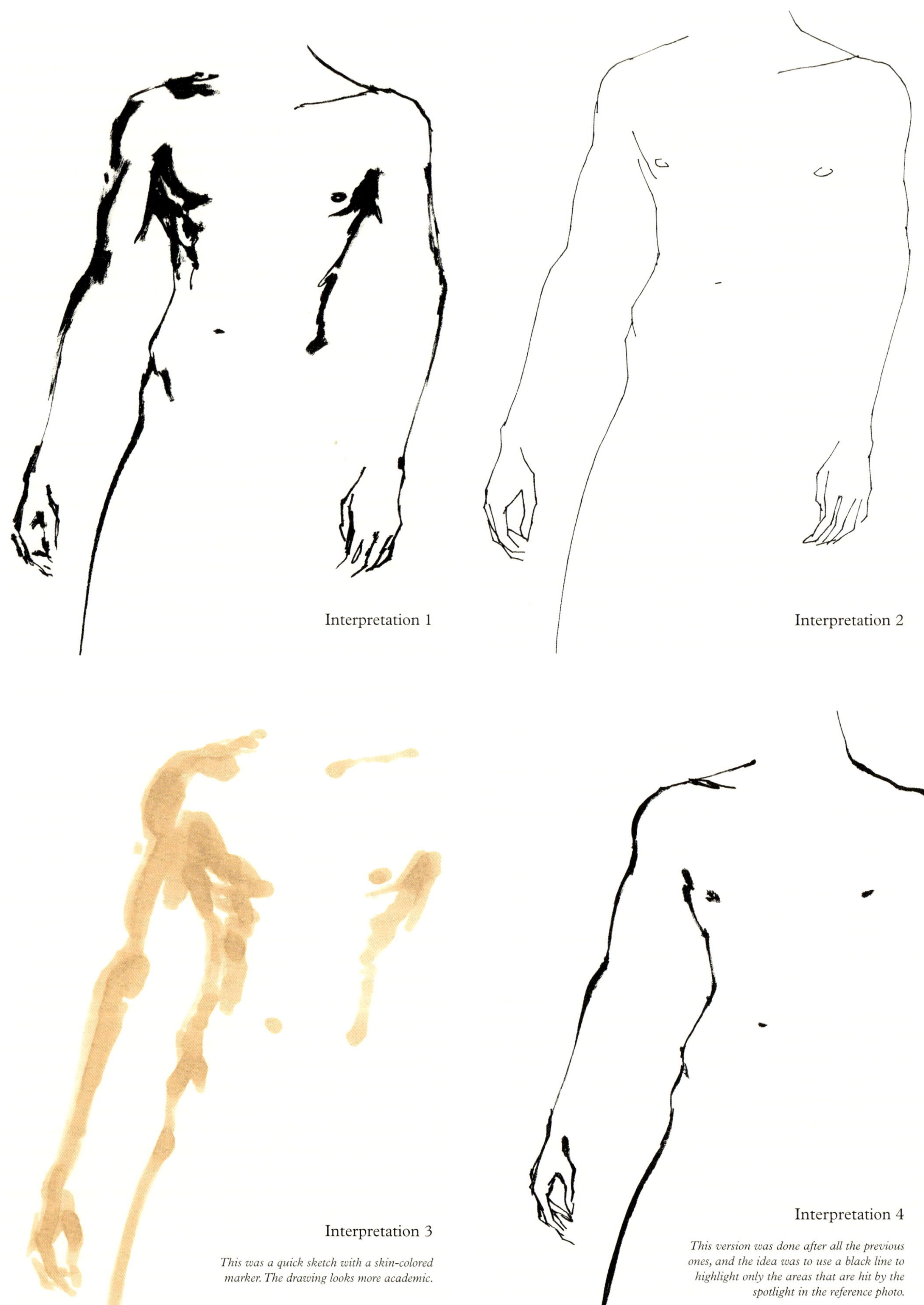

Interpretation 1

Interpretation 2

Interpretation 3

This was a quick sketch with a skin-colored marker. The drawing looks more academic.

Interpretation 4

This version was done after all the previous ones, and the idea was to use a black line to highlight only the areas that are hit by the spotlight in the reference photo.

A MAN'S PORTRAIT

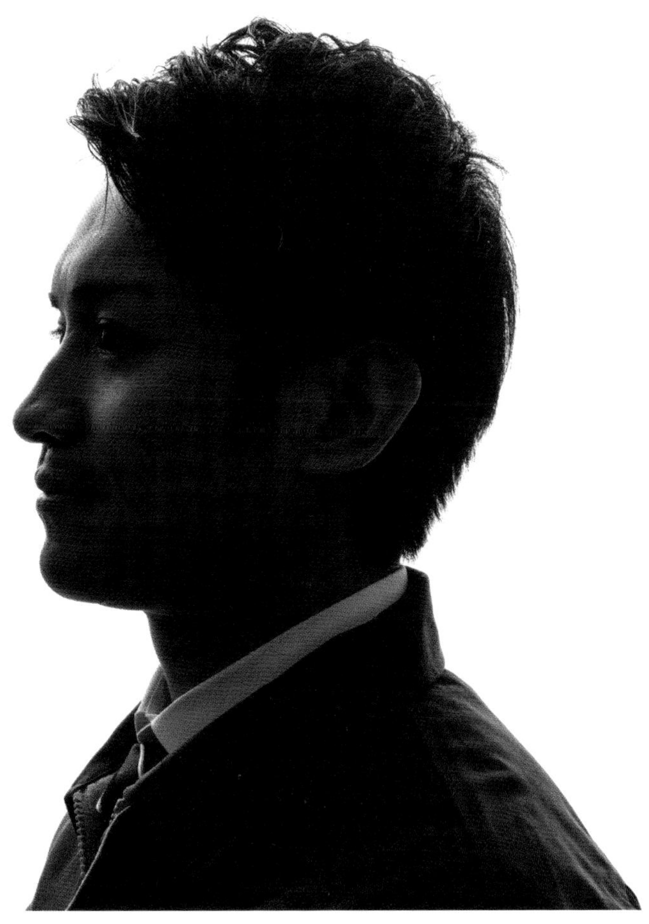

THE IDEA

Unlike the female portrait, I was looking for a backlit image for the male version. Using this face, which we can only partially discern, the drawing will have to give it a personality, an identity, while remaining sensitive.

WHAT I WANT TO EXPRESS

INTERPRETATION 1

A thin line will force me to scan the image. The portrait will have to emerge from this outline, highlighting a face and a gaze that I can only guess.

INTERPRETATION 2

A thicker line will force me to mark the facial features that appear to me.

STEPS

1—As with the female portrait, I begin by drawing and positioning one eye on the page. The gaze is decisive in giving personality to this portrait. I do the eye contour first, then the pupil. The eyebrow comes next. I then draw the arch, the nose, and the forehead.

2—I start from the nose to draw the outline of the mouth and tilt my line to create the chin.

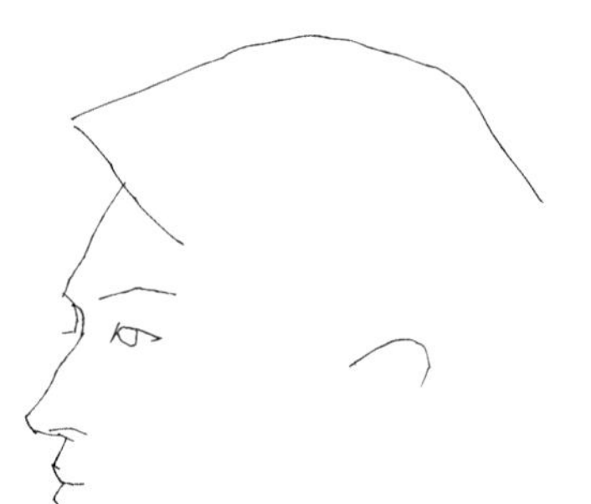

1

2

3—I add a very small line to signify a wise smile from a man who wants to keep his seriousness. I then draw the front section of his hair. I already get something from his face, maybe even the essence.

4—I continue anyway by adding the top of his hair and his ear.

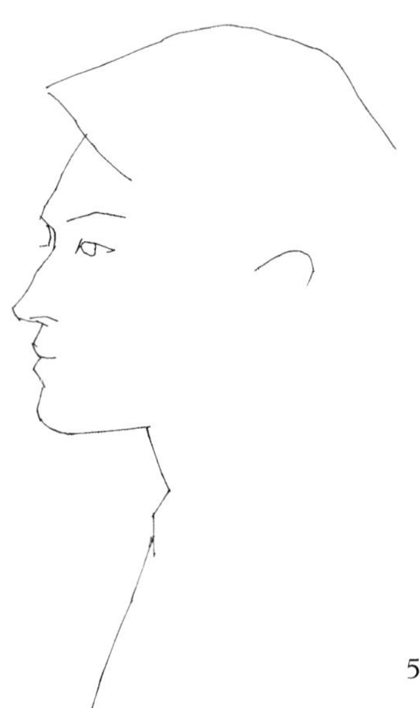

3

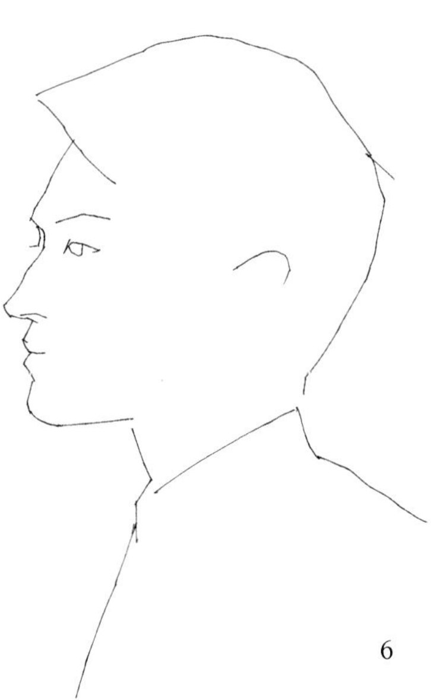

4

5—His face seems to float too much for me on the paper. I draw his neck and then outline his shirt collar and jacket. The portrait is already holding up much better!

6—I then finish with the back of his hair and his jacket. Only the line of the collar of his shirt is missing to raise his head in this portrait.

I am hesitant between steps 5 and 6 as the final portrait of this interpretation.

5

6

STEPS

1—Even if I am using a thicker and stronger line for this second interpretation, I still proceed to draw the eye first. On the other hand, this time, I start with the pupil, which I blacken immediately, then I contour the eye and add the eyebrow. I line mark the nose and forehead that are in the light. I then draw the brow bone and add the eyelashes of the other eye.

2—The first interpretation made it possible to scan the outline of this face, and I repeat this sequence of the nose, the mouth (which I am only suggesting this time), and the chin. I add two strokes for the front locks of hair.

3—I then illustrate the hairstyle by pursuing the wick of hair up to his ear and to the top of his head. I now have the face in place and the overall shape of his hair.

4—Then I push on my black brush-pen's tip to wake up the light caressing his face. I support my fine lines and play with the volumes of his face. It is a progressive work. It's a bit like walking in the dark. Do not rush into this action and the gestures associated with it. I start with what is happening around his eye.

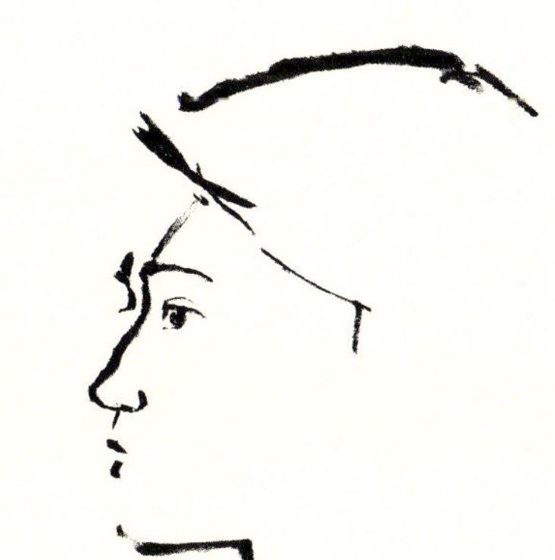

1

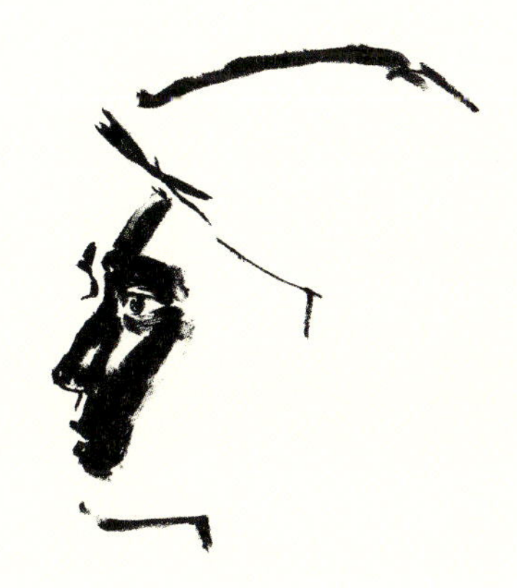

2

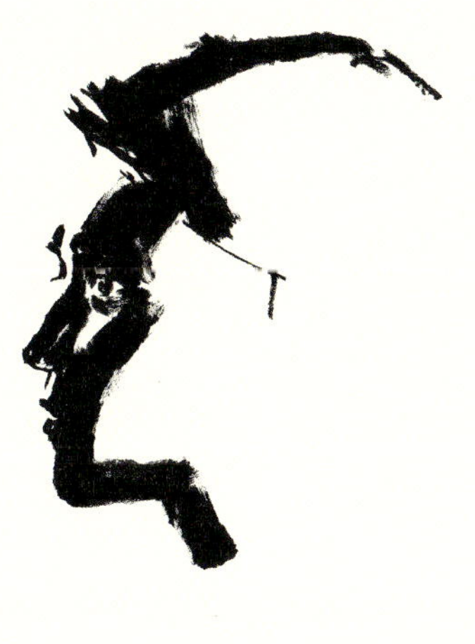

3

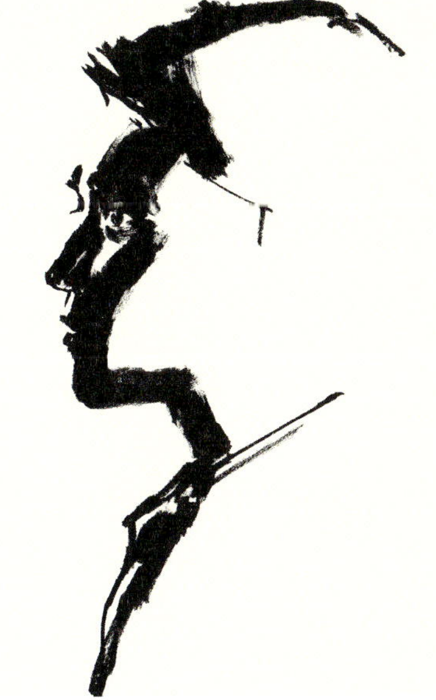

4

5—I continue this slow action to the mouth and chin. The neck is then done more quickly. I take up what is happening around the eye and the nose. The forehead and the hair should then be darker.

6—All that remains is to sketch the shirt's collar and the front of his jacket a bit more loosely.

5

6

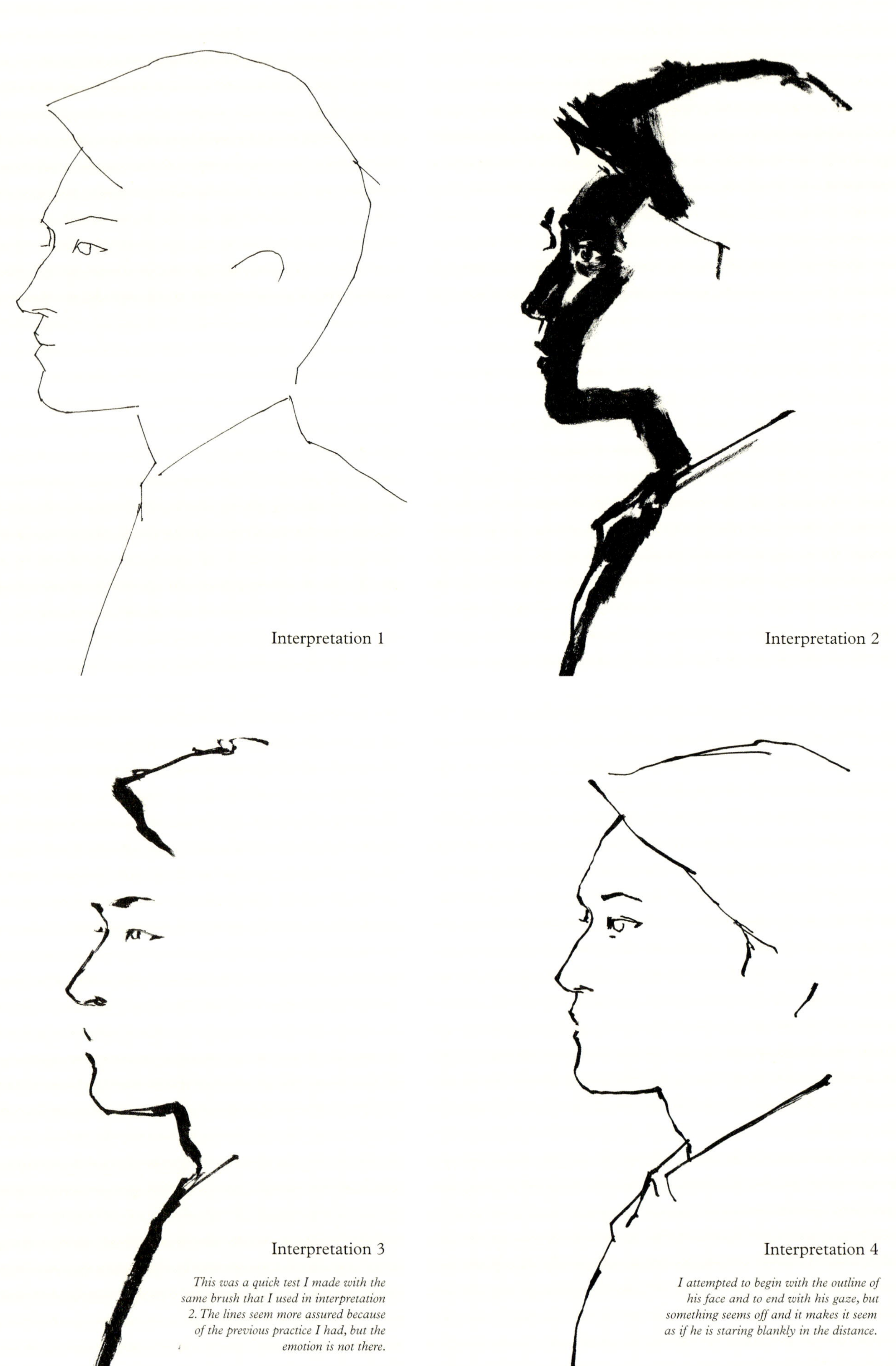

Interpretation 1

Interpretation 2

Interpretation 3

This was a quick test I made with the same brush that I used in interpretation 2. The lines seem more assured because of the previous practice I had, but the emotion is not there.

Interpretation 4

I attempted to begin with the outline of his face and to end with his gaze, but something seems off and it makes it seem as if he is staring blankly in the distance.

HANDS

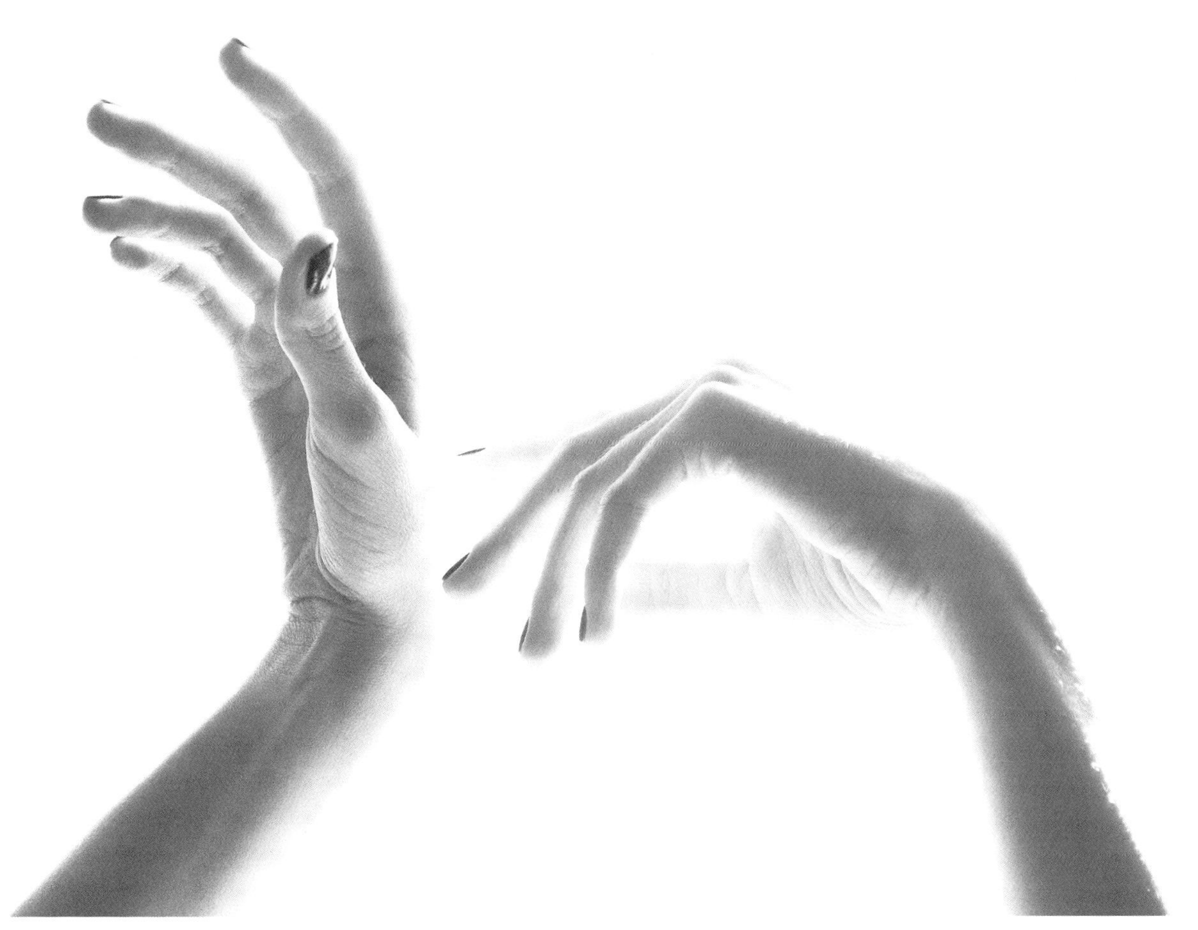

THE IDEA

Hands are an endless source of inspiration for me. Both strong and sensitive, they move me. They speak volumes and act like universal words.

As Auguste Rodin once said: "The hand reveals the man." I spend a lot of time working on the extremities of my figures, the hands in particular, to exploit their power of expression, whether attached to the body or isolated, as works in their own right and autonomous.

WHAT I WANT TO EXPRESS

INTERPRETATION 1

A fine line will be an obvious choice here to express the poetic aspect of this image.

INTERPRETATION 2

I will use a thicker line in a soft manner to be sensible.

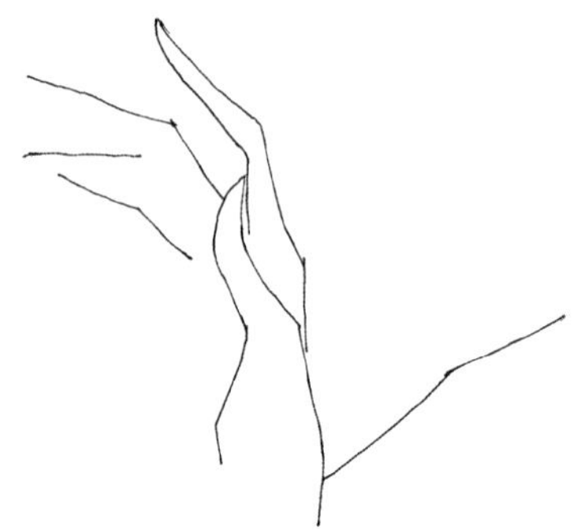

1

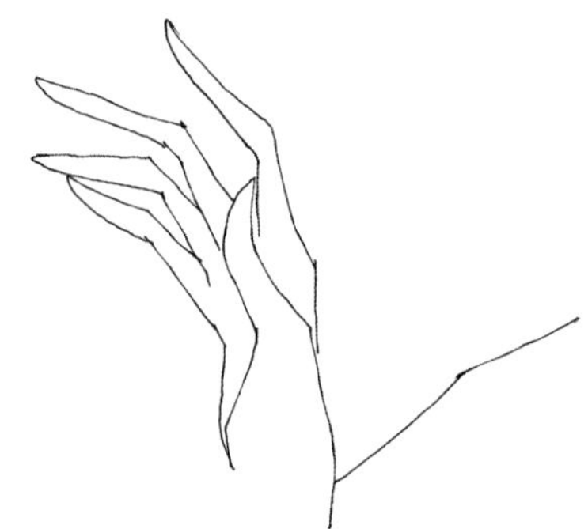

2

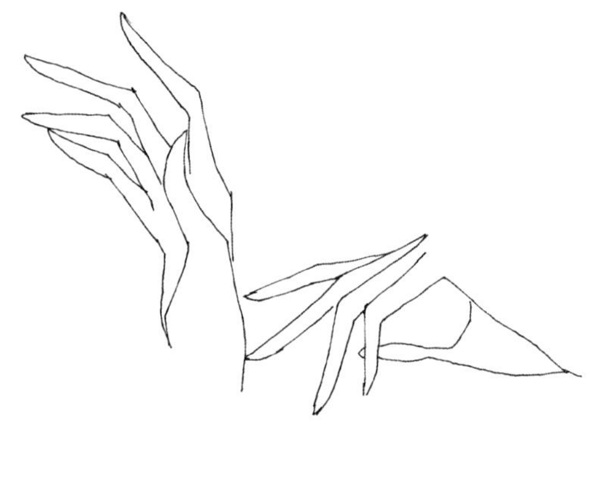

3

4

INTERPRETATION 1

STEPS

1—I start with the index finger, then immediately draw the thumb. A few lines are enough to place the phalanges and express how the fingers seem to dance. Then, I sketch the middle finger that comes to touch the wrist.

2—I can now draw the fingers of this first hand.

3—Like I did for the first hand, I draw the phalanges of each finger of this second hand delicately.

4—I can now draw the fingers of the second hand. The lines of the forearms remain to be extended and taken off the page to anchor the composition.

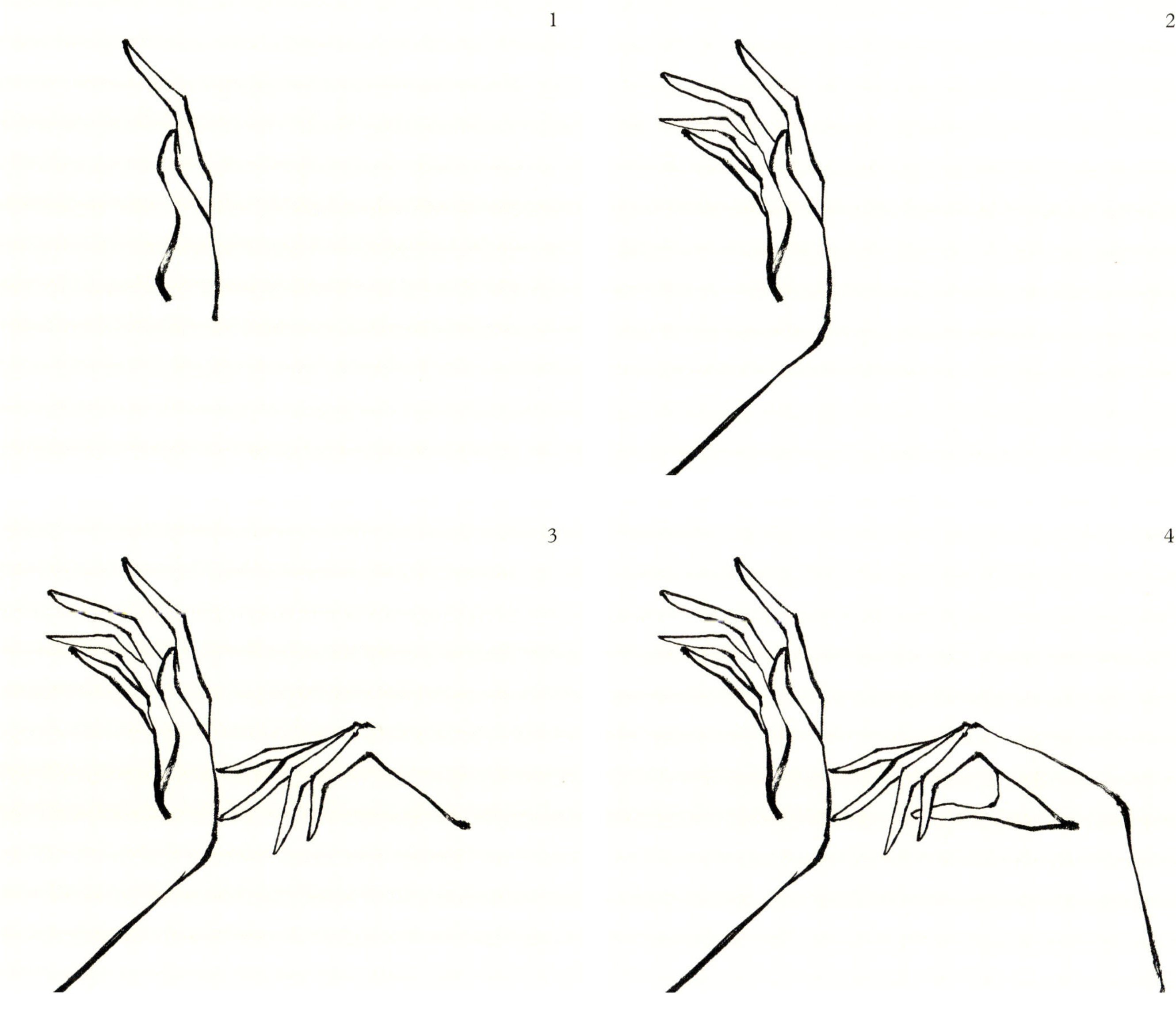

INTERPRETATION 2

STEPS

1—This time, I draw one hand after the other. The first interpretation allows me to draw these hands more confidently, and I draw the first one directly, finger by finger. I start with the thumb, then the index finger

2—I draw the next three fingers almost automatically. I let the brush of my felt pen dance and play with the thickness of its line.

3—For the second hand, I start with the middle finger, which touches the first hand. After the pinky finger, I draw the palm to indicate the position of the thumb behind it.

4—I can more easily draw the thumb as a result. From the beginning of the little finger, all that remains is to draw a line to reveal the wrist, pressing lightly to mark its angle with the forearm.

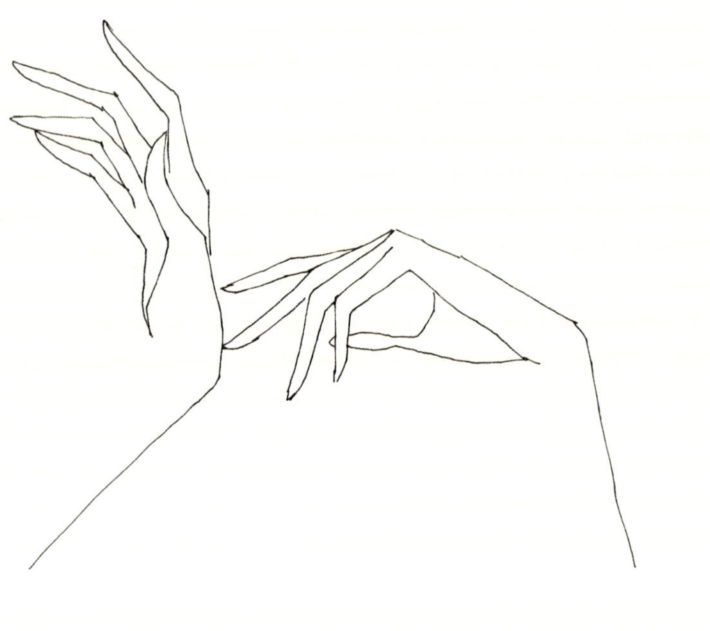

Interpretation 2

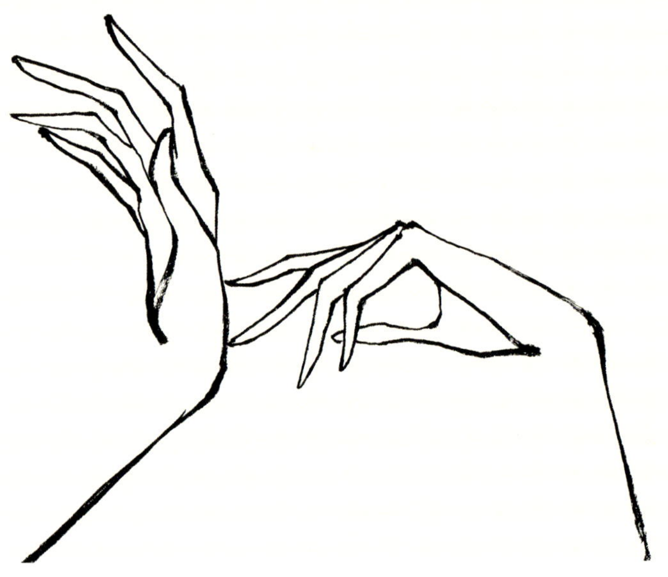

Interpretation 3

I tried using a colored marker for this interpretation, but I feel like the composition would work better if I showed more of the arms to emphasize their graceful, elegant pose.

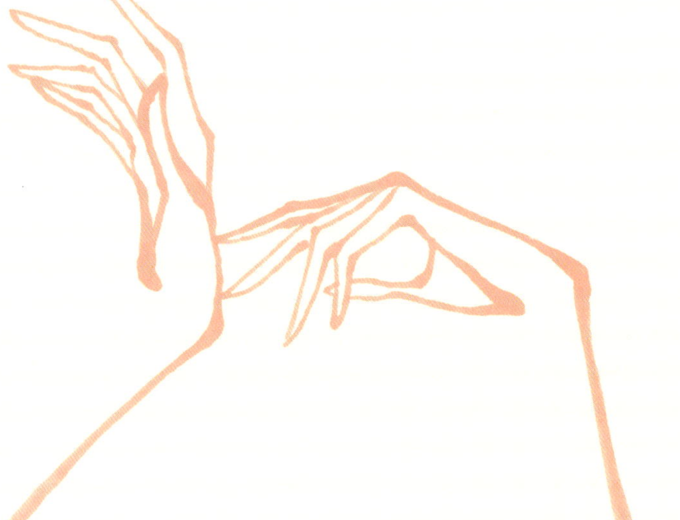

LEGS AND FEET

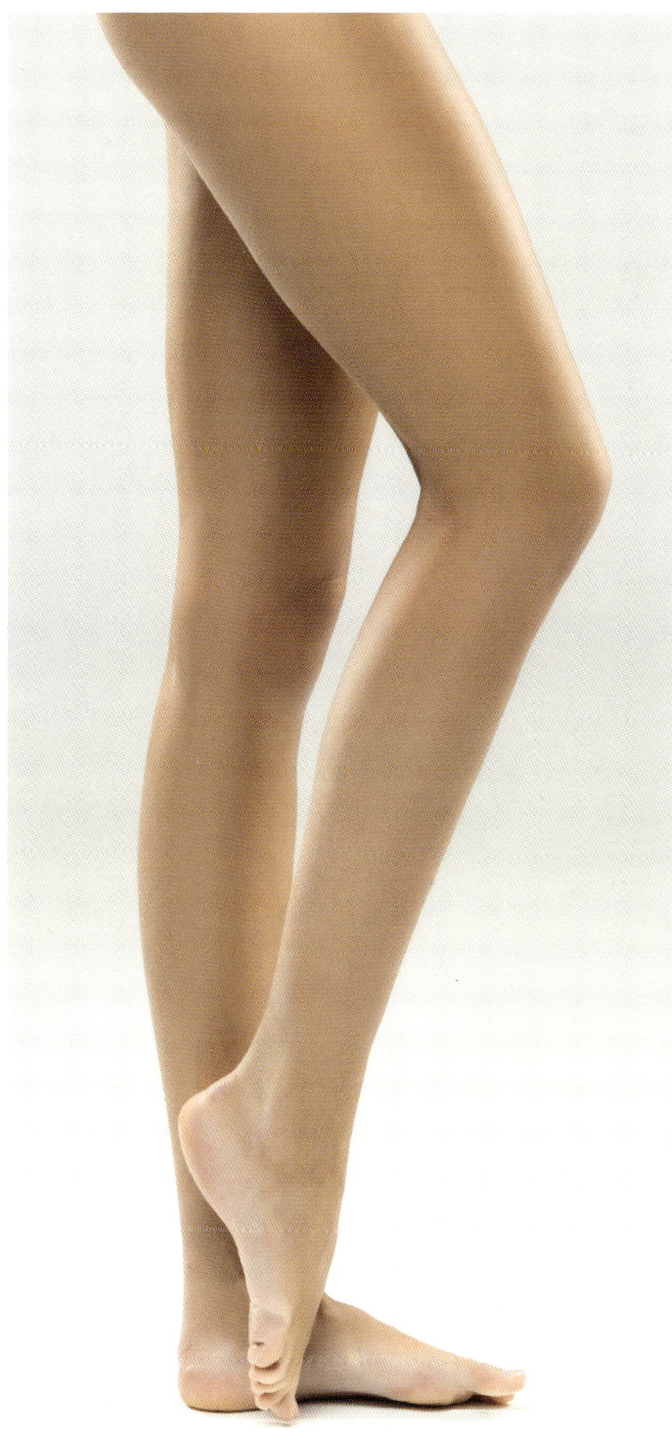

THE IDEA

After hands, the legs are a part of the body I really enjoy drawing. They offer a very broad language, from waiting to running, their link to the ground or their strength to project the body toward the sky. I chose this pose first for its elegance but also for the feet, which are together and have contrasting attitudes. One is anchored to the ground, while the other initiates movement. It could be a dance step or the start of something else.

WHAT I WANT TO EXPRESS

INTERPRETATIONS 1 AND 2

A thin line seems obvious to me for this pose. But I will follow different lines of these legs. This will allow you to see that the same technique can be applied freely.

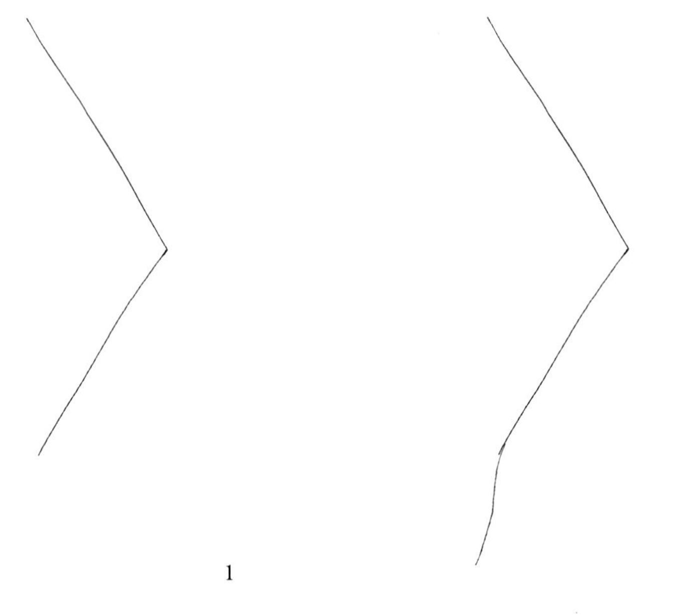

1

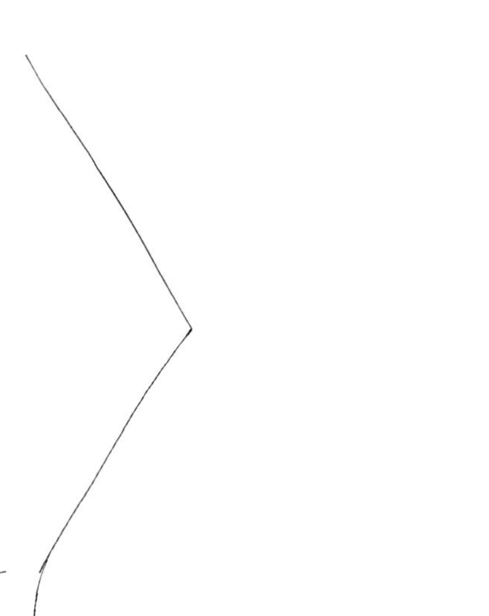

3

4

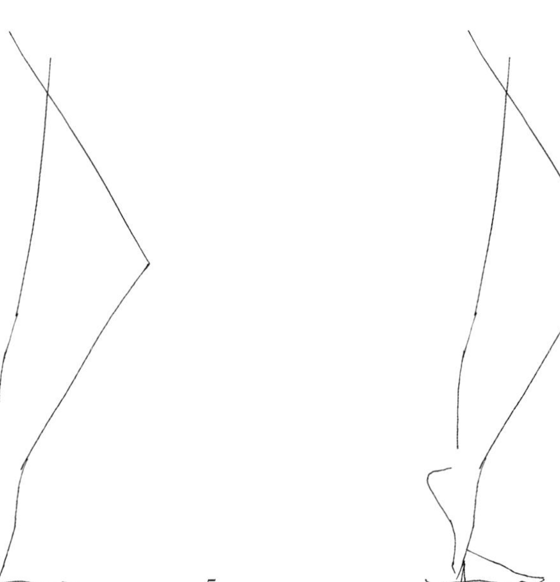

5

6

STEPS

1—I start by focusing on the front leg. The most important thing is to find the right movement and angle between the thigh and the tibia. I recommend starting with the thigh, stopping at the level of the knee, and then moving toward the tibia.

2—Once I arrive at the bottom of the leg, I search for the right movement to mark the curve on top of the foot.

3—Now I have to draw the curve of each foot's arch. The best thing is to start with the heel and continue the line down to reach the tip of the foot.

4—At this point, I create a slightly flowing line for the foot that is resting on the ground.

5—Then, I go back up to the top of the sheet. I draw a line that goes downward, along the hind leg, and lands at the heel.

6—The drawing is almost finished. All that is left is to draw the toes, which can be tricky, so I try to simply suggest them while remaining as accurate as possible. The idea here is to express the emotion of relaxation that comes from this pose. The final drawing should be both restful and dynamic.

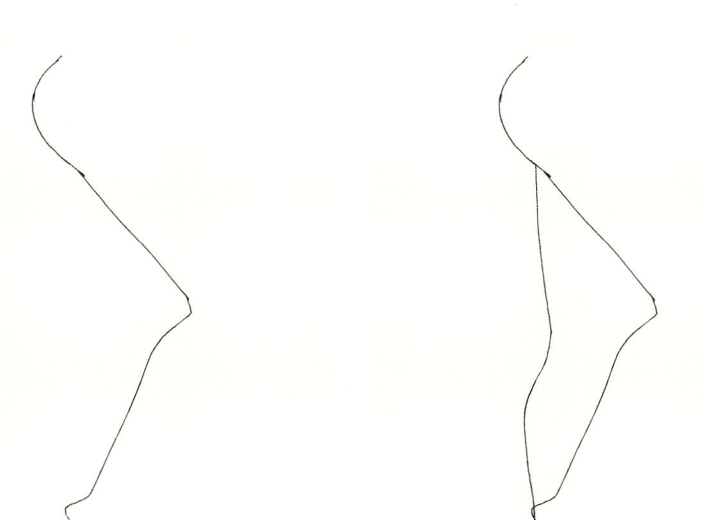

1

2

3

4

5

6

STEPS

1—This time, I start with the curve of the buttocks and keep going down to the thigh, stopping at the fold of the knee.

2—I go back along the calf, draw its curve, and proceed to draw the heel of the first foot.

3—Immediately, I continue with the curve of the arch of the foot all the way to the small toe.

4—I return to the back of the other leg and quickly bring my line down all the way to the ground.

5—Like I did previously, I try to find the right line for the arch of the foot on the ground. I could stop there. The lines seem sufficient to me.

6—I realize I could still add the toes, so I do that. Finally, I go on top of the foot to even out the drawing.

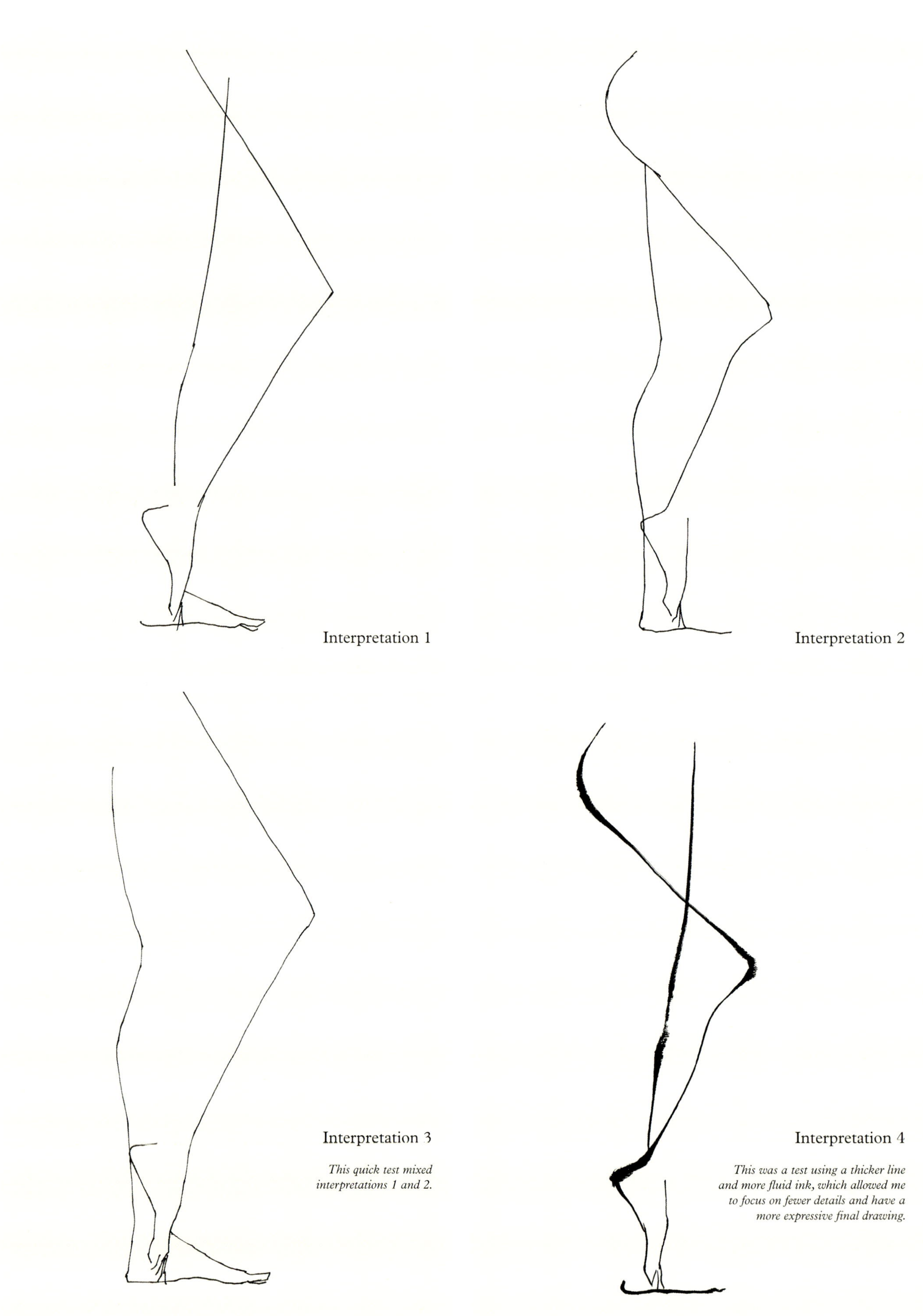

Interpretation 1

Interpretation 2

Interpretation 3

This quick test mixed interpretations 1 and 2.

Interpretation 4

This was a test using a thicker line and more fluid ink, which allowed me to focus on fewer details and have a more expressive final drawing.

FLOWERS

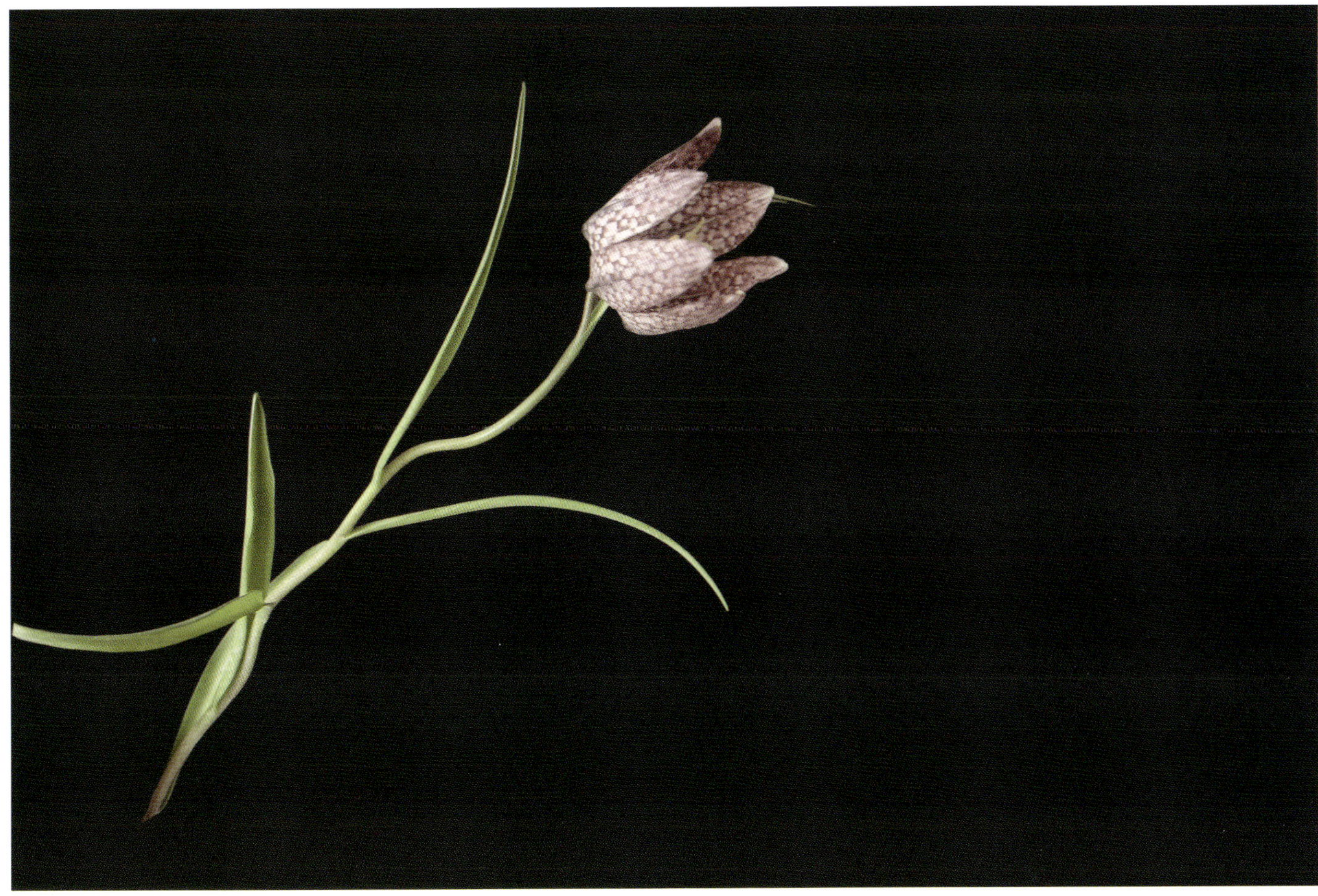

THE IDEA

Flowers have always been a source of inspiration to me, for both their shapes and movements. Nature offers free and constantly renewed sculptures. I am always fascinated by the work of great photographers like Robert Mapplethorpe or Nick Knight on this eternal subject. It is also always difficult for me to find the right expression that suits each of them, whether the flowers are alone or in a bouquet. Here is a photo that I took without pretension. It was the movement of the stem and the small flower that I am going to attempt to interpret.

WHAT I WANT TO EXPRESS

INTERPRETATION 1

I will use colored markers for the first attempt, working with very saturated inks on fine paper. I will take advantage of the thicknesses of the brushes to create the best composition.

INTERPRETATION 2

This very fragile flower also seems interesting to interpret in a more sensitive way, with a finer and more expressive line.

STEPS

1—I start by creating a petal on the left, using a single stroke. It seems simple, but this initial line will dictate the entire composition. Always imagine the finished drawing in your head before you start. In that way, half of the work is already accomplished. I add two other petals, both delicately and expressively by using the brush to play with the volumes and shadows of the petals. I can already begin to guess where the flower's leaves will land.

2—I go back over my previous lines to suggest a detail with fine brushstrokes.

3—I finish the shape of the flower, ending with its base. I ripple the pressure on the marker's tip.

4—I switch to the green marker and start the base of the flower by mixing the two colored inks. I then continue the line downward, undulating my gesture and marking the point where the two leaves will intersect.

5—With the marker, I make a swift bend and continue the line gently upward while pressing harder on the marker's tip to express the volume of the sheet.

6—I begin another line slightly further and pass over the stem to cross it and place the second leaf. The other leaves do not seem important or interesting to me in finishing this composition, so I decide to stop the drawing here.

STEPS

1—I begin, like last time, by drawing the first two petals that will act as the base of our flower.

2—I try to imagine the space that the next lines will take up on the page. I make a small petal to interrupt the rounded shape of the first two and give the flower more personality.

3—I then continue drawing the other petals in the same logic, alternating between round, soft, and pointy shapes.

4—Starting at the base of the flower, I draw the line of the wavy stem, keeping in mind where I imagine I will place the two leaves.

5—I start tracing the first leaf by cutting through the stem and leveling with the flower on the sheet of paper.

6—I start from a higher point for this second leaf, but for this one I double the line to create a slight volume.

1

2

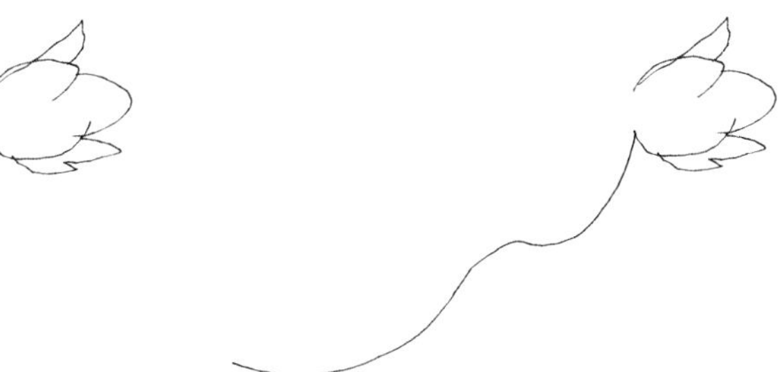

3

4

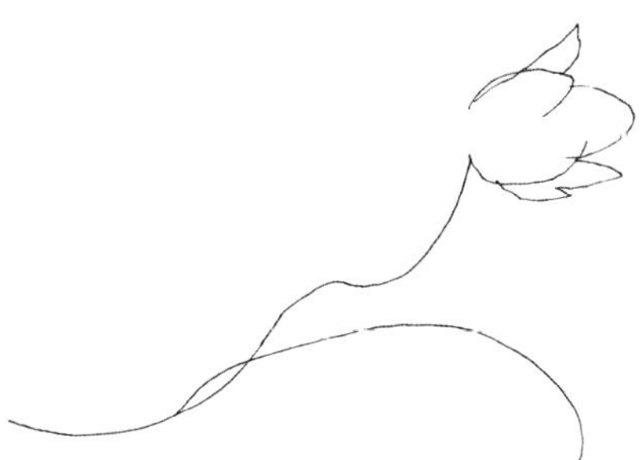

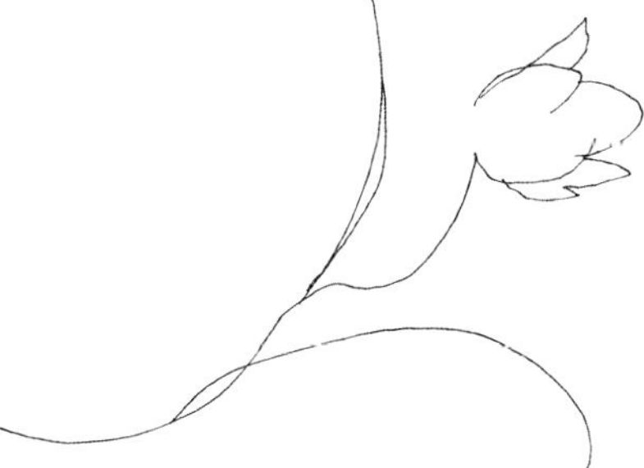

5

6

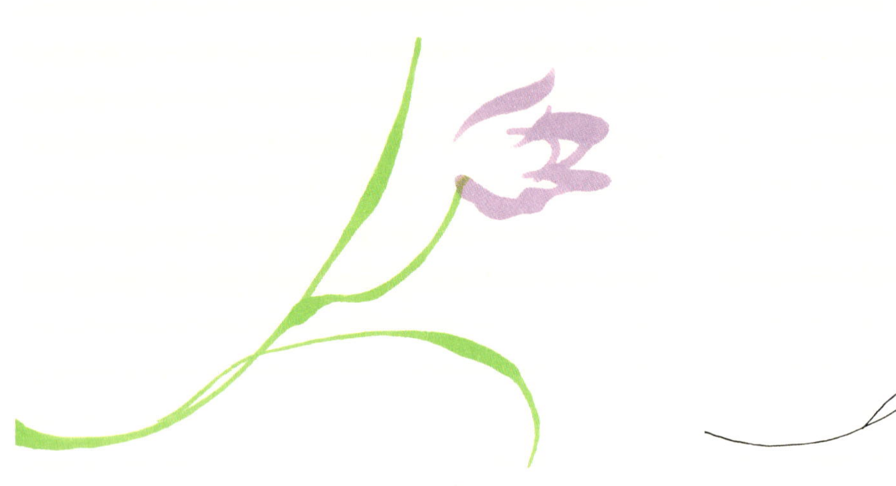

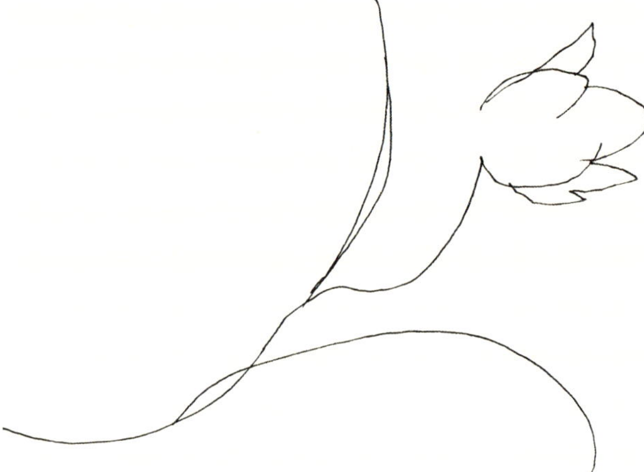

Interpretation 1

Interpretation 2

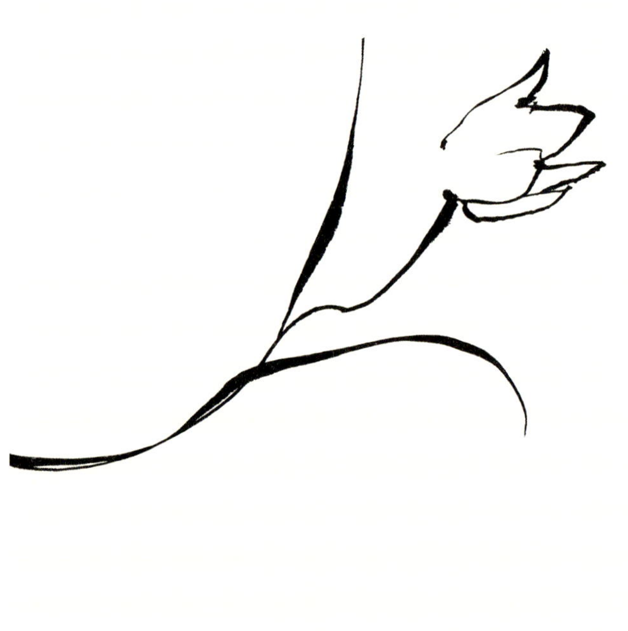

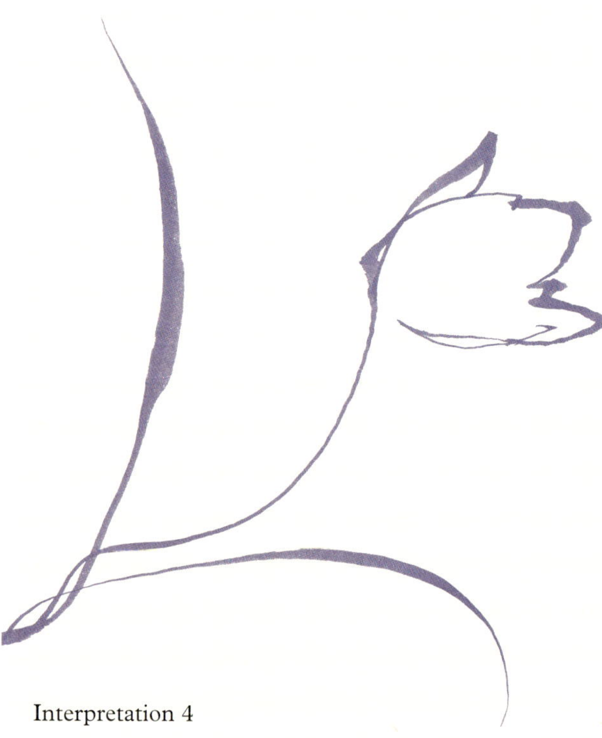

Interpretation 3

Interpretation 4

This was a test I made using a thicker black stroke. With this technique, the leaves become the focus of the drawing.

Using a colored marker, I attempted a cropped version of the same composition.

STILL LIFES

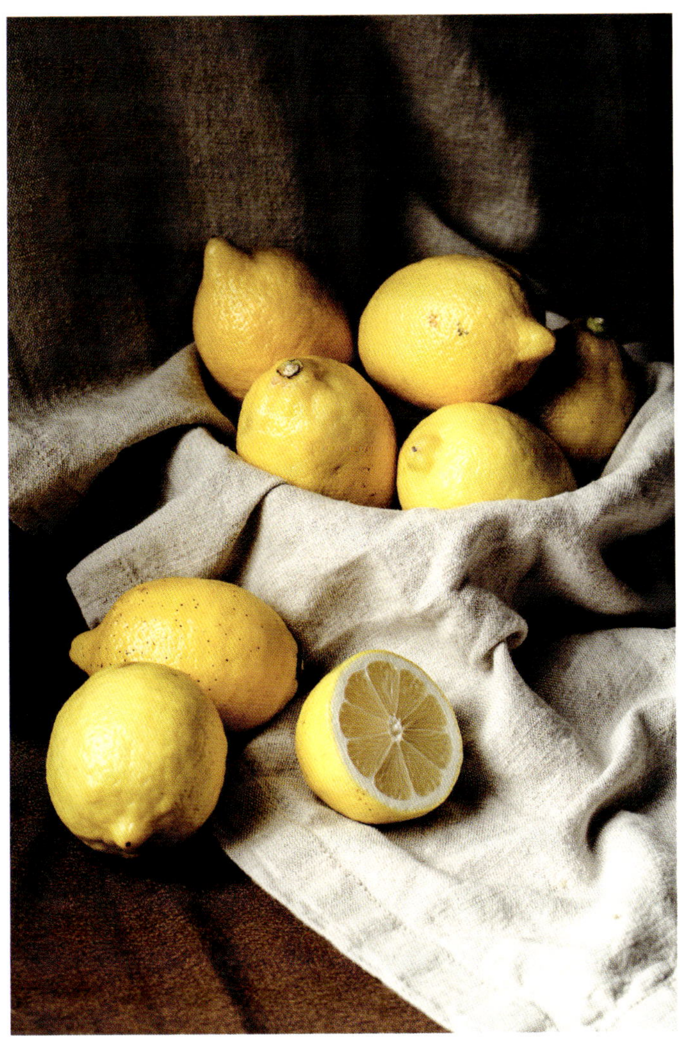

THE IDEA

Drawing still lifes is an exercise I do very little despite the fact that I really like this subject. I am fascinated by artists such as Henri Matisse or Giorgio Morandi, who manage to make these small harmless scenes into sensitive artworks. I chose this image for its graphic rhythm and its soft staging, which feels natural and not too posed.

WHAT I WANT TO EXPRESS

INTERPRETATION 1

It seems obvious to create a colored piece for this composition. I will reduce this approach to the yellow of the lemons and a nude color to express the shadows.

INTERPRETATION 2

I will use a very thin line to see how it will flow in the overall composition.

STEPS

1—I start with the lemons that are in the basket. I vary the pressure I place on the tip of the marker to obtain a nice rhythm throughout the drawing. The lemon with the thinnest line takes in slightly more light. I do the second with a thicker line because it is placed more in the shade.

2—I maintain the same pressure to draw the other two lemons with similar line qualities. I do not finish the fourth lemon to leave room for the possibility of another line.

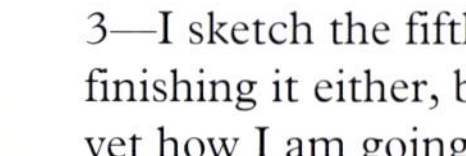

1

2

3—I sketch the fifth lemon without finishing it either, because I don't know yet how I am going to draw the basket that contains the lemons I have just drawn.

4—I deport my hand down slowly and sketch the three lemons with a softer line, thus rendering them in a more graphic style. I decide to draw almost entirely the second lemon even though it is hidden in the image.

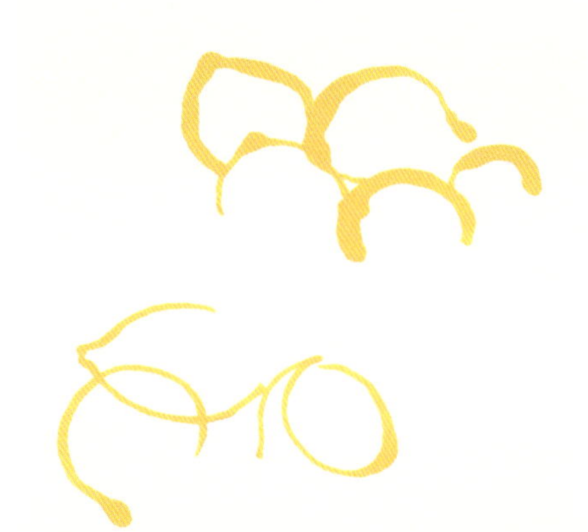

3

4

5—I pick up the nude-colored marker, which seems both softer in tone yet slightly stronger in presence than the yellow I just used. I trace the edge of the basket starting with the left side, applying stronger pressure on the tip of the pen. Then I make a very thin arc to keep the importance of the lemons in the composition.

6—Now, I draw the shadows of the lemons that are placed in front with a thicker line. This allows me to have a contrast between the yellow lines and the nude-colored ones, which creates a complementary optical effect.

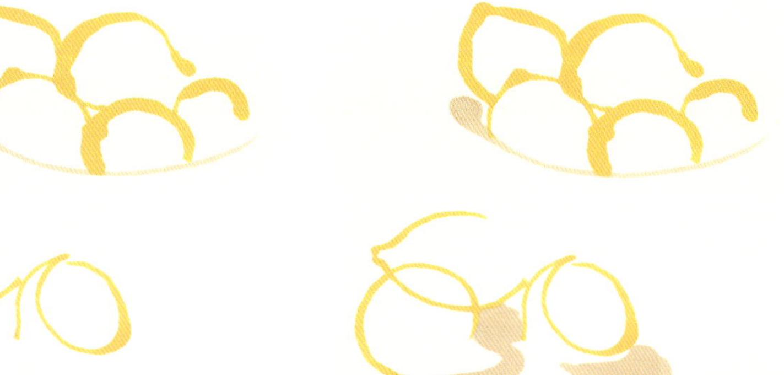

5

6

STEPS

1—Like I did with the previous inter-pretation, I begin by sketching the first two lemons in the basket. The one in the foreground first with a soft and sensitive line to express the shape of the lemons to its fullest.

2—I then place a third lemon by adding a simple half-circle that I keep open on the end. I'll see later if I want to draw the tip of the lemon or not.

3—To finish the fruits in this basket, I trace the fourth small lemon. I'm not looking to be consistent in terms of the fruits' volumes. On the contrary, they must be varied more or less noticeably so that the composition seems as natural as possible. Remember, perfection is not our goal!

4—I now move to the other lemons located a bit lower, outside the basket. I start with the one in the foreground by making a slightly awkward circular shape before adding the lemon behind it, placed on its side.

5—For the third lemon of that group, I start with the part that rests on the table-cloth, showing that it is cut with a single line. This last lemon makes it possible not to repeat the closed shapes of the fruits.

6—All that remains is to sketch with one line the edge that covers the basket. I don't finish the line and stop before I go full circle. This is both to lighten the drawing and to be coherent with the composition.

1

2

3

4

5

6

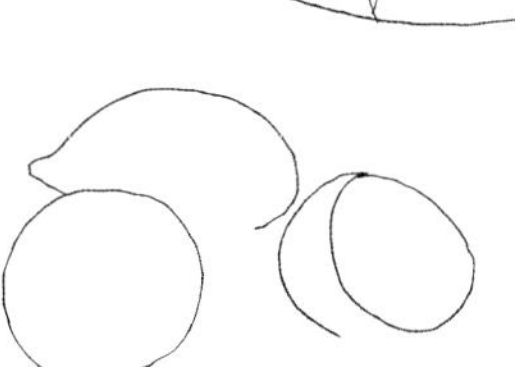

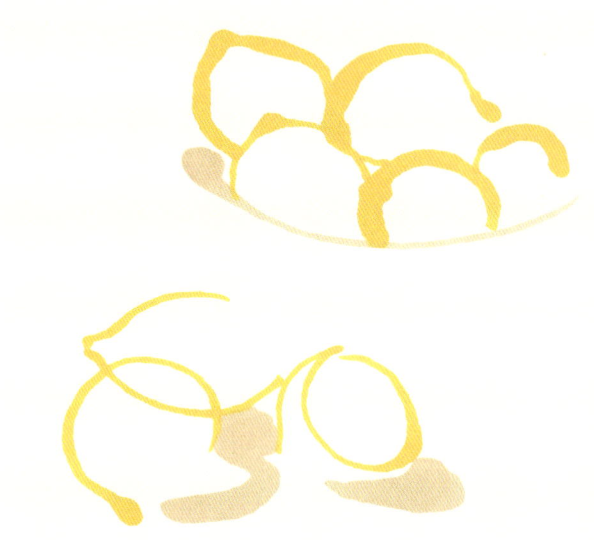

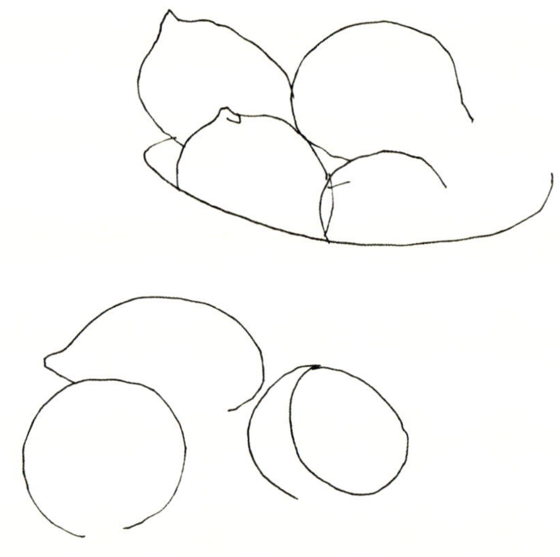

Interpretation 1   Interpretation 2

Interpretation 3

Here, I used a thicker and stronger line to be more expressive.

Interpretation 4

In this drawing, I started with the composition of interpretation 3, but I decided to add leaves to the lemons. They are not pictured in the reference image, but I wanted to see how the final piece would look if I added them in. It feels more organic to me.

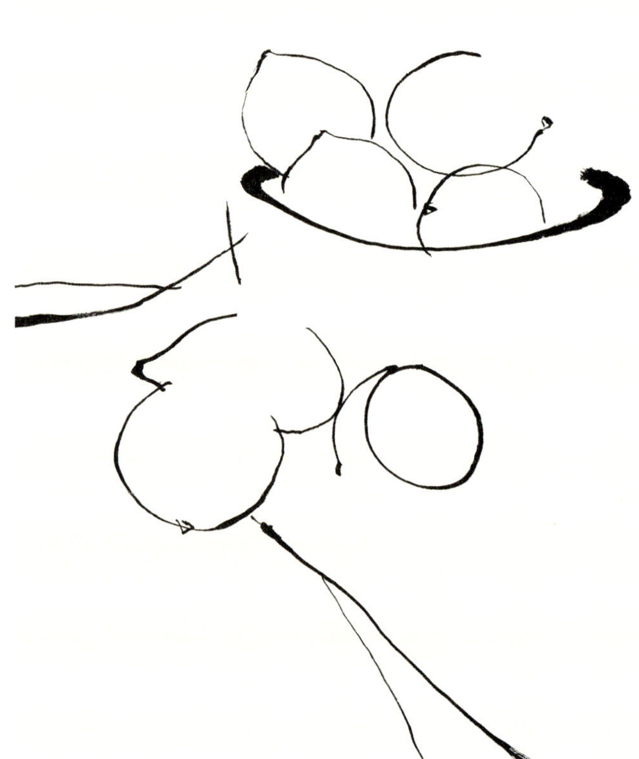

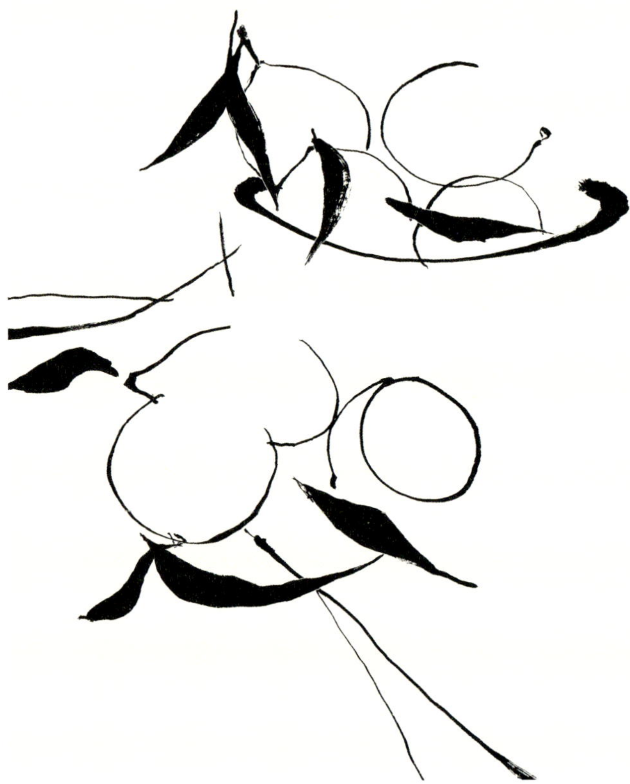

LANDSCAPES

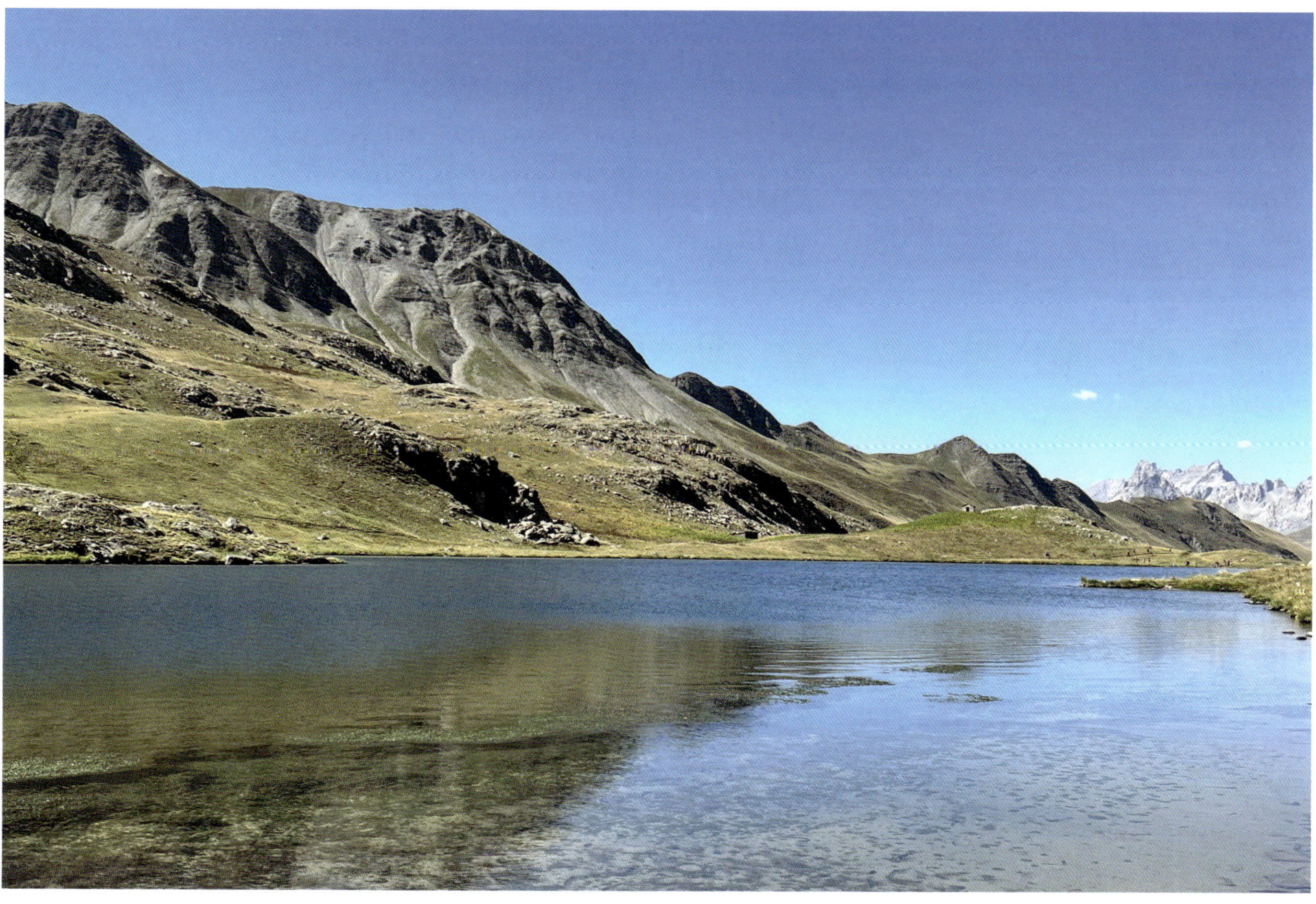

THE IDEA

I shot this particular photo with my iPhone during my summer vacation. Make sure to save any images you enjoy to an album on your phone or computer so that you can easily access them when deciding to create a drawing.

WHAT I WANT TO EXPRESS

INTERPRETATION 1

I will try to convey how the mountain becomes one with its reflection in the lake, with varying intensity. I will highlight the contrast between these two elements by using two different colors as well as two varying techniques of line art. I will keep the lines that express the water similar in style.

INTERPRETATION 2

I will attempt to vary the thickness of the lines depicting the lake's water to see if it is more effective.

STEPS

1—Using a soft-tip green marker, I start at the top left and work my way down. The best thing to do here is to lightly push down on the tip of the brush to convey the beginning and then progressively release the pressure to let the relief of the mountain take shape.

2—I progressively draw the mountain ridge going down and across the sheet of paper while continuing to vary the thickness of my line according to your own sensitivity.

3—I repeat the above steps by adding a second line outlining the mountain in the background. Here, I subtly add a third slightly thicker line to give the feeling that there is something larger and grander in the back.

4—Using the soft-tip blue marker. I begin with a line that feels like the lake's shore. I use shorter lines to adjust the length of the next parallel lines. I could also place a shorter one above if my first line feels like it is too low in my composition.

5—I continue tracing my lines as evenly as possible. They will naturally vary with the sensitivity of the brush and my hand. This is what will give the slight variations that will ultimately make my drawing more interesting and appealing.

6—I add a new series of intermediate lines that follow one another but create a different form. This will vary the intensity of the blue and the reflection of the mountains.

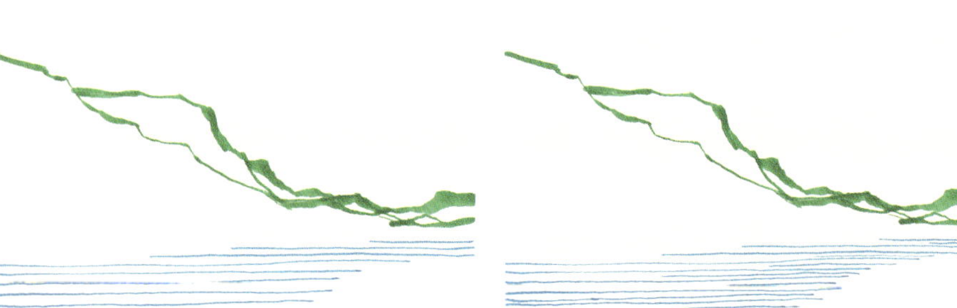

1

2

3

4

5

6

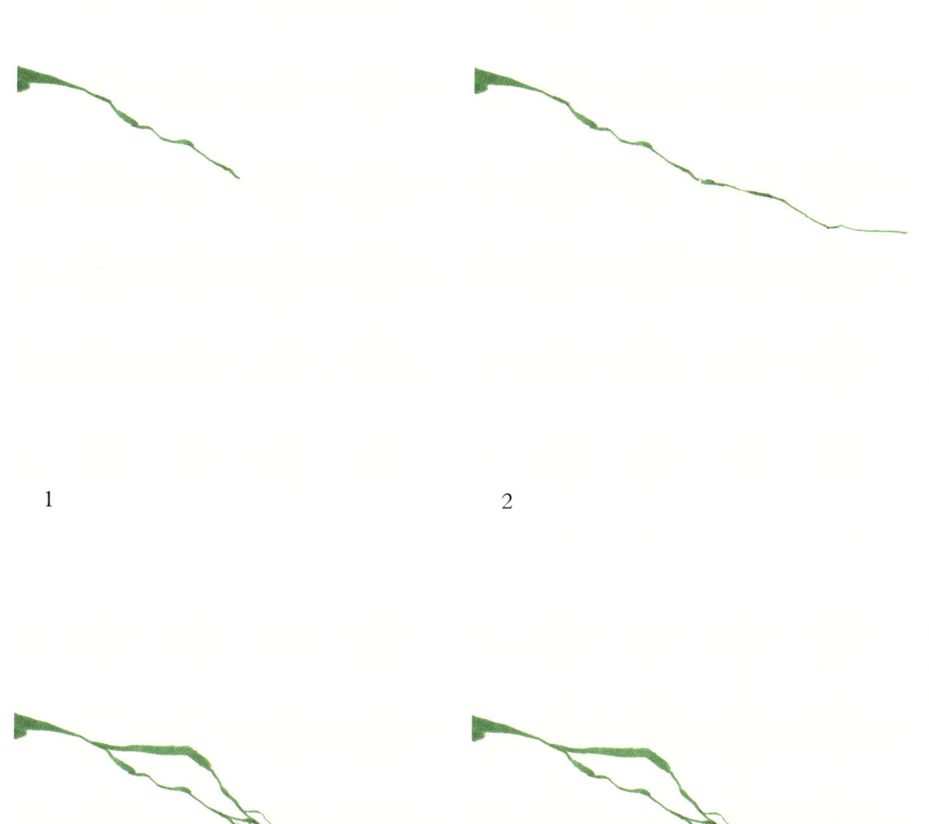

STEPS

1—Working with a soft-tip green marker, I begin my line at the top left of the sheet as I work across and down. The best thing to do here is to lightly push down on the tip of the brush to convey the beginning and then progressively release the pressure to let the relief of the mountain take shape.

2—I progressively draw the mountain ridge going down and across the sheet of paper while continuing to vary the thickness of my line.

3—I repeat the above steps by adding a second line outlining the mountain in the background. Here, I subtly add a third slightly thicker line to give the feeling that there is something larger and grander in the back.

4—Using the soft-tip blue marker, I begin with a line that feels like the lake's shore. I use shorter lines to adjust the length of the next parallel lines. I could also place a shorter one above if my first line feels like it is too low in my composition.

5—I continue tracing my lines as evenly as possible. They will naturally vary with the sensitivity of the brush and my hand. This is what will give the slight variations that will ultimately make the drawing more interesting and appealing.

6—I Add a new series of thicker lines that follow one another but create a different form. This will vary the intensity of the blue and the reflection of the mountains.

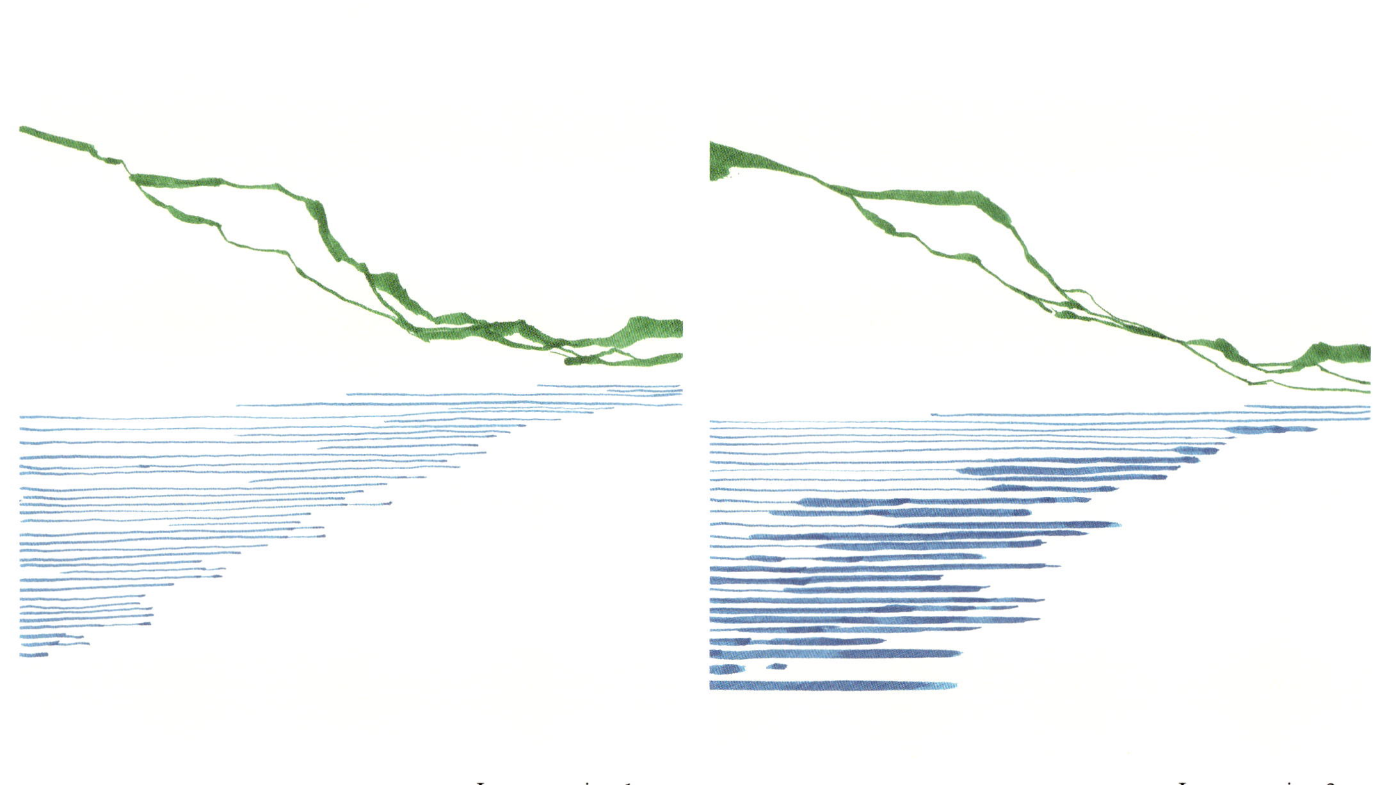

Interpretation 1   Interpretation 2

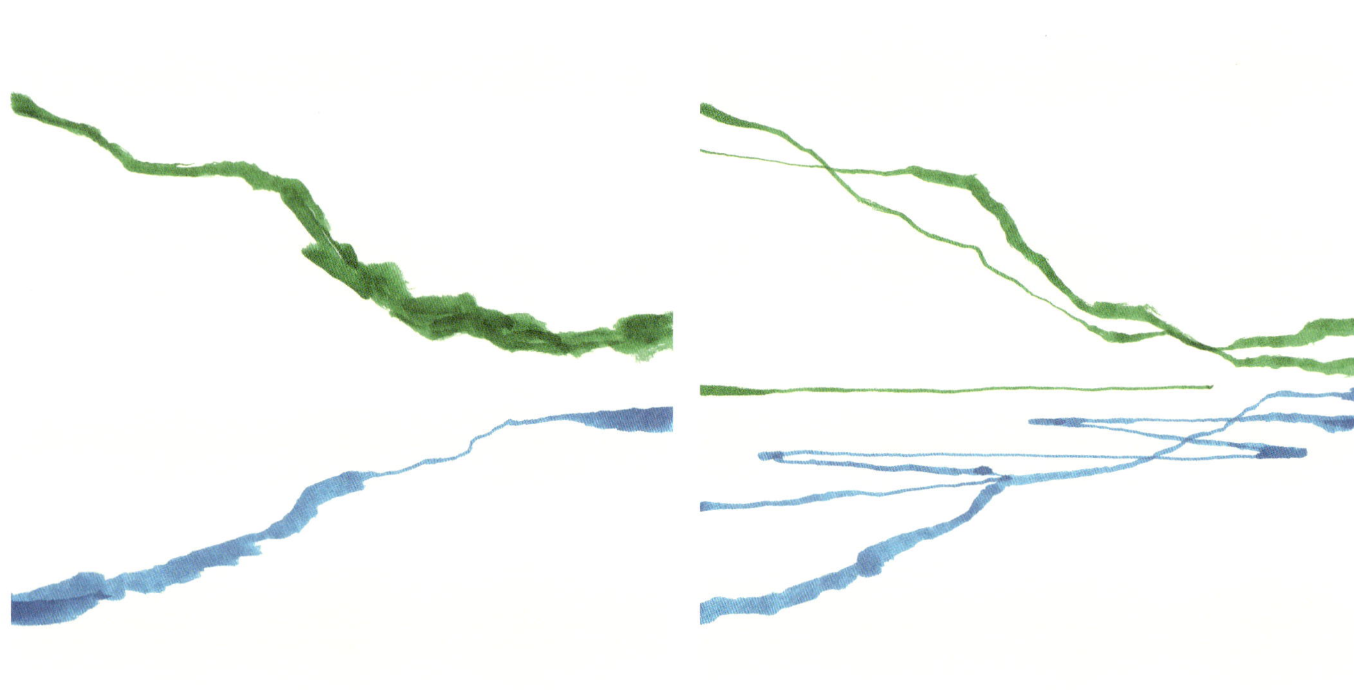

Interpretation 3   Interpretation 4

Here, I tried to use only two colored lines,
but the rendering was not legible enough.

Here, I tried using multiple colored lines, but
I found the final result to be too busy and abstract.

CATS

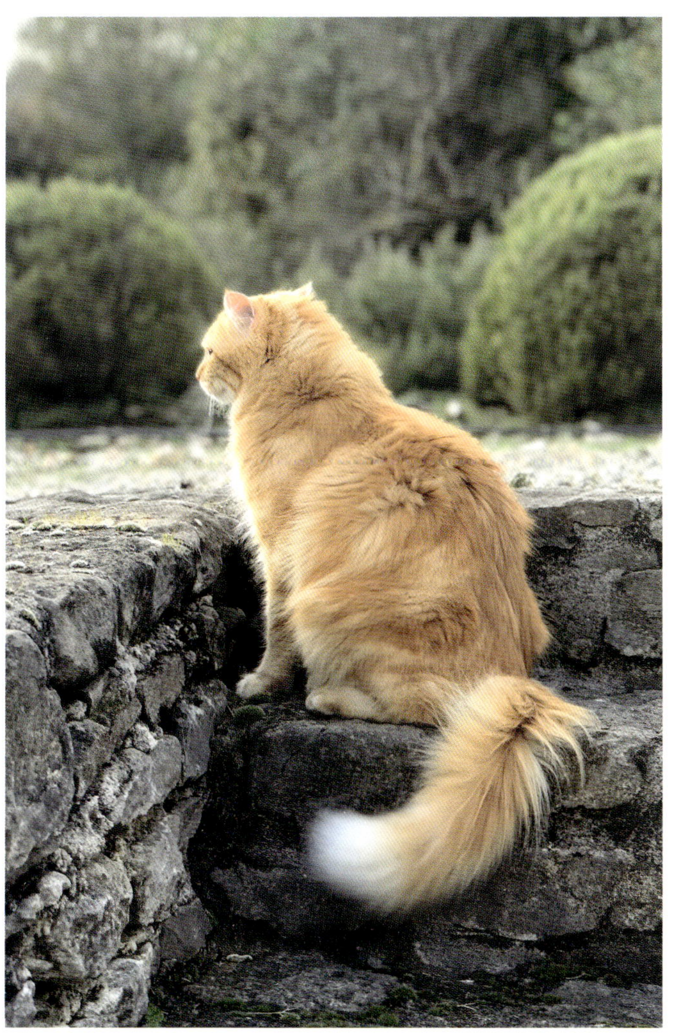

THE IDEA

I've never personally had a cat, but I come a family where cats have and are still quite present, meaning they do play a role in my life as well. This particular cat is not mine. It is one of the many cats that belong to the family of my agent Athina Perrin, who manages Cura, the agency that represents me as an artist. She says she doesn't play favorites, but I know this is her little protégé!

WHAT I WANT TO EXPRESS

INTERPRETATION 1

A swift, orange line seems like an obvious fit to me to capture this pose. The most difficult aspect will be to render the cat's fur and gaze that, we can only assume, is quite piercing.

INTERPRETATION 2

I will use a similar approach, but with a black brush-pen. This will force me to slightly modify more or less the shapes and lengths of the lines that will make up the drawing.

STEPS

1—I begin the drawing as if it were a portrait, placing the eye first on the page. Then, I very slowly make my way to the cat's muzzle and continue to mark his chin. I very lightly draw the lobe of his ear.

2—I continue with the top of his head, to his neck, marking the thickness of his fur with a thicker hairline, which creates a fairly soft dynamic.

1

2

3—I then sketch his second ear. It seems easy, but it indicates precisely the orientation of his head, so it's okay if it takes a couple tries to reach the correct position.

4—I resume my line from the fold of his neck. I quickly move down his back until I reach the bottom of his tail.

3

4

5—Then, I move away slightly to start the curve of his tail, keeping almost the same finesse of line that I used for the end of his back. With a quick gesture, I trace the movement of his tail, ending it with a thicker tip to signify the movement of his fur. I could stop there.

6—I decide to add the front leg to ground the cat on the page. I start at the top and go down marking his shoulder. Then, using a thinner line, I give direction to the leg and end with a slightly thicker line for his paw.

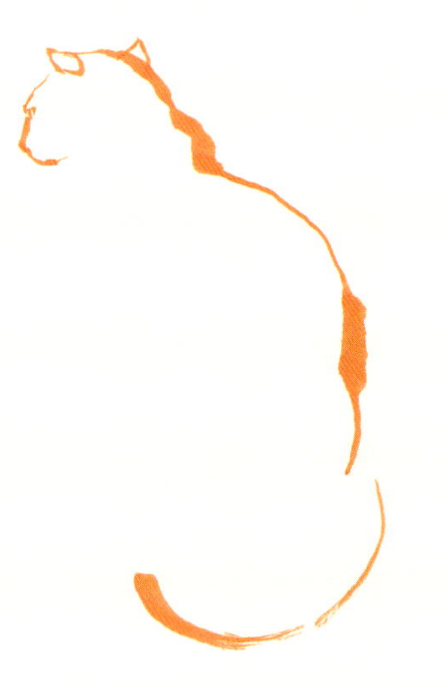

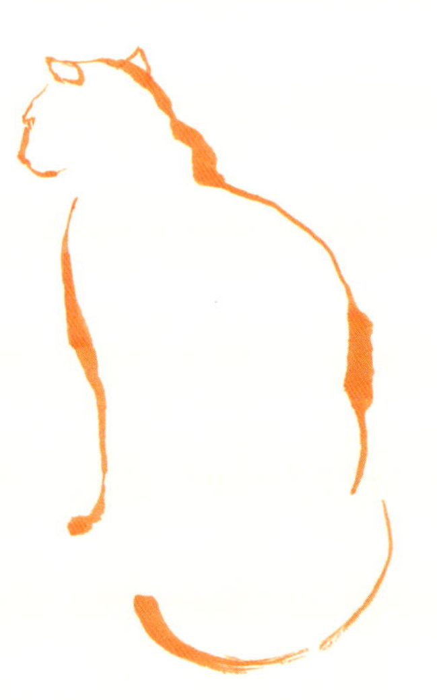

5

6

STEPS

1—Similarly to the first drawing, I begin by drawing his eye, then his muzzle, and finally his ear.

2—This time, I place the tip of his second ear first, which helps me draw the top of his head down to his neck.

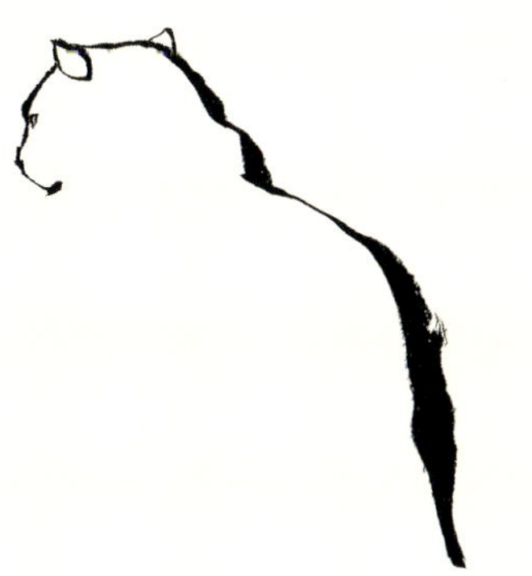

1

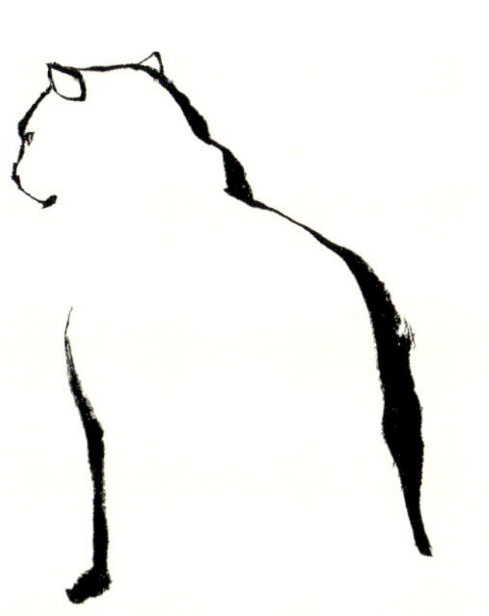

2

3—I draw an almost continuous line from the curve of his back to the bottom of his silhouette.

4—I don't draw the tail right away, and I sketch the front leg differently with a shorter yet thicker line ending with its leg.

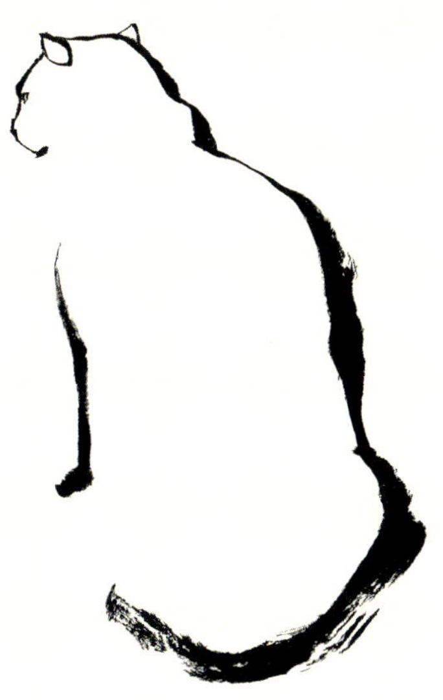

3

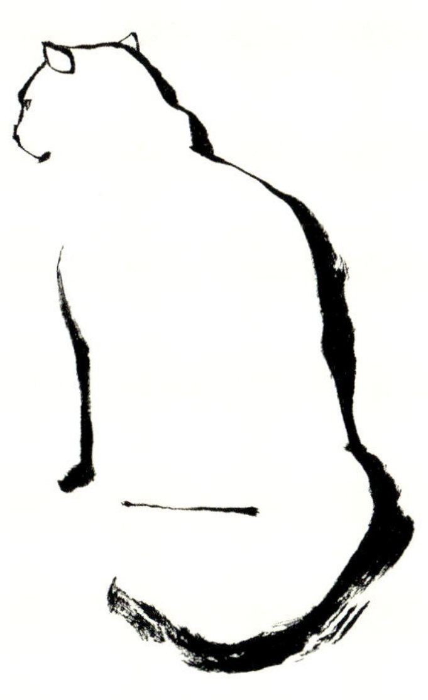

4

5—I then draw his tail with a faster, almost wild line, pushing the thickness of the brush to the maximum to obtain a brushed effect that I find interesting in rendering the movement of his fur.

6—I add a thin line for the hind leg, thus finishing the drawing. I prefer the drawing without this last line!

5

6

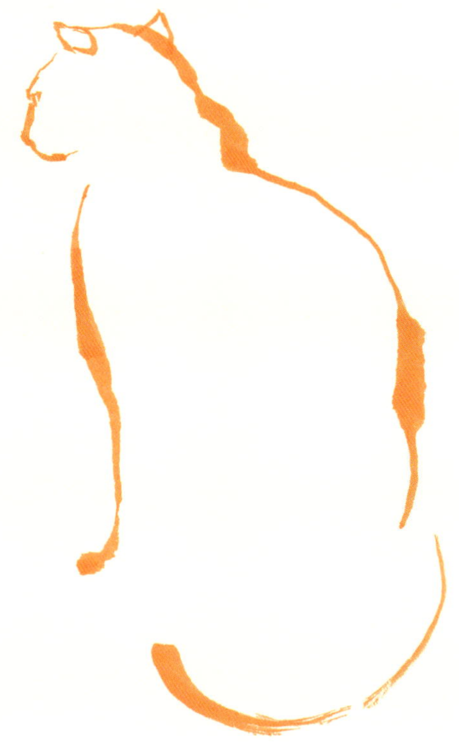

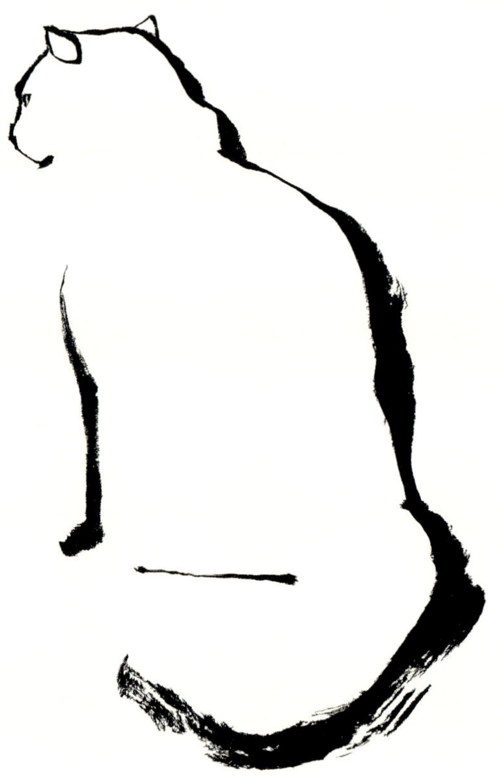

Interpretation 1

Interpretation 2

Interpretation 3

Interpretation 4

I tried using a fine line but found the final result less interesting and we lose the information of the cat's fur.

Here, I tried imagining the same pose from a different angle.

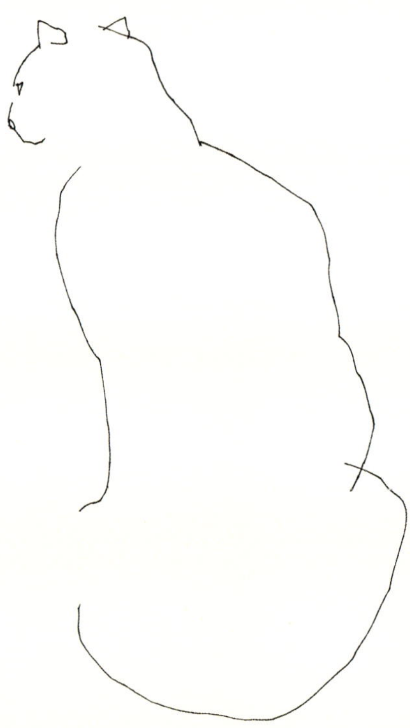

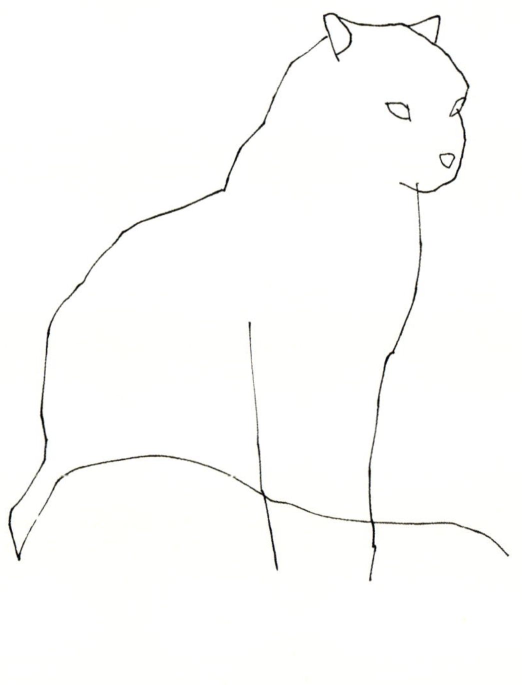

HORSES

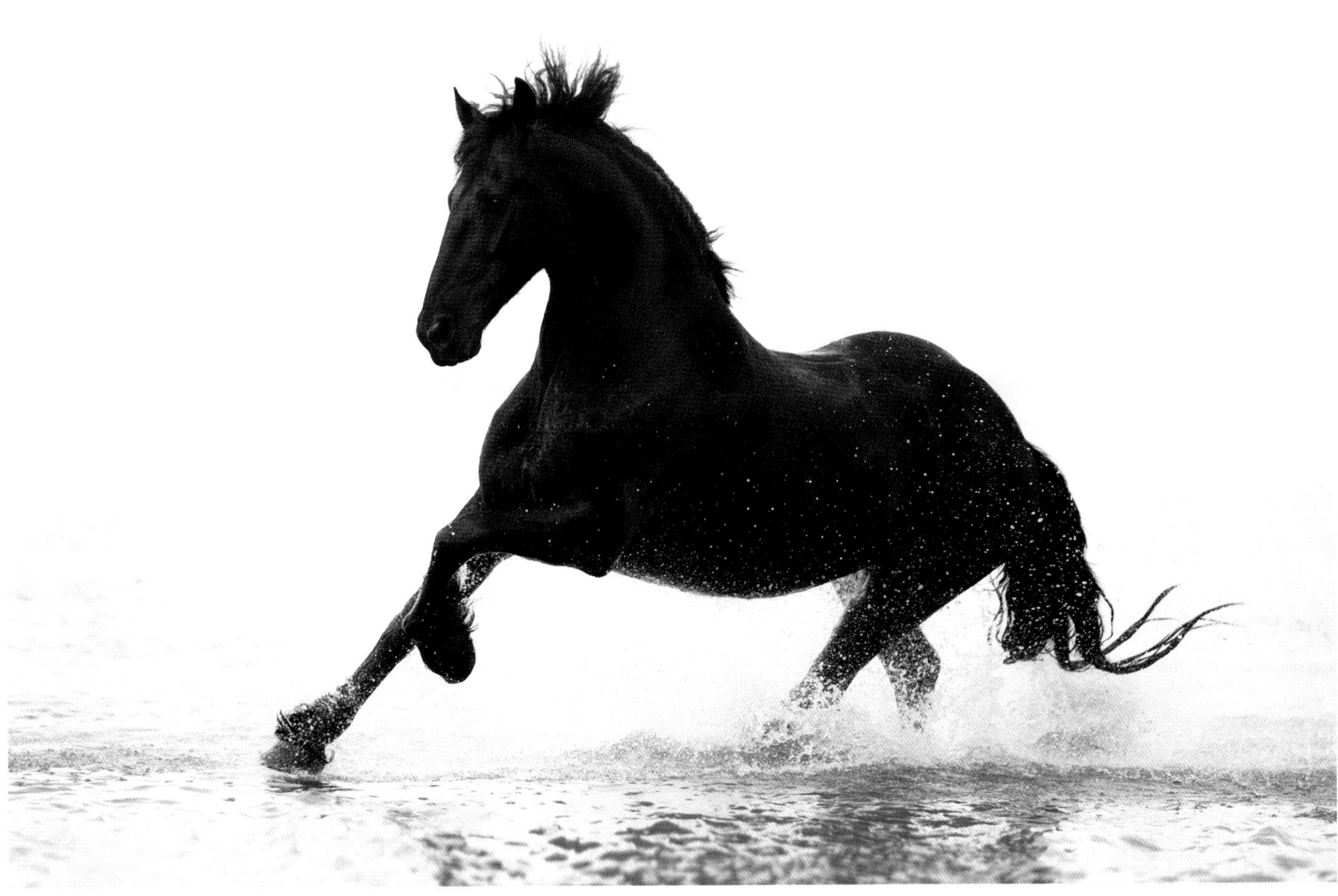

THE IDEA

I am not a rider, but I like to draw horses. Their grace and power fascinate me. The image that almost immediately comes to mind is that of my wife galloping on a vast beach in the Finistère in Brittany, France. When I came across this image, that memory came back to me quite vividly!

The horse is, to me, a difficult animal to draw. If the horse is not well drawn, it will very quickly resemble another animal, vaguely a dog or a donkey. After drawing this animal several times, you will see that your attention will be focused on the head, the ears, and the placement of the eyes. The musculature comes next. The legs must appear to dance, and the tail should energize the silhouette.

WHAT I WANT TO EXPRESS

INTERPRETATION 1

I will focus on the horse in its entirety. The pose will force me to use a horizontal format.

INTERPRETATION 2

I will focus on the front part of the horse.

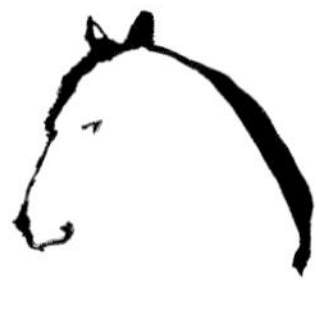

1

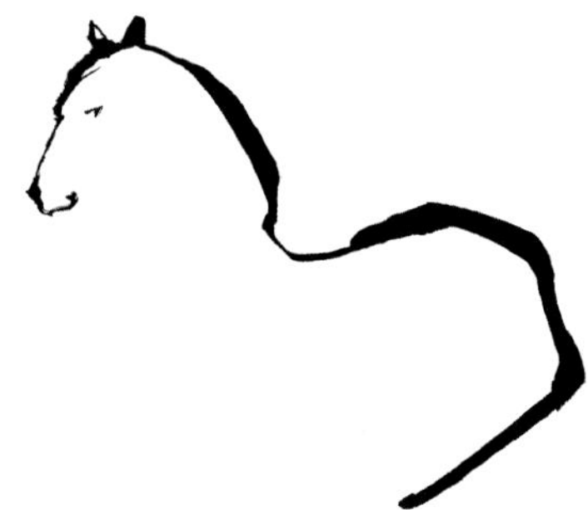

2

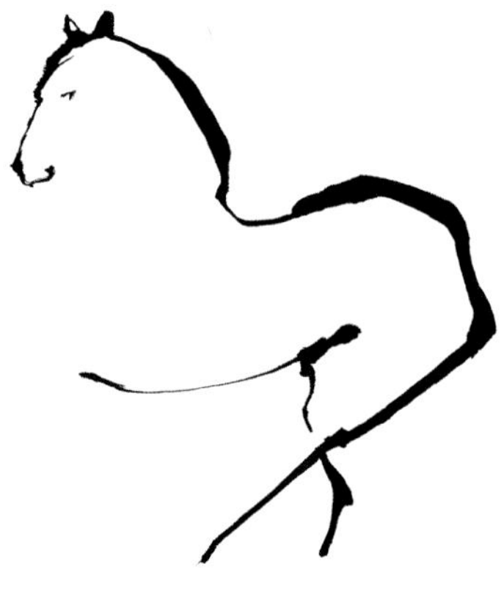

3

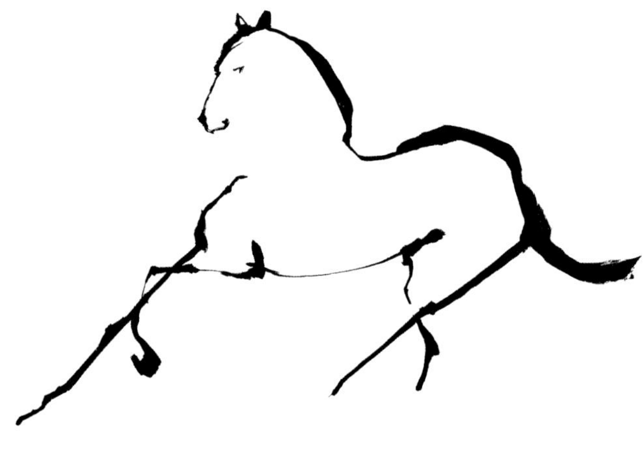

4

INTERPRETATION 1

STEPS

1—I start with the part that seems to me the most difficult and technical: the head. I draw the muzzle, then the nostrils. Then, I go up to the ears, barely drawing them, as if I were only marking their location. Then I continue with the eyes, the trickiest thing to do because if you get the wrong placement or shape, it will be very difficult for the figure to look like a horse. I make a dot, decide if that dot is on the top of the animal's eye or somewhere else, then score the continuation.

2—Then I let my line run over the withers, back, and croup. Once I do that, the horse is starting to take shape. It should feel like you could saddle up and go!

3—I continue the left hind leg to the ground, then draw the curve of the belly moving forward. Then I sketch the horse's right hind leg by lifting the line to hint at the thickness of the other hind leg.

4—I proceed with the outline of the horse by drawing the front legs. I begin with the bent left foreleg, then the right foreleg, which should appear to be outstretched. The tail is now all that remains. I draw it from the rump by dropping the line and then going back up. It is necessary to express the rebound of the hind legs and the energy of the horse.

STEPS

1—For this second drawing, I also begin with the head, but this time I place it in the center of a vertical page. I start with the ears first, then proceed to outline the mouth.

2—I keep the line going to sketch the chin. From there, I begin to draw the neck, all the way down to the horse's shoulder. I go back to the mouth and sketch the nasal passages. I leave them like this so that I can go back and reinforce them later if necessary.

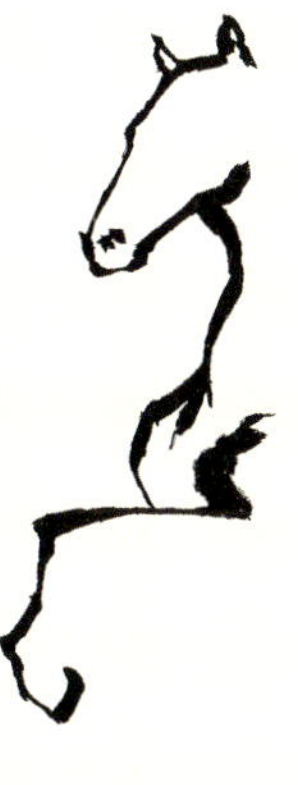

1

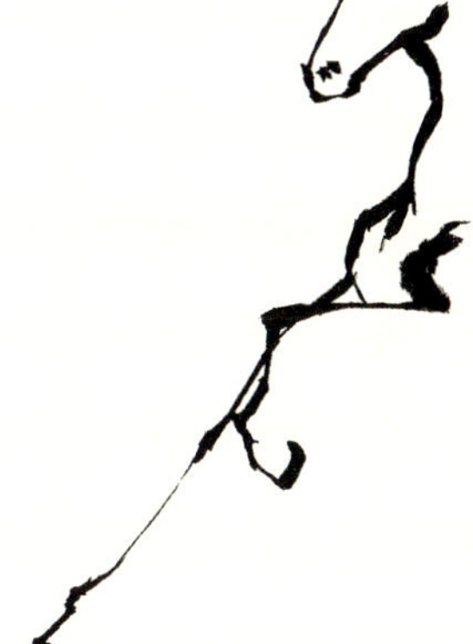

2

3—I go back down to the shoulder and draw the arm, elbow, and knee of the bent leg. I end with the hoof. This will serve as a reference for the second leg.

4—I start from the shoulder of the horse to start the line of the elongated leg. You have to mark the knee either by pressing harder on the brush-pen or by making a slight gap. I then have to continue to the hoof. This is what allows me to position the horse on an imaginary ground.

3

4

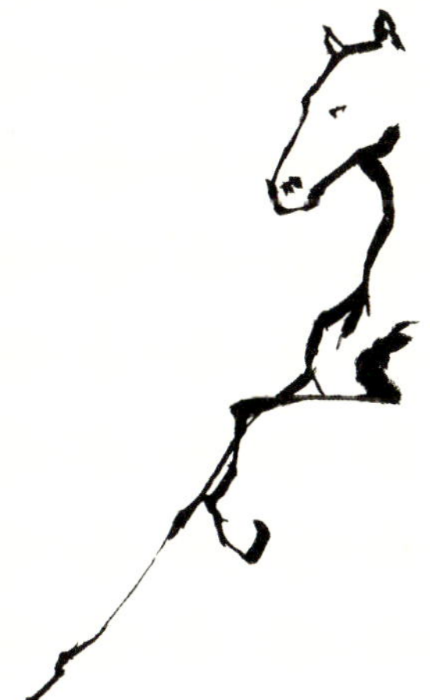

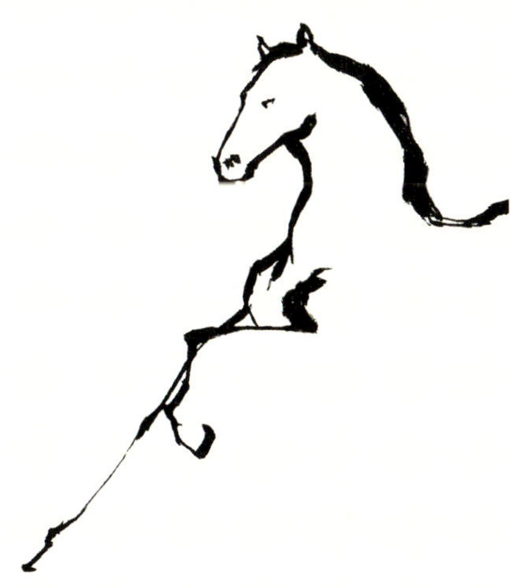

5—Just like the previous interpretation, the placement of the eye looks like nothing but it personalizes the horse in detail. With just a slight suggestion, a brief line, a very small brushstroke, the gaze is created. This is an important moment in this drawing.

6—Now I have to finish the horse's mane, withers, and back. I could have also stopped at the mane as in interpretation 4 on the following page.

5

6

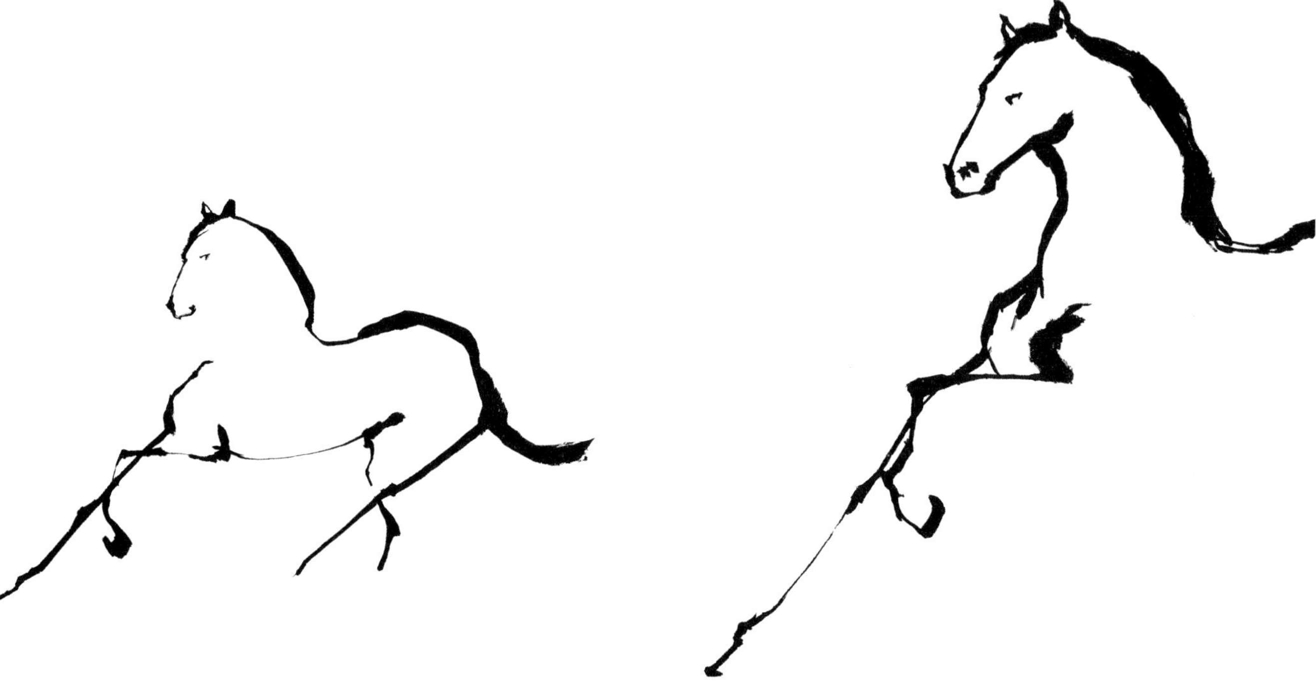

Interpretation 1

Interpretation 2

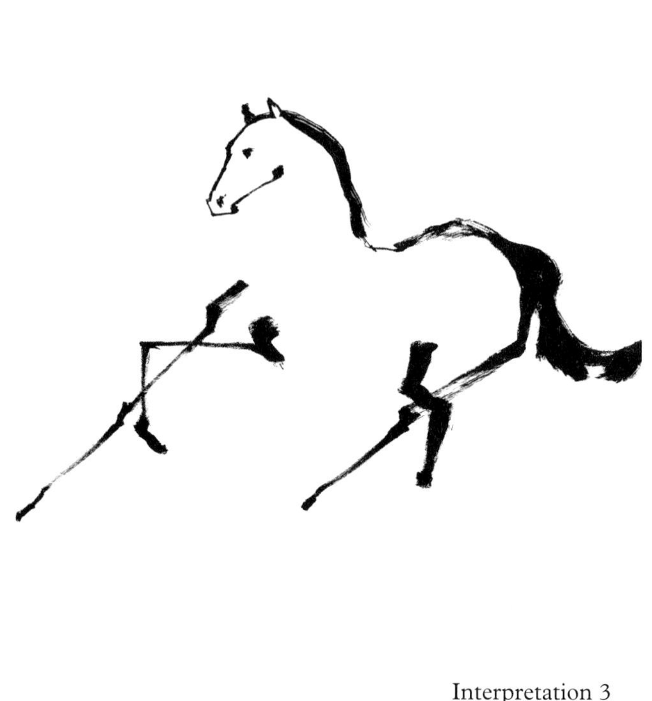

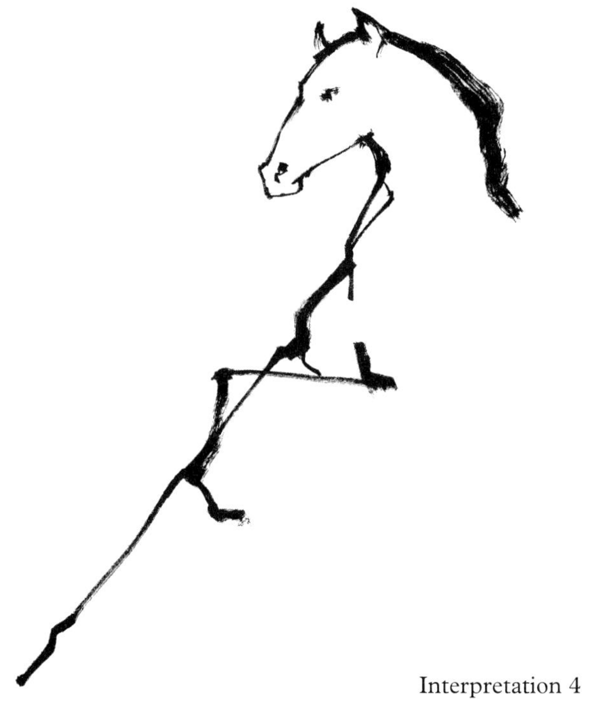

Interpretation 3

Interpretation 4

Here, I wanted to stay close to my first interpretation while using a thicker brush. I also created my lines faster because I knew the pose and my hand remembered it well. The belly and the neck were not necessary, but I decided to focus more on the tail.

In this drawing, I started with my second interpretation, but my lines were faster and steadier. I also decided to stop at the mane to focus fully on the front section of the animal.

SWANS

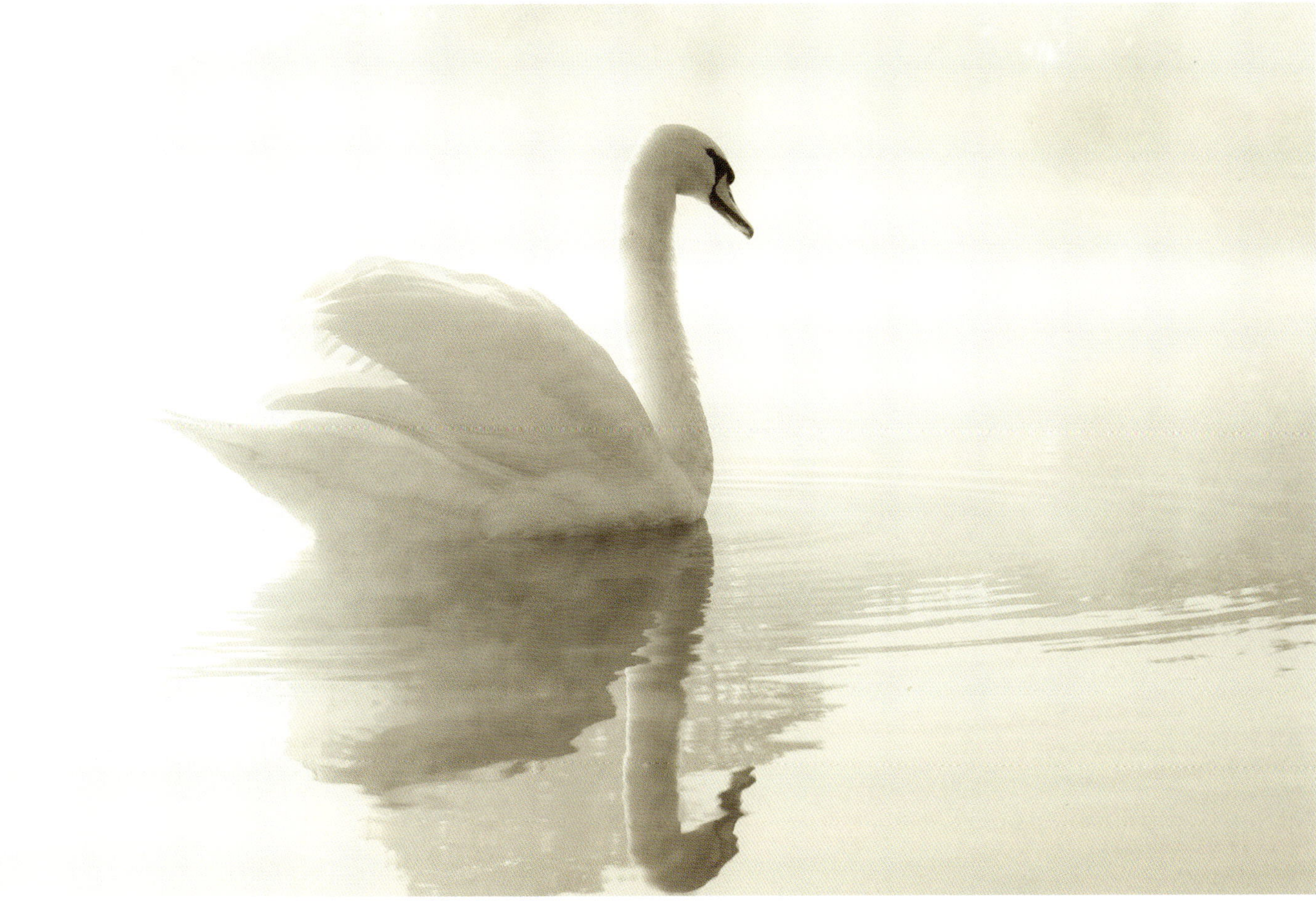

THE IDEA

I was born and raised in Annecy. The swan is one symbol of its lake. It is a bird as elegant as it is unsympathetic. I remember some Sunday mornings, I was rowing on the very still water of the lake in a misty ambiance similar to the one present in this image. I remember peacefully and silently gliding on the water as swans passed and flew by. It's a very fond memory of mine.

WHAT I WANT TO EXPRESS

INTERPRETATION 1

I will try to illustrate the majestic aspect of this swan by using two colors: one for the beak and a soft pale blue for the feathers and reflection.

INTERPRETATION 2

I will see what happens if I use a black brush. The reflection will have to be created in a different manner.

STEPS

1—I start with the swan's beak. It is necessary to have in mind the size and the place that will take up the rest of the bird on the page. I begin with the wide part near his eye and finish toward the tip. When you put the marker on the paper, the ink can settle quickly, which can be troublesome if you start with the thicker part.

2—I change to the light blue felt-tip pen and begin without waiting by positioning the eye, and I go over the ornament of the beak once more to give it more dimension. The inks mix. Then I go back over his head and draw everything in a single line.

3—I style the plumage by varying the thicknesses of the brush-pen. I lift the brush so as not to be constant and return to the level of the water and the point of his neck. I could stop there.

4—I add a few lines to mark the reflection. The lines should remain fairly parallel but vary in thickness, like the ripples of water.

5—You have to continue like this slowly enough to see how far you can go.

6—I continue the lines of the reflection while finishing placing those of the swan's neck and head.

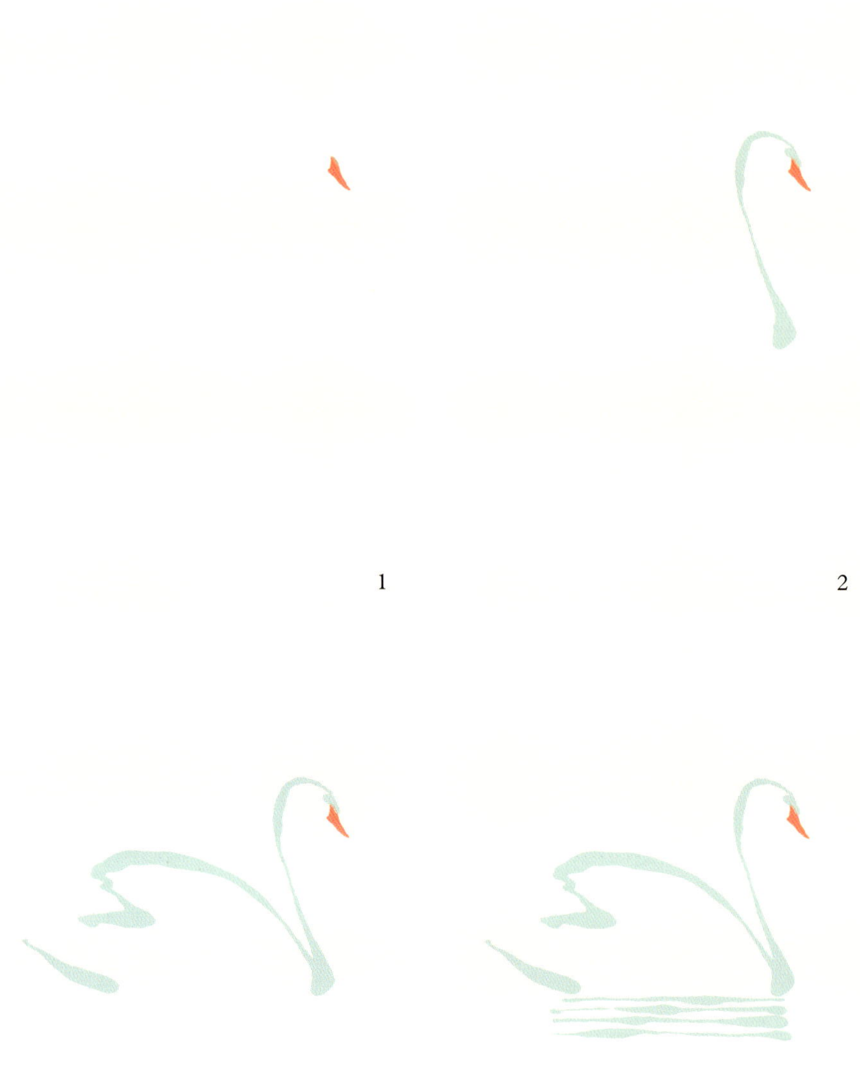

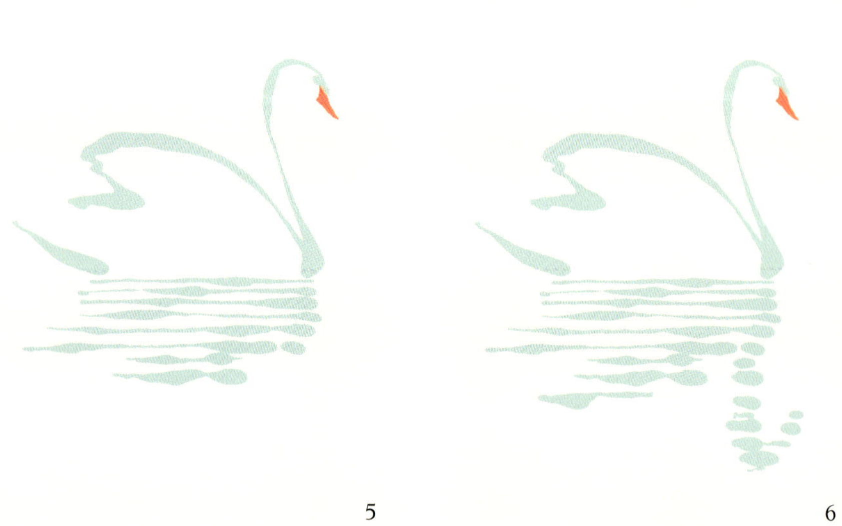

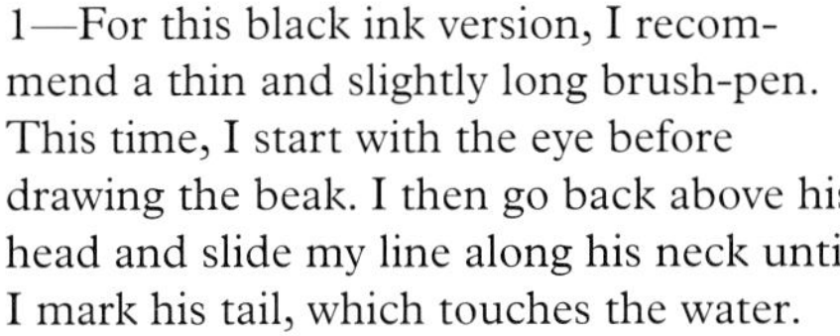

STEPS

1—For this black ink version, I recommend a thin and slightly long brush-pen. This time, I start with the eye before drawing the beak. I then go back above his head and slide my line along his neck until I mark his tail, which touches the water.

2—I go back immediately to the wing, suggesting a few feathers.

3—Like I did in the previous interpretation, I lift the brush so as not to mark the entire outline of the wings and finish with three lines for the shape of the wings and the feathers of the tail.

4—I continue the contour lines by doing the same with the reflection. A few softer lines like water respond to the swan's silhouette.

5—Before continuing, I do the same on the front with the reflection of the neck. I could potentially stop there.

6—I decide to continue by lifting the brush. You have to imagine the horizontal lines of light and lift the brush in the same levels. I finish by adding the head and beak in the reflection.

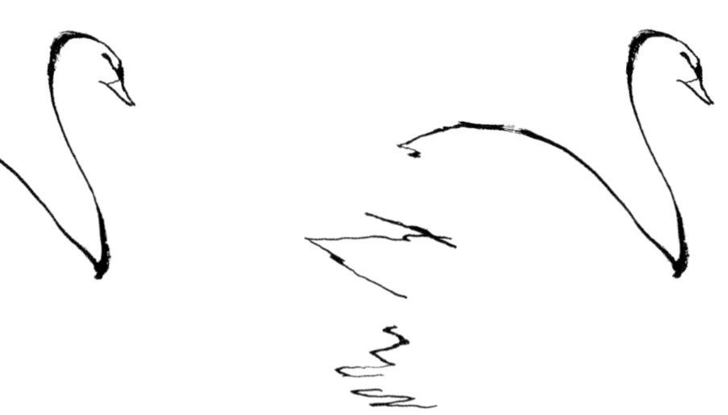

1

2

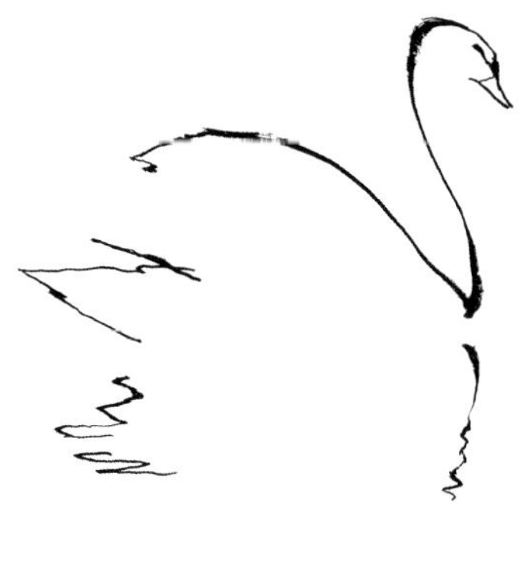

3

4

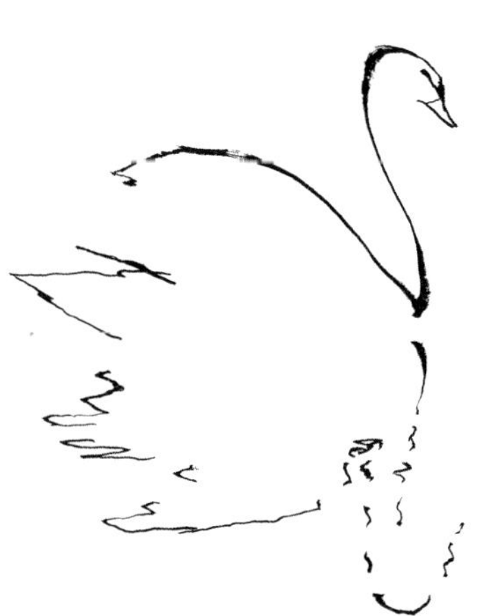

5

6

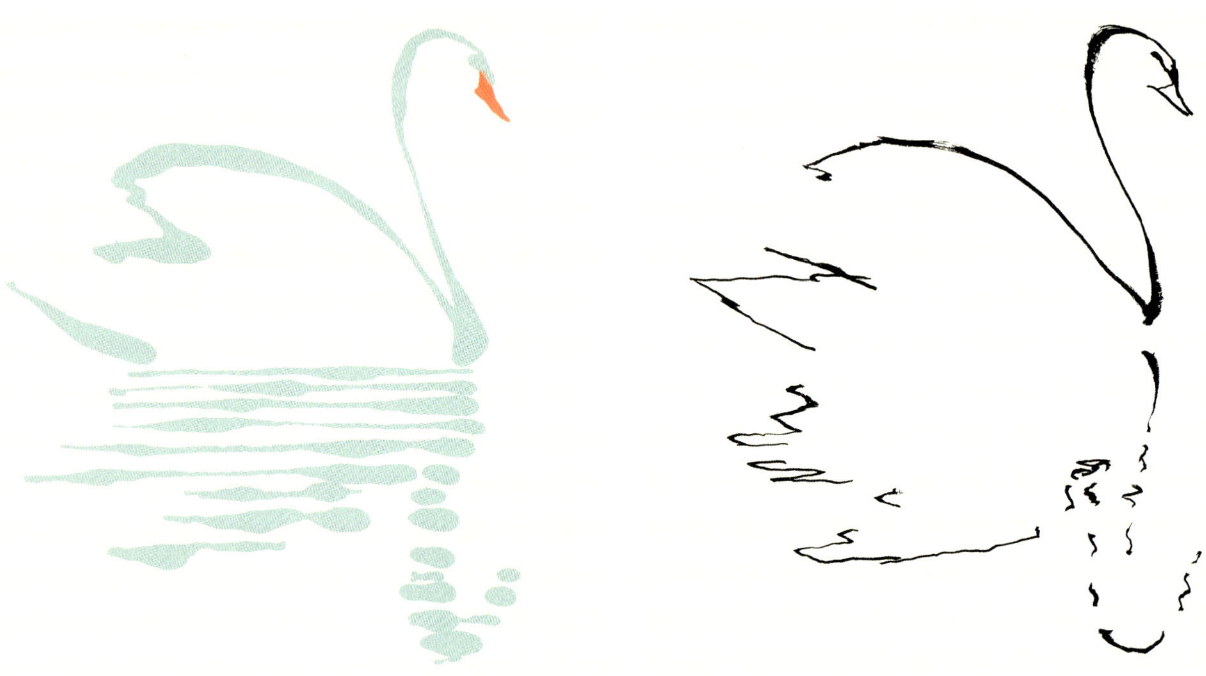

Interpretation 1

Interpretation 2

Interpretation 3

Interpretation 4

I created a silhouette with a single line, almost never picking up the pen from the paper. The reflection is no longer necessary.

In this drawing, much like my first interpretation, I created a silhouette of the swan, but my lines were less detailed and I did not finalize certain aspects such as the swan's beak. I also decided to keep the reflection, but I opted for simple, fine lines.

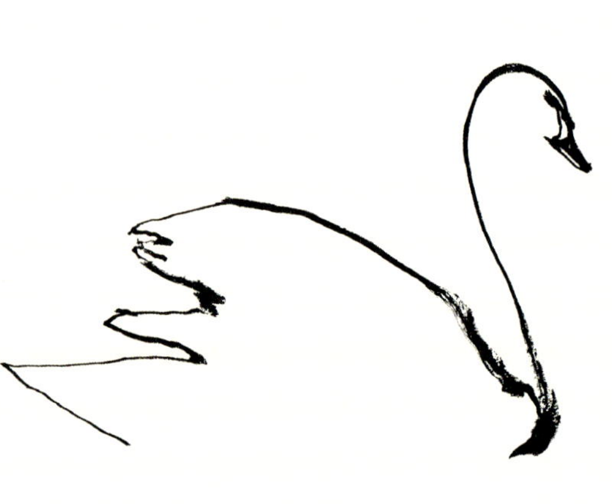

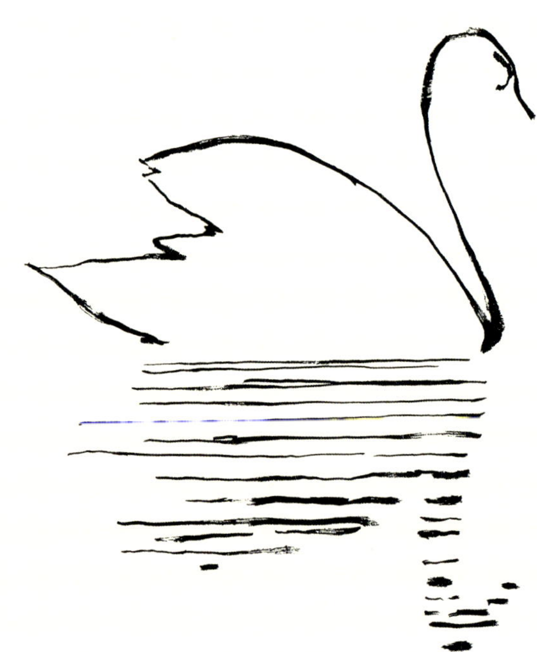

OBJECTS

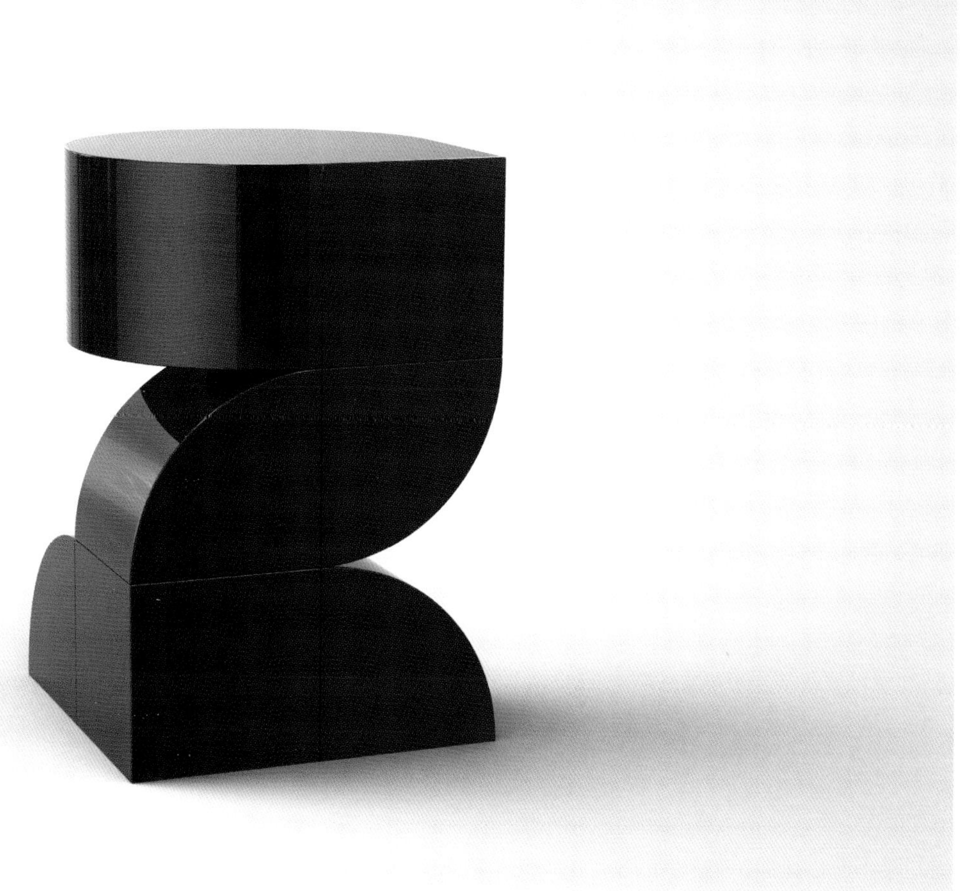

THE IDEA

Alongside art, I also run Forest&Giaconia, a highly sought-after consultancy studio and a design office with interior and product designer Clémentine Giaconia.

I've always been interested in product design and using drawings for greater projects. I admit to being equally intrigued by design and drawing, each field providing me with a new set of eyes to look at the other. Where drawing stops on the paper, paper is the starting point for design. With our studio venture, I have learned to never place any limits on myself or my creative desires.

The object pictured above is Totem 01, a stool that is part of a larger furniture collection that we designed with Archimobilier in Paris, including a dinner table and consoles.

WHAT I WANT TO EXPRESS

INTERPRETATION 1

It will be a fun exercise to redraw an object that my wife and I have imagined and drawn before its manufacture and distribution. I will start first with an interpretation that is quite representative of the actual image.

INTERPRETATION 2

I will have a little bit more fun and interpret the object in a more abstract and dynamic manner. I would like to use a set of lines to express the construction of the volumes.

STEPS

1—I start by creating a thin line for the seat. From there, I can play around with varying thicknesses to give it the correct proportions.

2—I try to reproduce the first line as parallel as possible.

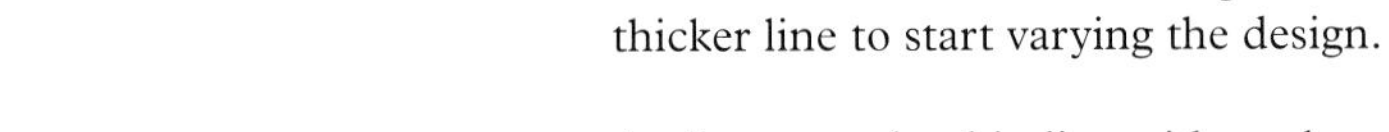

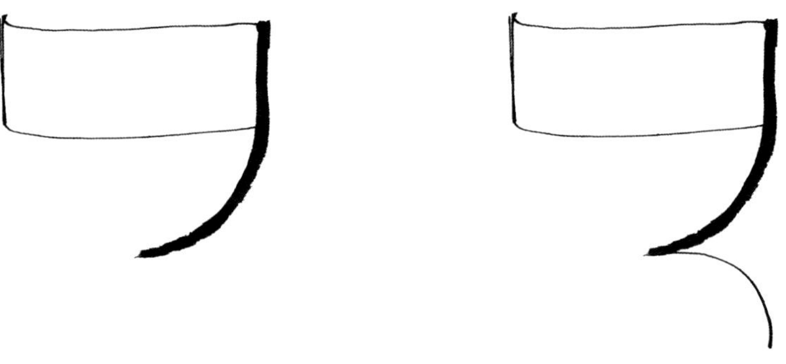

1

2

3—Now it's time to draw using a much thicker line to start varying the design.

4—I go over the thin line with my brush-pen to create this small curve, which must go all the way down to the ground.

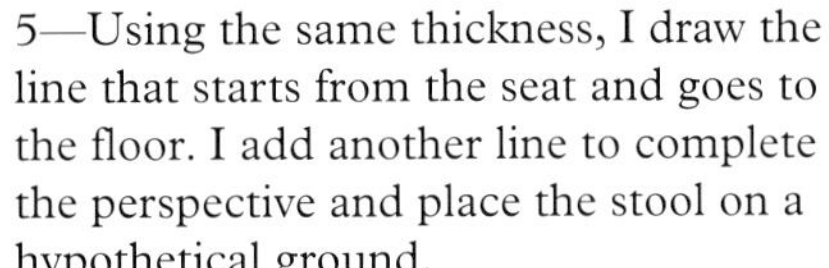

3

4

5—Using the same thickness, I draw the line that starts from the seat and goes to the floor. I add another line to complete the perspective and place the stool on a hypothetical ground.

6—I resume the counter-curve using more force to complete the drawing.

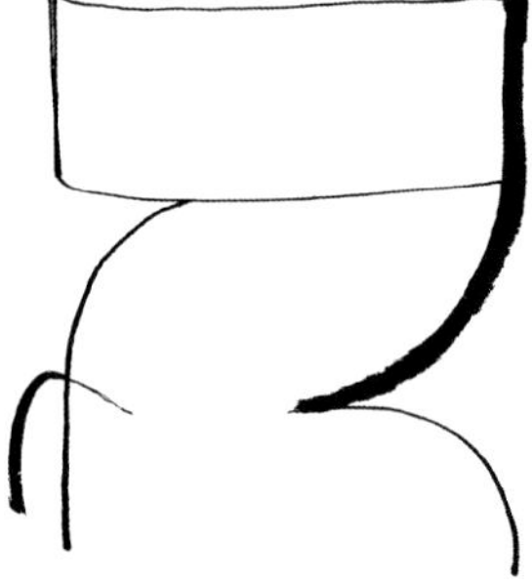

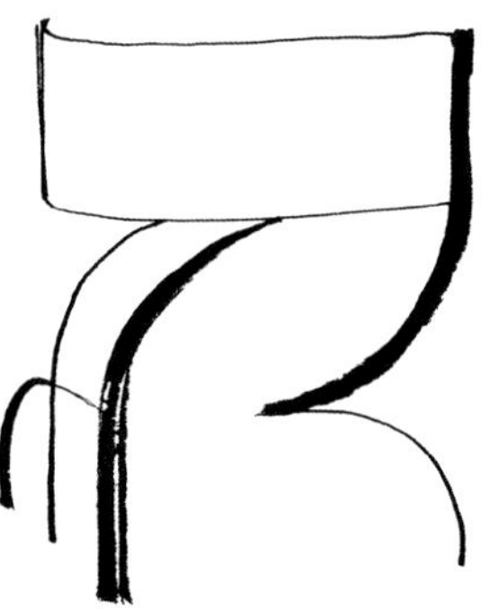

5

6

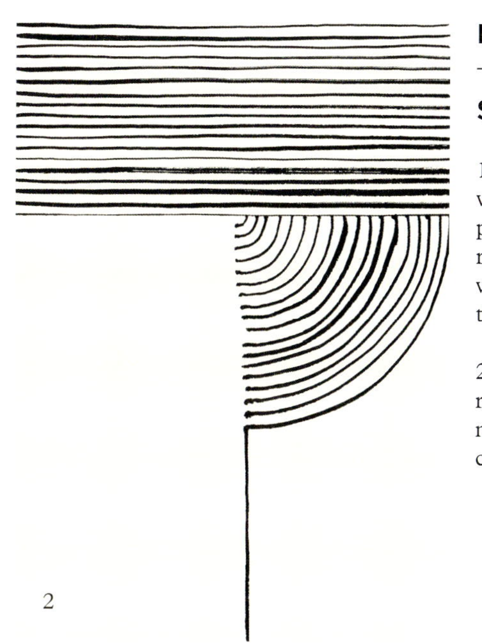

STEPS

1—The best thing to do is to have a sheet with vertical and horizontal lines that you put under your paper. This will help you be rigorous and constant in your tracks. I start with a series of horizontal lines, varying the thickness of the strokes slightly.

2—I keep this same frequency to draw repeated quarter circles, which already give me the rhythm of the drawing. I stop each circle section in the center of the page.

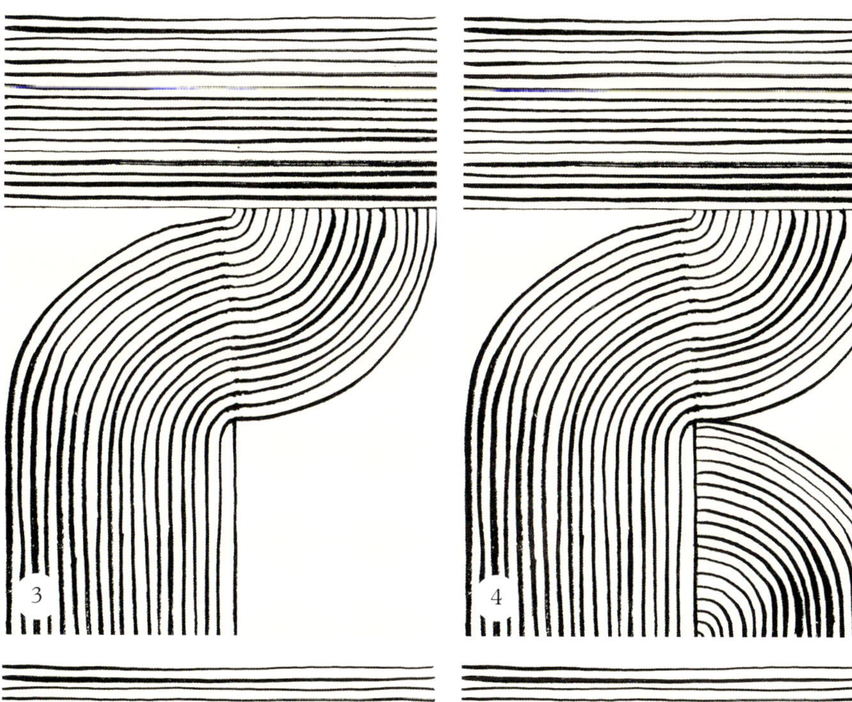

3—I continue this movement by tilting the circular curves down to the left and ending vertically.

4—I go back over the first curved lines, continuing the same rhythm and finishing all the way to the bottom of the page.

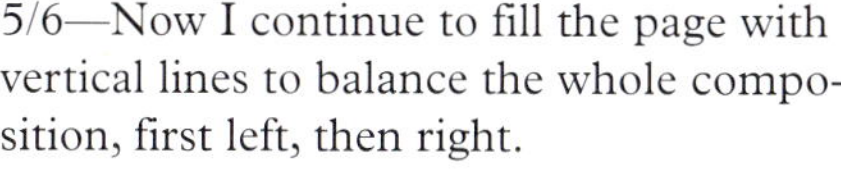

5/6—Now I continue to fill the page with vertical lines to balance the whole composition, first left, then right.

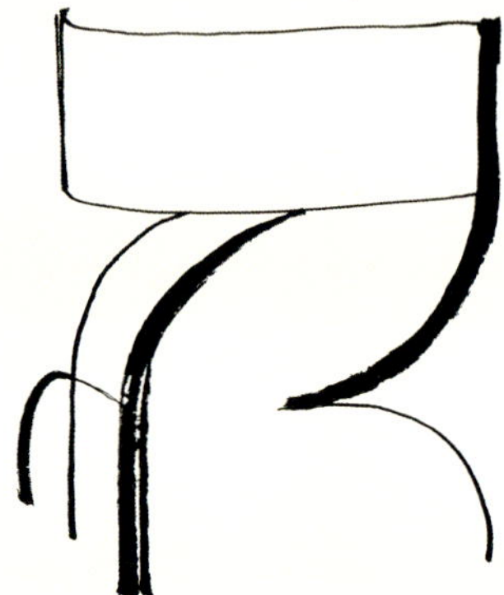

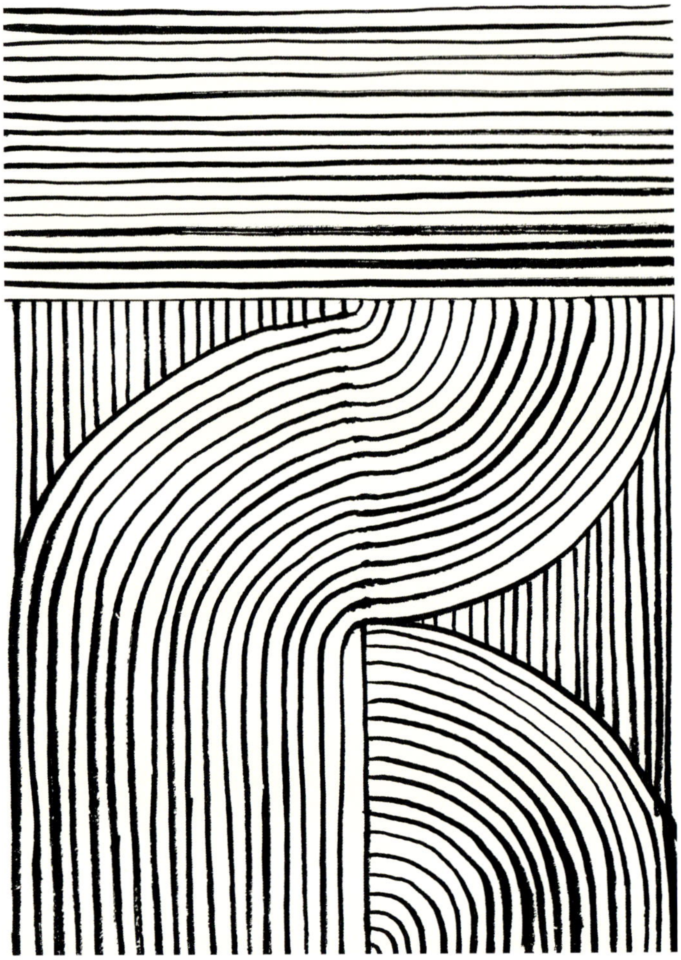

Left: Interpretation 1
Right: Interpretation 2

Interpretation 3

I was going to make an improvement of interpretation 2, but finally decided to stop and focus on the hands and what they express.

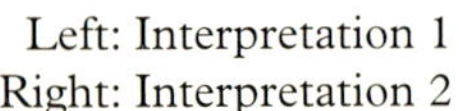

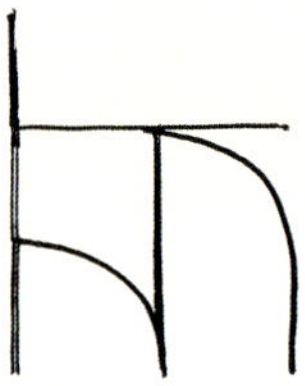

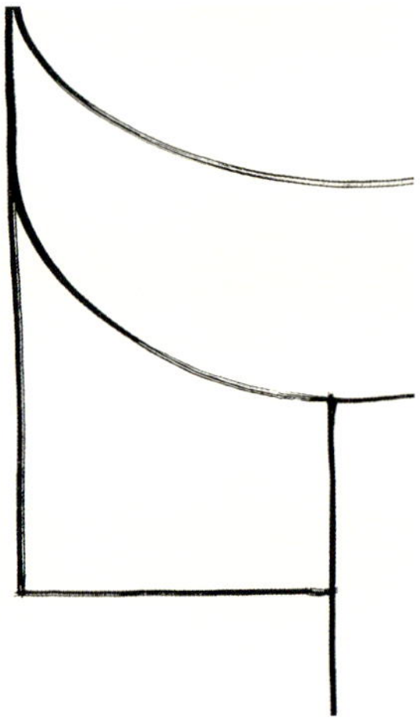

Further explorations

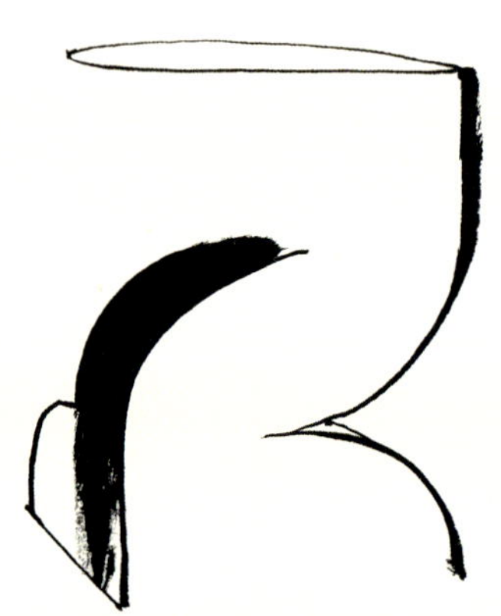

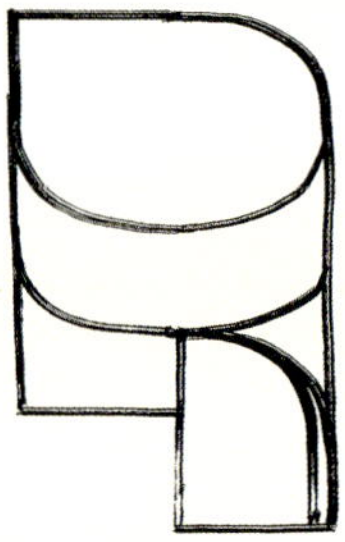

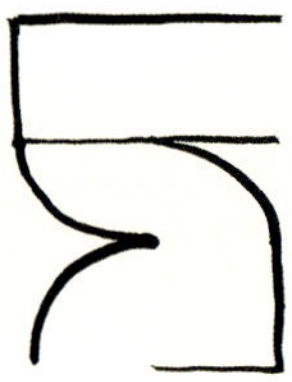

INTERIOR (Using One Color)

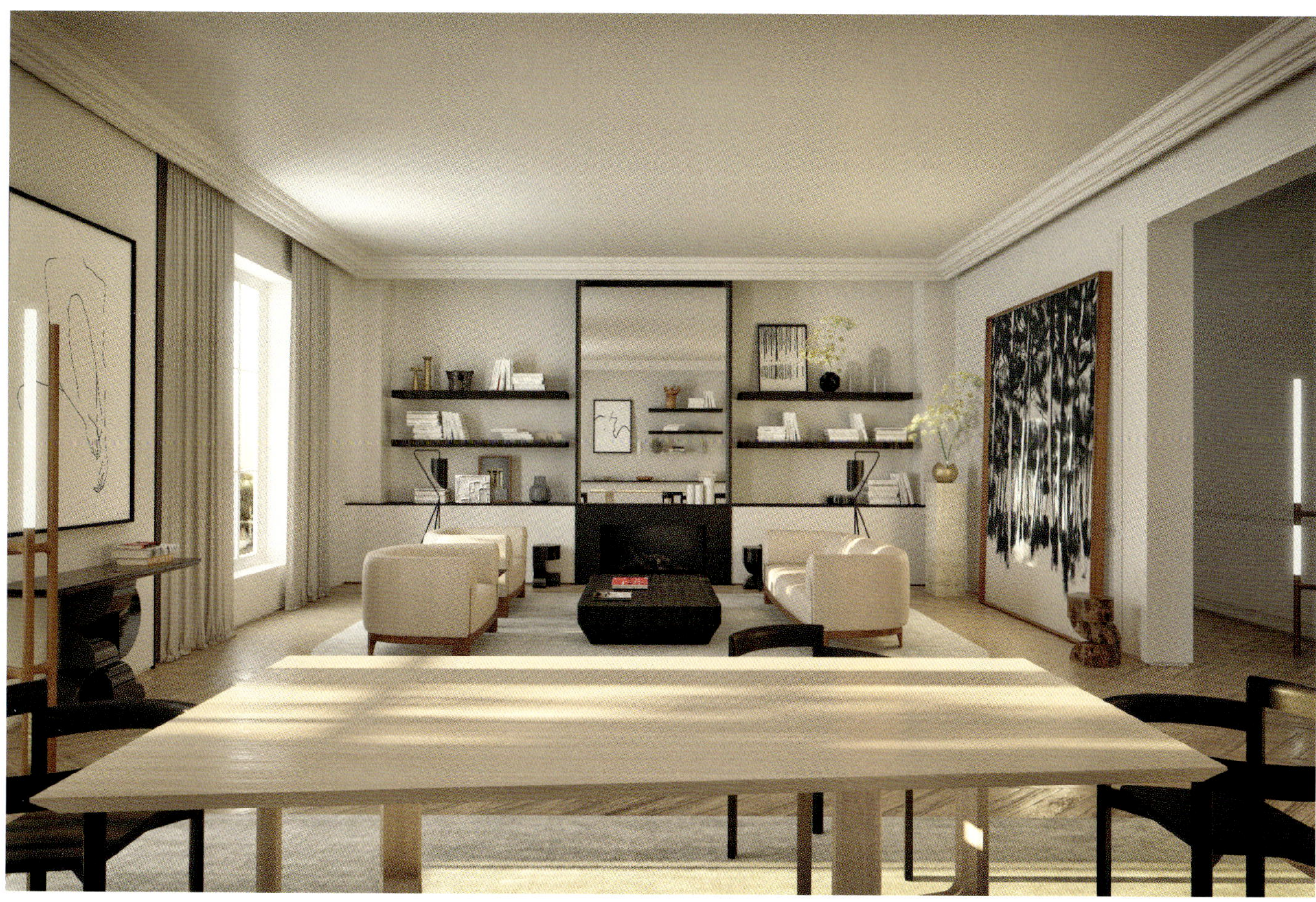

THE IDEA

This rendering is of the private residence project in Paris that my wife and I designed for one of our clients. Here, you can see a view of the living room from the dining room. The interior design is by Clémentine Giaconia.

All the pieces of furniture that are pictured were designed by us. The dinner table, armchairs, sofa, and lamps are edited by Delcourt. Consoles and stools are produced by Archimobilier. These pieces are all distributed worldwide.

WHAT I WANT TO EXPRESS

INTERPRETATION

A thick brush will allow me to graphically punctuate the page. It will be necessary to alternate the line widths to bring this space to life and make the space understandable.

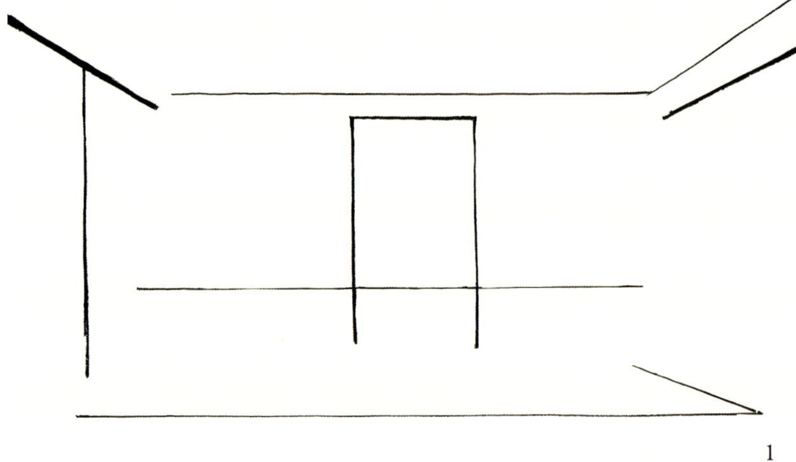

1—The most important thing to keep in mind while designing an interior, which is also true in architecture in general, is to sketch the most important construction lines first. I therefore begin with the horizontal line of the ceiling, then add the one that signifies the edge of the fireplace, and finally sketch the horizontal line of the carpet. I then trace the fireplace and the frame of the mirror placed above it, following up with the perspective and vanishing lines of the ceiling and carpet. I end with a vertical stroke to mark the curtain. This allows me to begin to understand the rhythm that the drawing will have and structure the overall space.

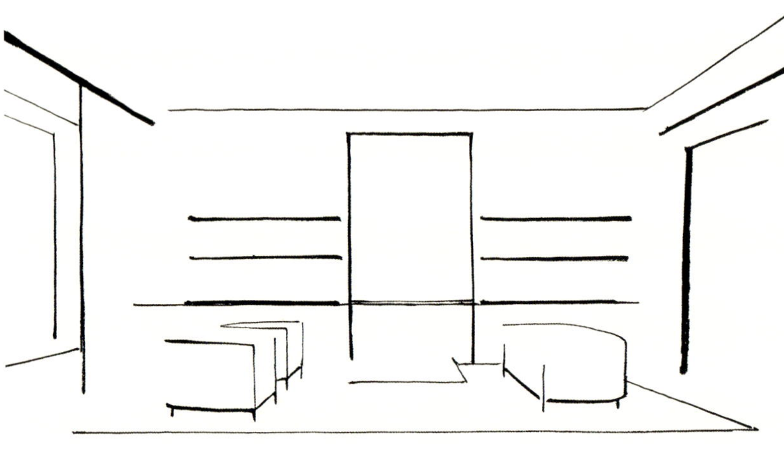

2—From there, I add the details of the space that interest me. I suggest the outline of the window and shelves. I sketch the pieces of furniture and the coffee table, and draw part of the picture frame that is placed behind the sofa.

3—I can then mark the shadow of the coffee table and the dark frame of the fireplace. I sketch in part of the forest of the painting and add a few vertical lines from the curtain on the left to echo the painting. All that is left to do is to highlight the legs of the armchairs and the sofa, and add a thicker line for the stool.

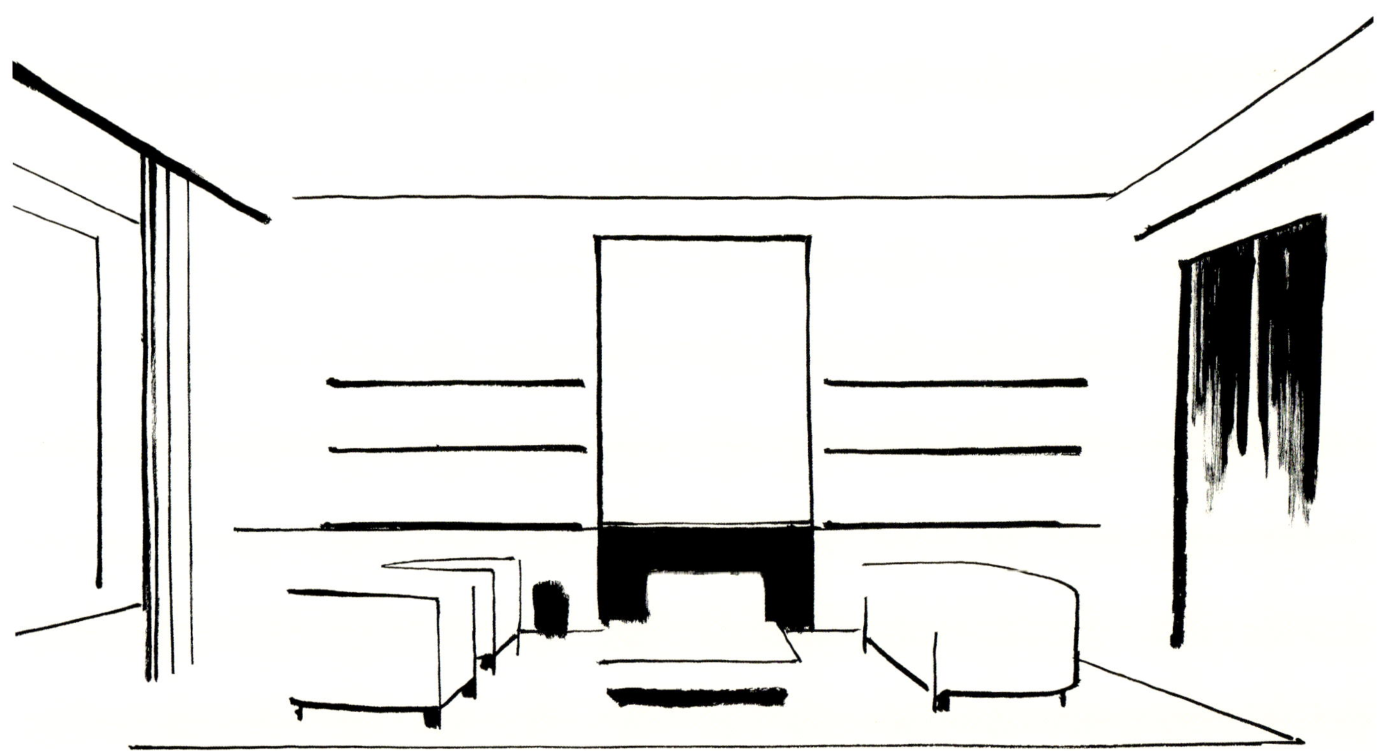

INTERIOR (Using Two Colors)

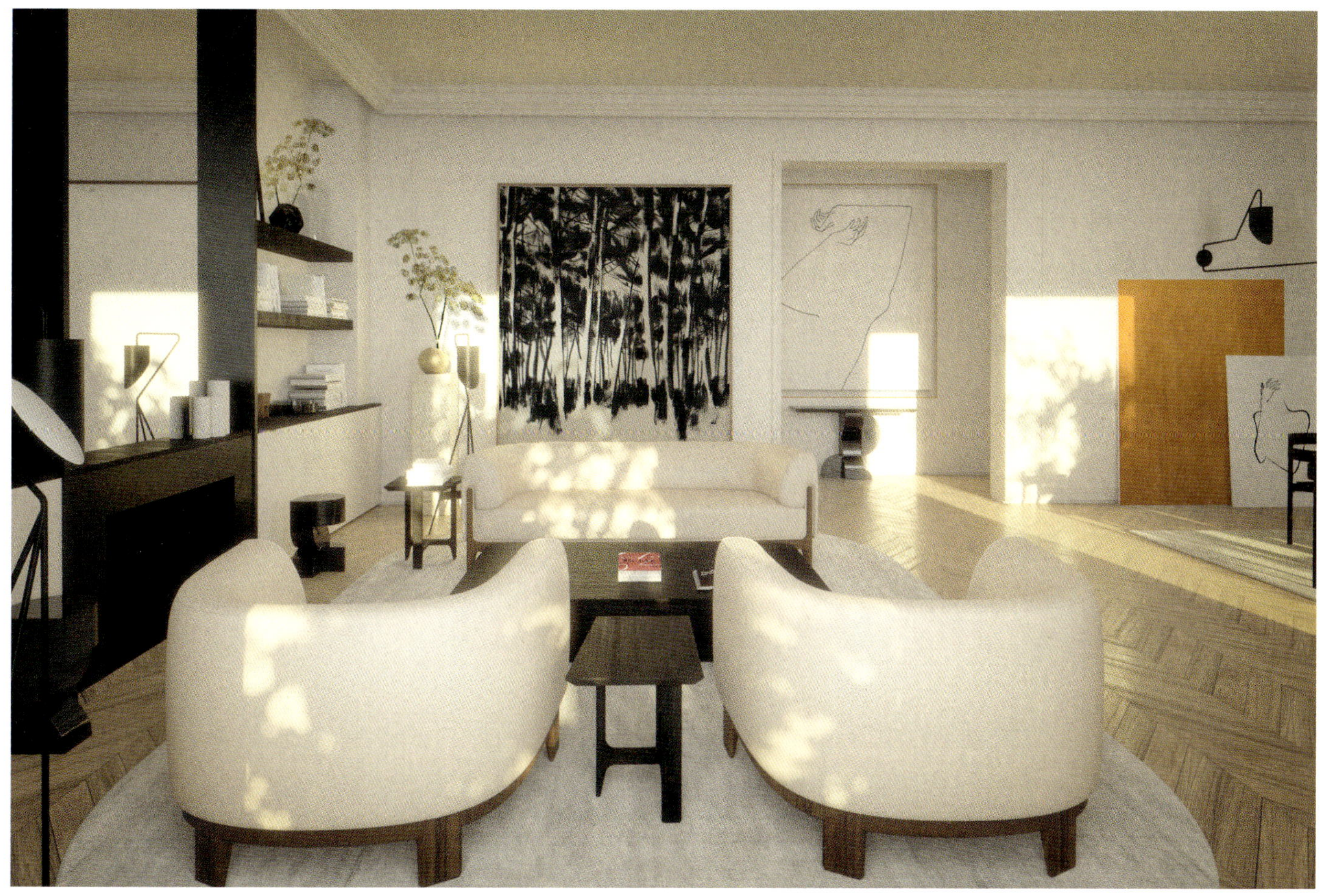

THE IDEA

Still in the same space, here is a different angle of the living room to work on.

WHAT I WANT TO EXPRESS

INTERPRETATION

I will use two colors to give more depth to the elements that make up the space

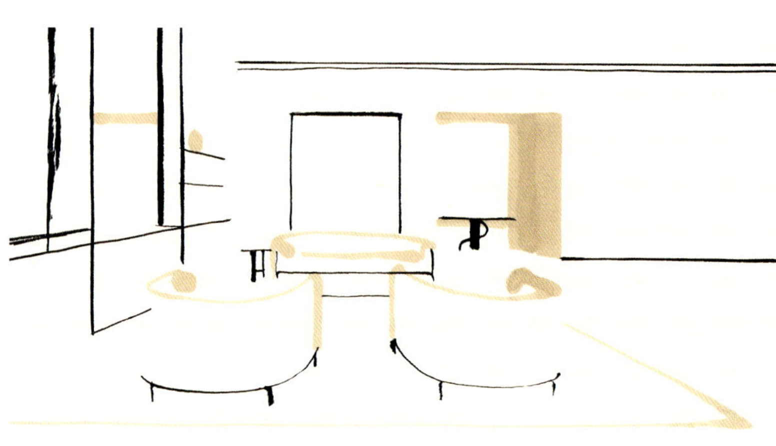

1—This time, I try to think like a photographer and begin by shading in the softer tones to define the space and its decor. I start at the bottom with the outline of the carpet, then quickly sketch the top of the furniture with a very thin line. I then go over these same lines using a stronger line to express soft shadows. At this time, I can also mark the shadow of the opening onto the hallway.

1

2—Switching to a black brush-pen, I start with the left side of the composition and add the vertical lines of the fireplace and the mirror above, following with the vanishing lines of the trays. I then draw thin lines to express the graphic moldings of the ceiling. I add a line for the ground on which the entire composition is held. I still have to add the details of the furniture and the console in the hallway. I go back to light felt to place the shadow of the console in the hallway and the reflection of the hallway in the mirror above the fireplace.

3—From there, I then have to fill in with black the fireplace and the frame above as well as the furniture legs. I then sketch the framed painting behind the sofa using a sheet of paper over it as a mask to keep the rest of the drawing intact.

2

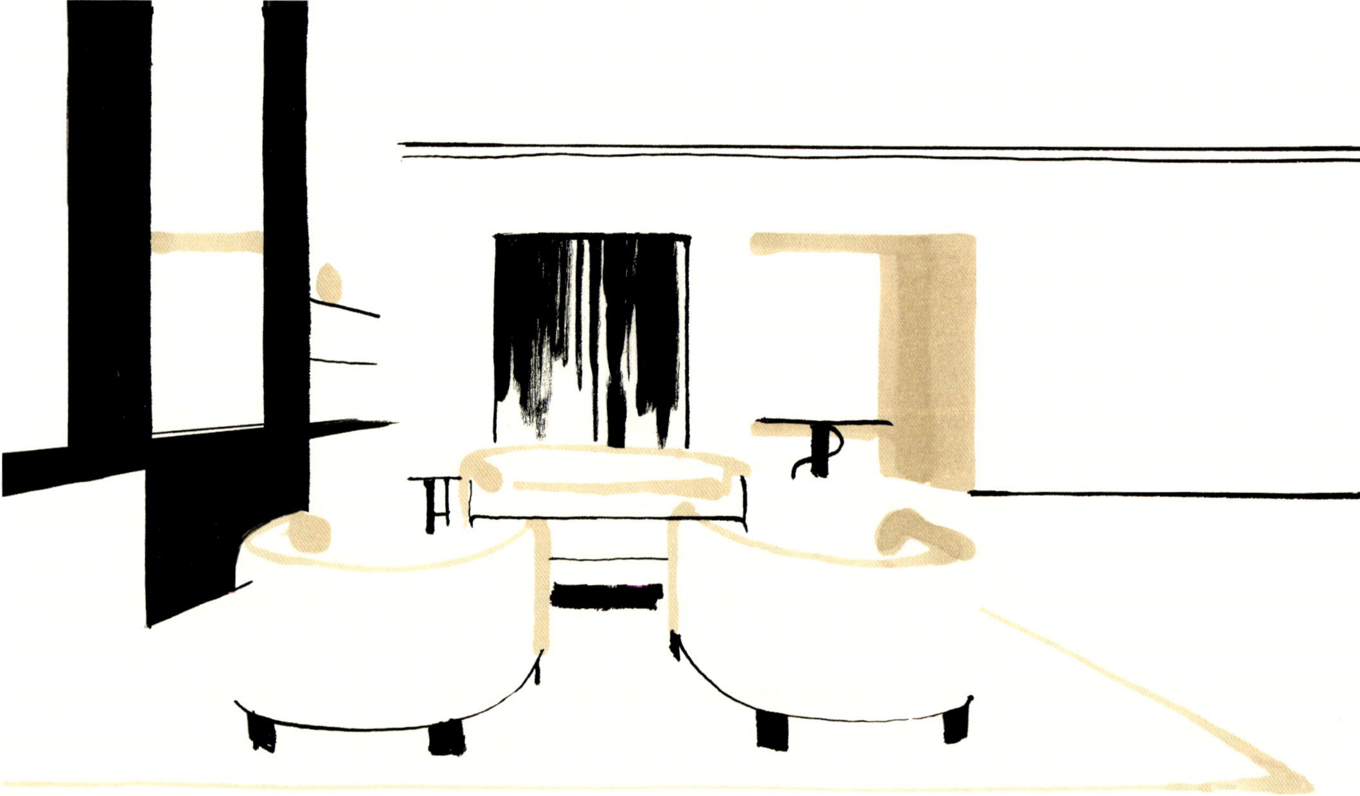

3

HOUSES

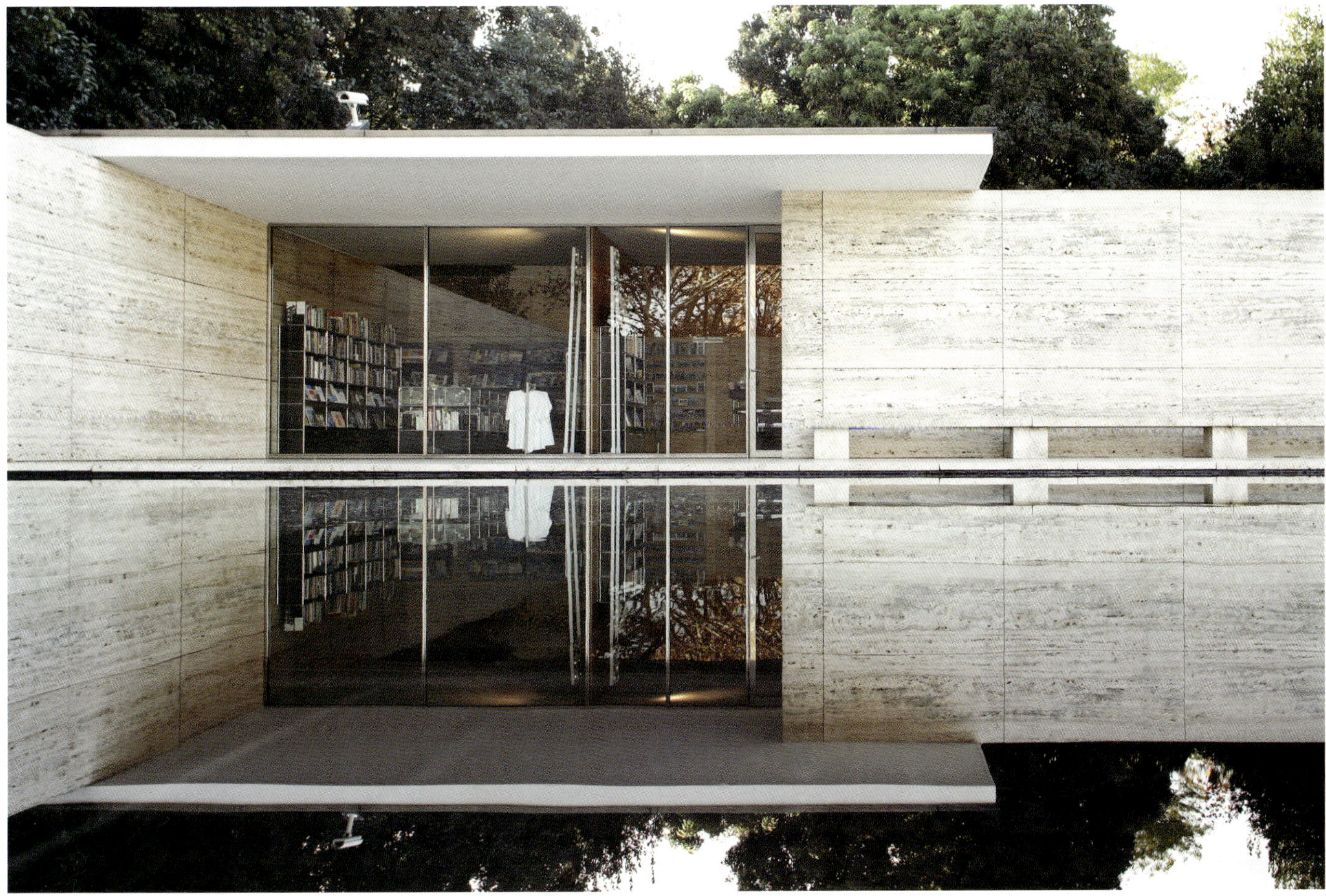

THE IDEA

Architectural drawing is very similar to music in that you must keep your lines in rhythm on the paper. This image was taken at the Barcelona Pavilion, designed by Ludwig Mies Van Der Rohe and Lilly Reich, for the 1929 international exhibition. It is a major work of the Bauhaus movement, which redefined architecture as we know it today.

I had the opportunity of collaborating with the photographer Quentin Simon on a visual essay made up of his silver gelatin photography prints and my drawings for an exhibition that was held in Paris in 2019 and was the subject of the publication of a book "Alba."

Interestingly enough, I have never been to this place and yet it fascinates me so much. The works of this architect are so fundamental. I could not pass up the opportunity of making a new tribute to this wonderful space.

WHAT I WANT TO EXPRESS

INTERPRETATION 1

I will use thin lines made with a soft brush-pen.

INTERPRETATION 2

I will give the house more character by also drawing the surrounding nature and its reflections in a more contrasting way.

STEPS

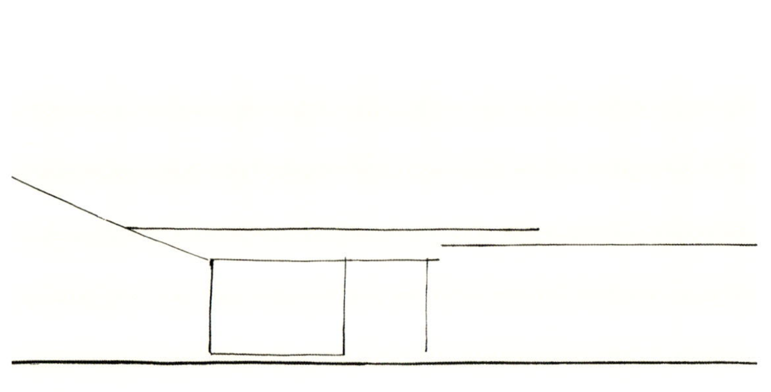

1—For this type of drawing, it is important to keep in mind the space that the composition will take up on the page and to choose your paper's format accordingly. I begin by drawing a few important horizontal and vertical lines. These will serve as my base and determine the placement of everything else in the final drawing.

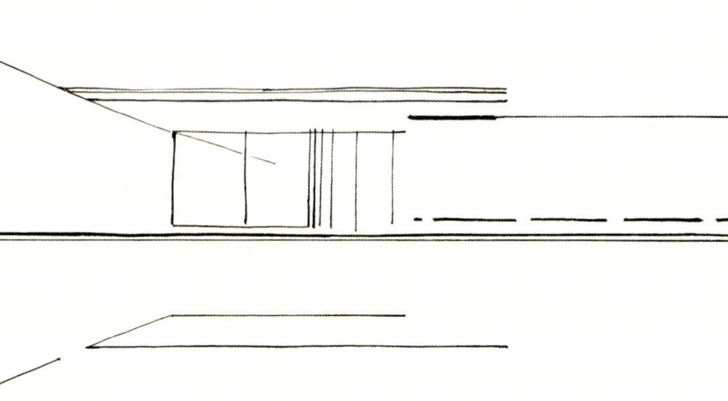

2—From there, I can add the additional lines that I find interesting or important and a few small details that are specific to the construction or building that is pictured.

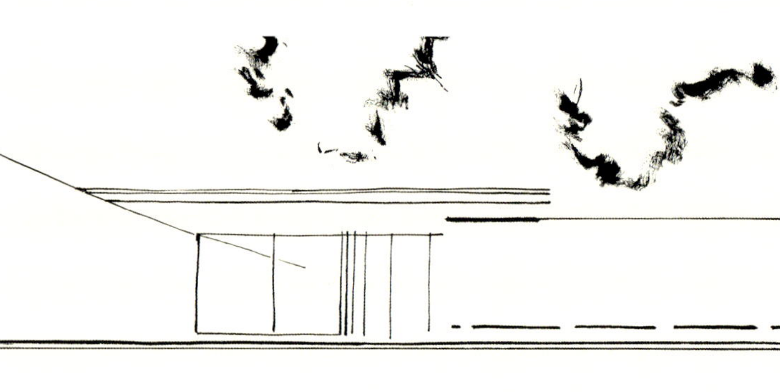

3—Still using the same brush-pen, I remove a little bit of ink by drawing on a separate sheet of paper until I obtain the brushed effect that I am looking for. I then draw the contours of the trees above the house.

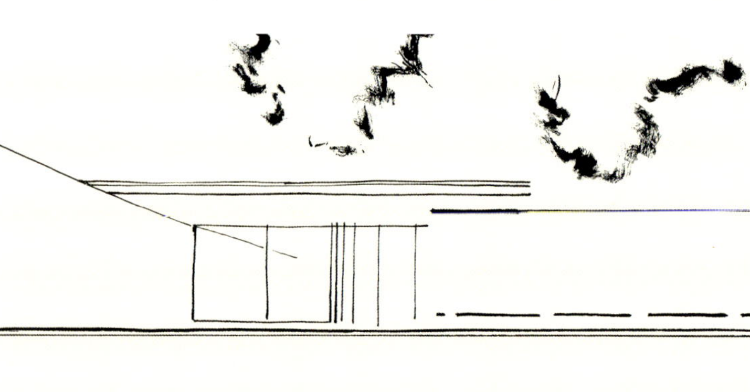

4—To be coherent, I work on the symmetry of the contours of the trees and the brushed effect of the water for their reflection.

STEPS

1—This time, I begin with the central line that acts as our horizon line. This line embodies the symmetry of this drawing and image. I place it almost in the center of the page. From there, I quickly place the construction lines around the windows. I then add the line of the roof and the diagonal line, which marks the left wall.

2—Right after doing this, once I've mastered the way I handle my brush-pen on the paper, I sketch in the shadows on the large windows. To do this properly, I place a blank sheet of paper on top of my drawing and use it as a frame so that I do not run over the lines while shading.

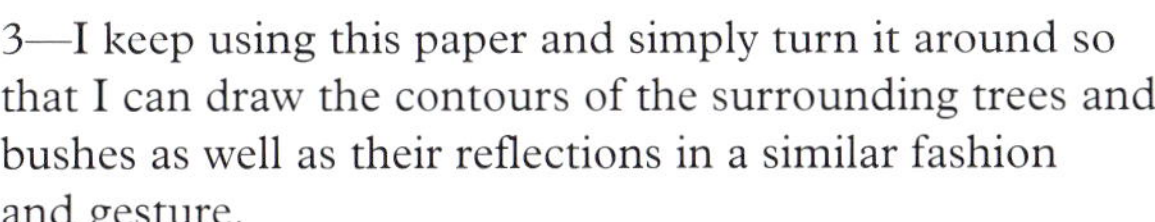

3—I keep using this paper and simply turn it around so that I can draw the contours of the surrounding trees and bushes as well as their reflections in a similar fashion and gesture.

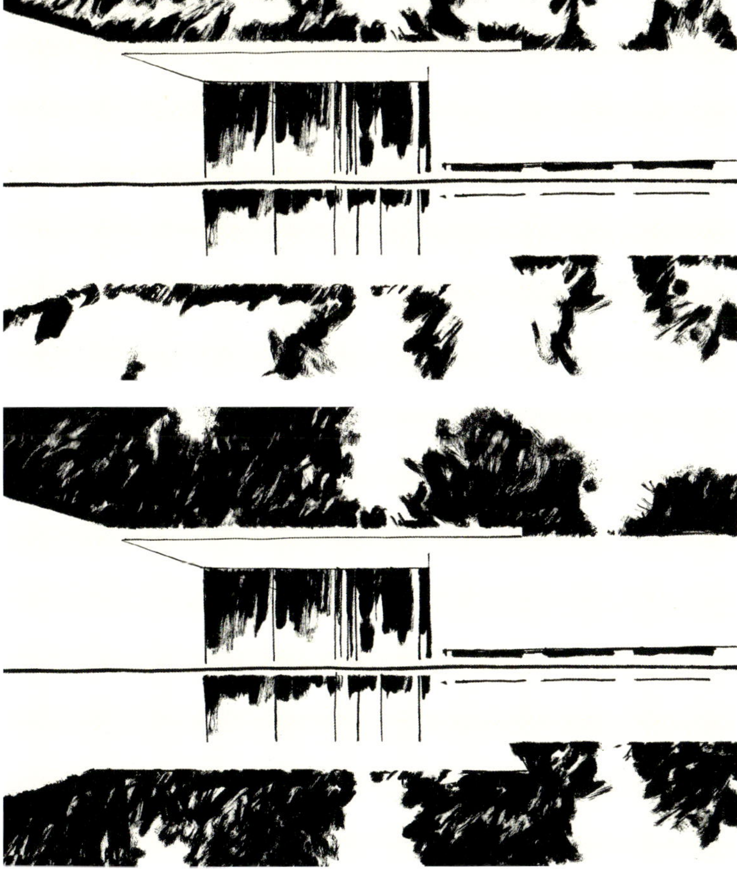

4—I now have to focus on finalizing these shapes by adding a brushed effect, still using my blank sheet of paper as protection when needed. By playing with this negative space, I've successfully rendered the volume of the walls and the house without adding extra lines.

Interpretation 1

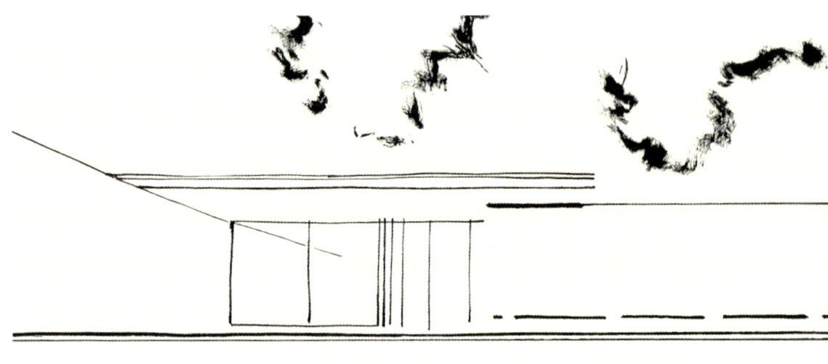

Interpretation 2

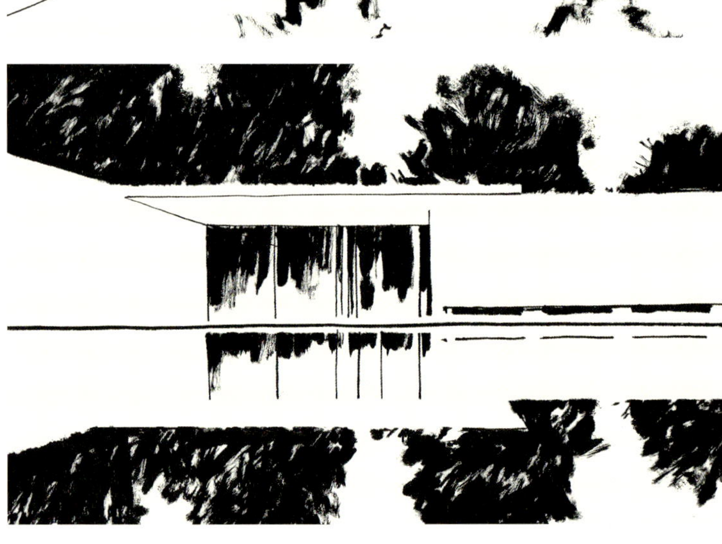

Interpretation 3

This test was done using very fine lines. I personally find this drawing less convincing and appealing.

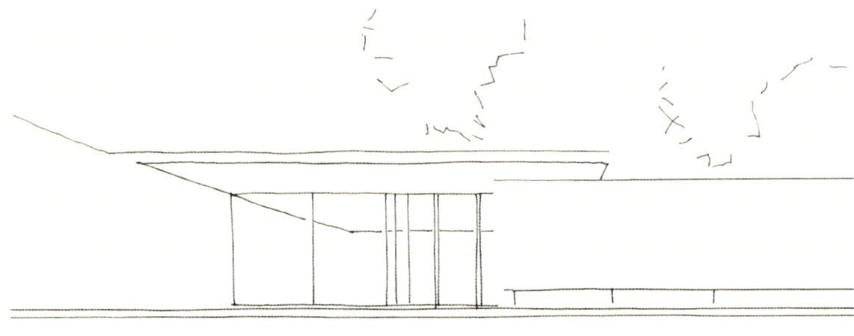

Interpretation 4

Here, I wanted to see what would happen if I used thin colored markers.

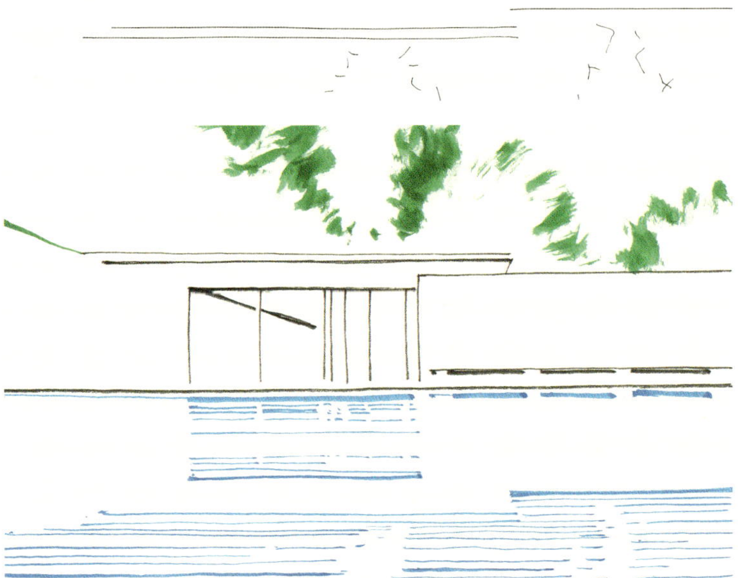

LOOKING AT WHAT YOU'VE MADE

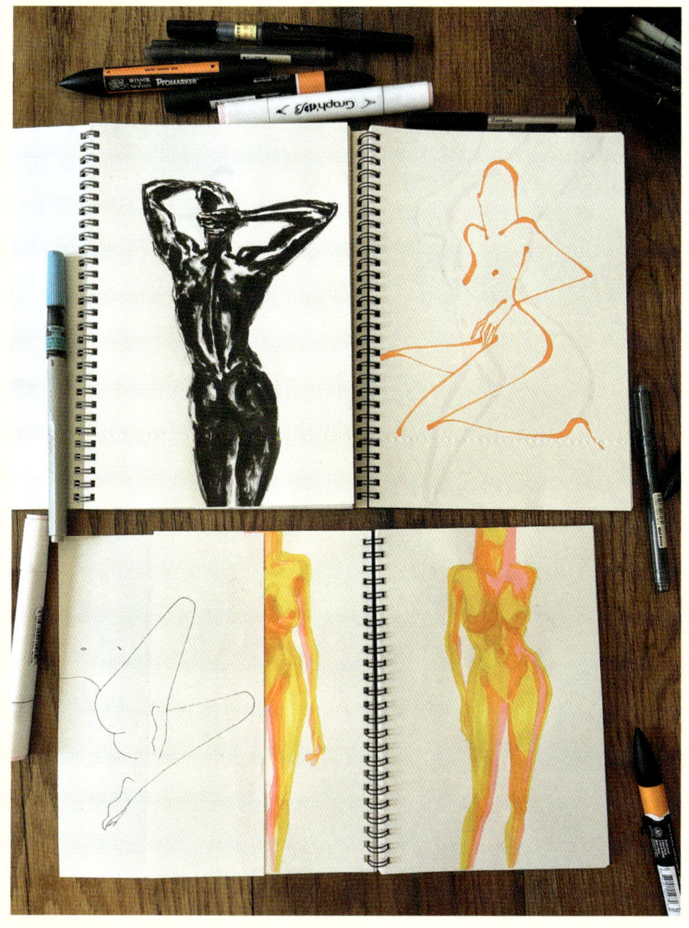

Is the format the most appropriate for the subject? Would it have functioned better as a colored drawing, a painting, or something else? Try to be as objective as possible. For each negative aspect you find in the work, it is important to counterbalance it with positive feedback because a critique should feel constructive.

Taking pictures of what you've made and looking back on them once time has passed is valuable because you will no longer be in the production stage of the works and this will allow you to look at them with a refreshed gaze. You can also install your works on a wall in your workspace using thumb tacks or clips to look at them differently than if they were in your sketchbook.

Once you've done all the work, it's time to sit back and look at what you've done! For me, I found that the best way to be successful at critiquing my own work was to pretend like my work was going to be critiqued by someone else who did not know me, my intentions, or my abilities. Instagram proved to be a great tool in doing this so that I could post my work, see how it looked when it was photographed, and allow others to react and respond to the drawings objectively, without context.

If you are not ready to share your works with others around you, you can also self-critique your work, which is valuable step in finding your way as an artist. When doing this, treat yourself as two different people: the artist creating the project and another artist who is critiquing the project. If you were the client or collector, would you be happy with the final result? What could be perfected, what is missing, what could be edited or removed?

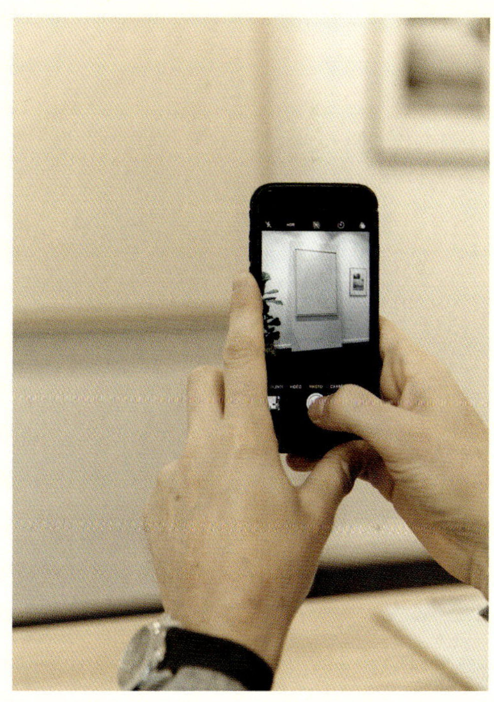

CHOOSING THE FINAL PIECE

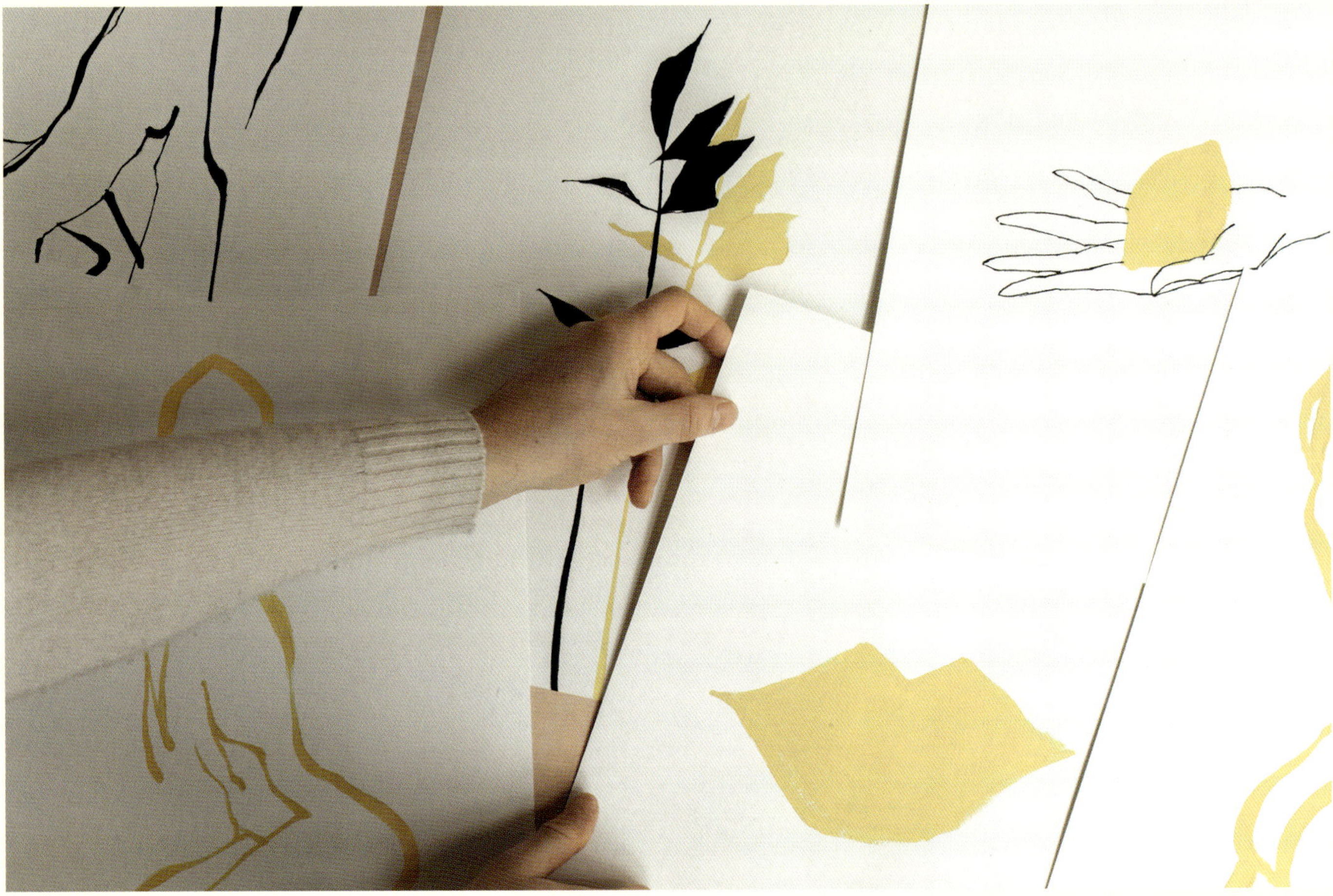

Now that you've selected your favorite drawings, how do you choose the final one? Personally, I like to really set aside time to look at the works, observing them in my studio but also in natural light. If it's a work belonging to a series, does it function well with the other drawings when placed side by side? If the work stands on its own, what does it make you feel when you look at it? Once you've picked your favorite, make sure you also examine it fully before deciding to frame and share it. Inspect the work for any paper defects, dust or specs present on the page, ink bleeds, leaks, messy lines, or crinkled paper. Treat the final piece as you would treat a work in a museum: Wash your hands before handling it, store it in an acid-free archive box with appropriate protection from sunlight, and if you are framing the work yourself, ensure the frame and glass are clean and dry before inserting your drawing.

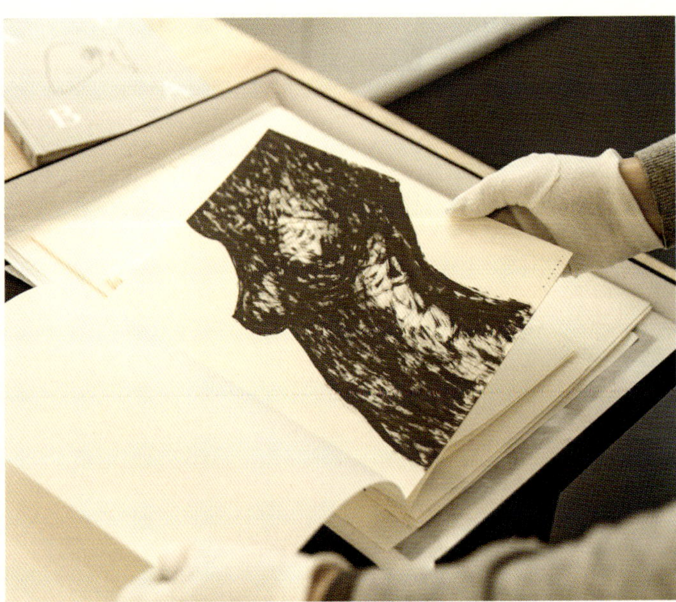

SHOWCASING YOUR ARTWORK

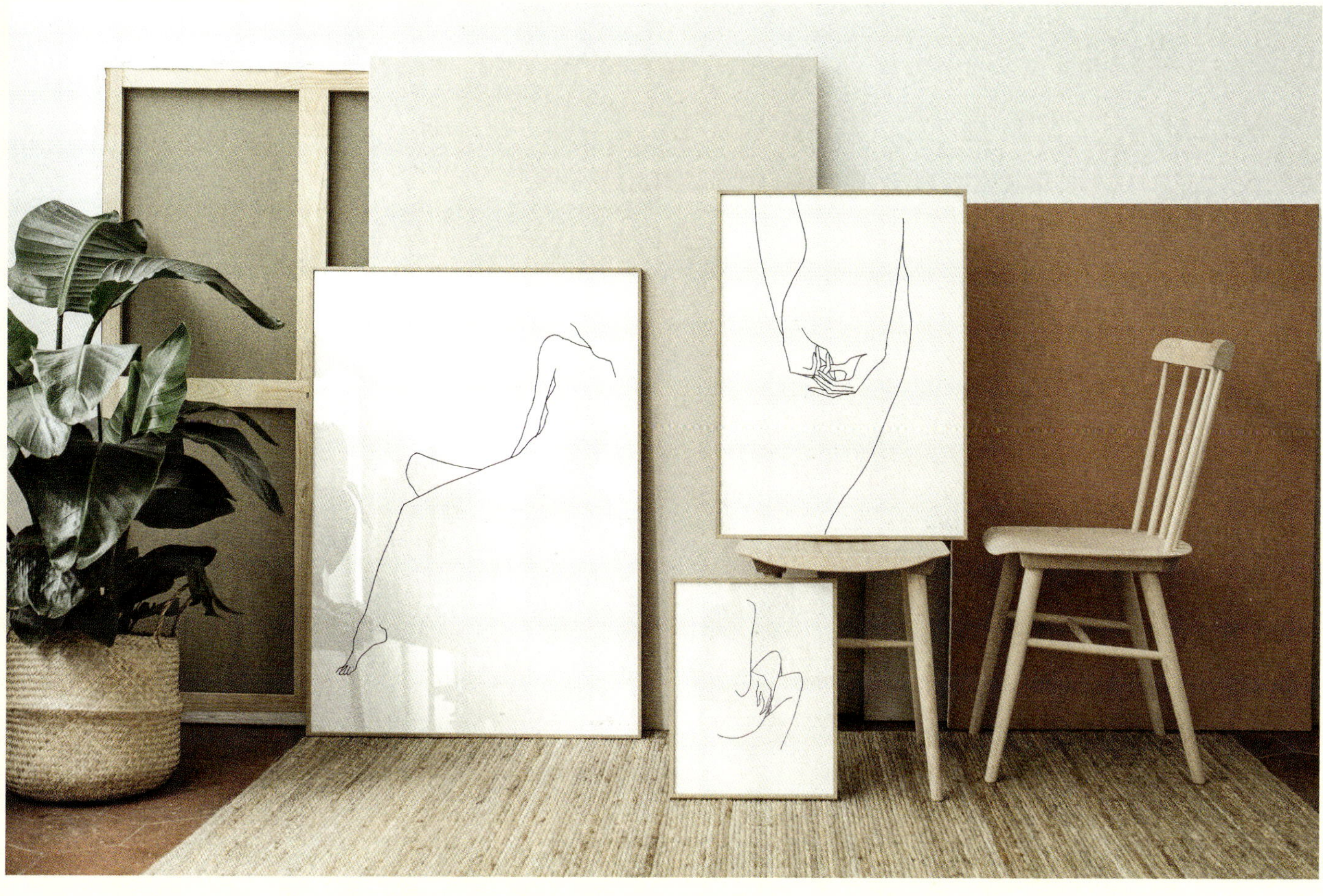

We are finally at the best part: sharing what you've done!

Showcasing your work doesn't have to be for an audience. It can also be for your personal pleasure, in the comfort of your own studio or home. There are many ways to show works on paper nowadays, so feel free to pick whichever one fits your style the best. For example, if you decide to frame your works, do you prefer frames that perfectly fit your drawing sizes as shown above or mats, also known as mounts? These thick pieces of paper or board sit between the artwork and the framing glass to protect the surface of the work. Colored mats and frames can accent your art, and small pieces thickly matted can make for a dramatic display, as seen in the bottom left photo on the next page. If you made digital prints, you can handle the works in a less "precious" manner by hanging them with clips or, like I did, show them on hangers so that clients can browse through them in the studio much like you would browse through a rack of clothes at your favorite store.

Keep in mind how you want your audience to interact with your work and if you want that interaction to be personalized or more traditional.

Once you've decided how to show your works, decide if and how you want to share them with your surroundings. Organize an exhibition, host a meet and greet in your studio, display your works on a website, share them on social media, or open an online store—the possibilities are endless and the only thing to consider is to pick what makes you happy and brings you the most joy when sharing your works.

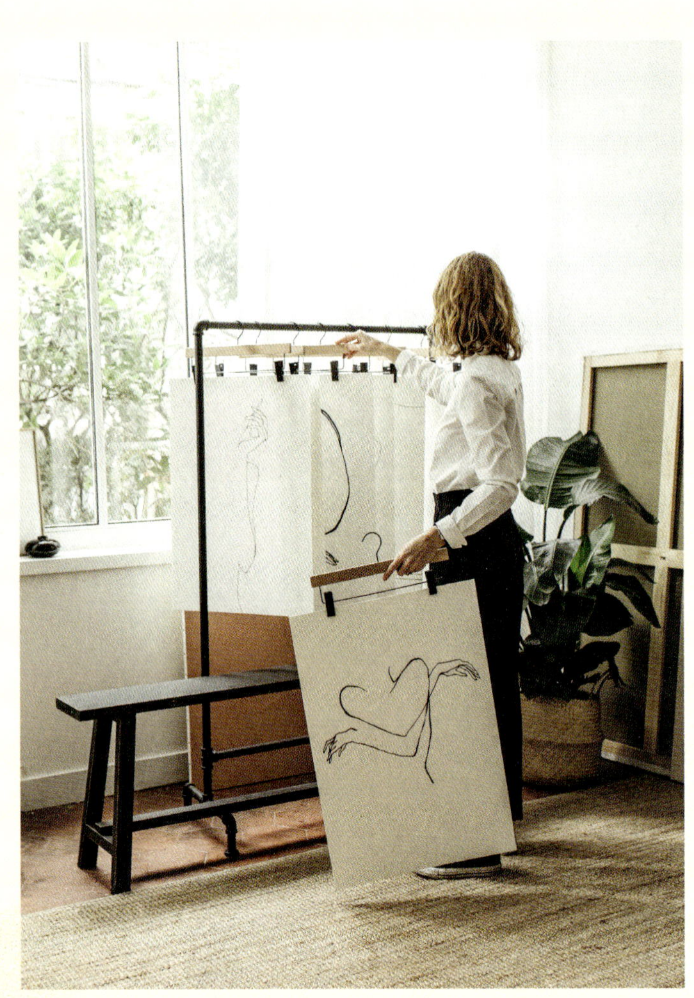
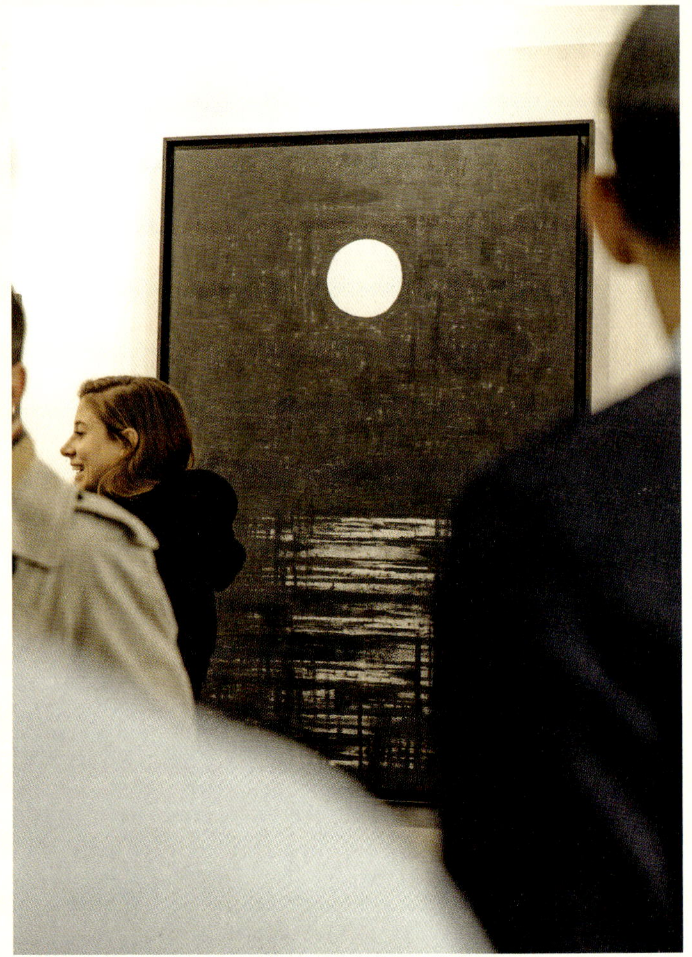
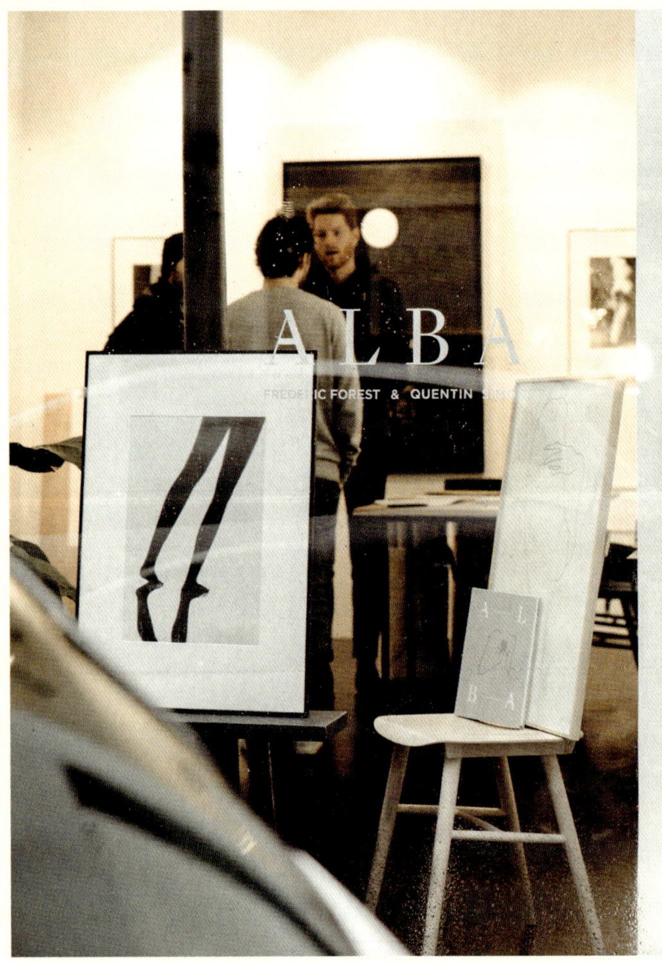
ALBA
FRÉDÉRIC FOREST & QUENTIN
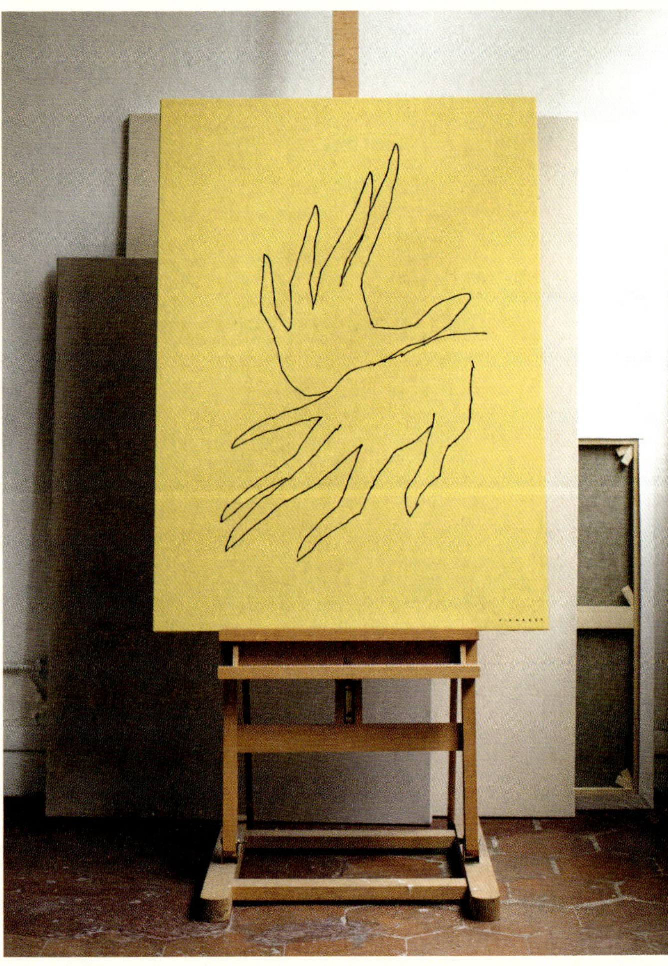

ACKNOWLEDGMENTS

In addition to the dedicatees, deepest thanks to:

Joy Aquilino, Athina Perrin, David Martinell, Elizabeth Weeks, Lydia Anderson,
and—of course—Heïdi and Clémentine Forest-Giaconia.

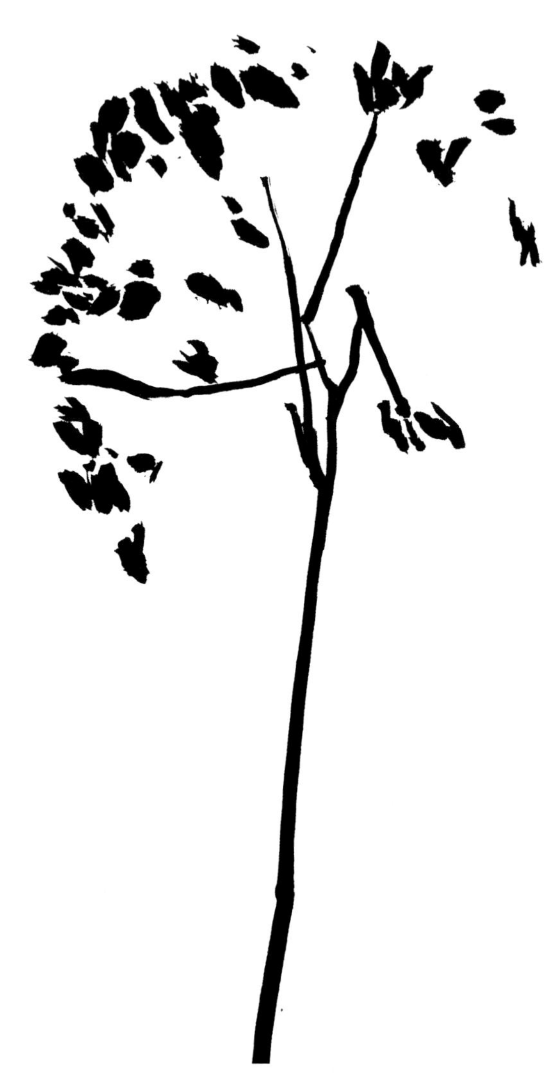

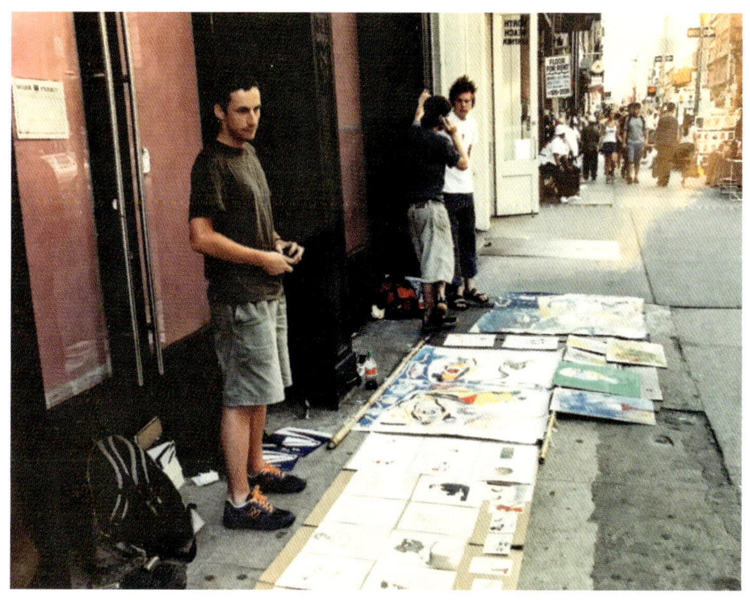

Frédéric Forest selling his drawings on 5th Avenue, New York City, July 2001

ABOUT THE AUTHOR

"As a child, I always had a pencil in my hand and sheets of paper to draw on. I would skip meals because I would be cooped up in my room, focused on drawing. I never took drawing or painting lessons. I learned on my own."

Frédéric Forest grew up in Annecy, a city often referred to as the "Venice of the French Alps." This picturesque hometown quickly became a subject of much exploration for Frédéric, an imaginative child who spent his free time taking in everything that the world around him had to offer. "Growing up, I drew inspiration from my town's mountains and streets," Frédéric says. "We didn't have exhibitions there; my artistic eye was shaped by everyday activities, like snowboarding, skateboarding, or surfing while on vacation." Printed press and magazines played another important role in Frédéric's artistic education. "As soon as something new landed at the newsstand, it was hysteria. I would travel to Geneva just to read fanzines—they were imported and too expensive to buy. My eyes would scan everything I saw and accumulate all these new images and art in my head, re-creating what I saw on paper."

Pursuing his passion has carried him a long way. Today, Frédéric is an artist, designer, and creative director based in Paris. In 2008, after various experiences working with Erwan and Ronan Bouroullec, Noé Duchaufour-Lawrance, and Jean-Marie Massaud, he and Clémentine Giaconia set up their own design consultancy studio FRST (partner with luxury brands), and an eponymous studio Forest & Giaconia (furniture, interior design with editors, and private projects). Alongside the cooperations with international luxury firms, he creates his own art. Evocative and precise, yet minimalist in nature, his drawings have landed him international collaborations with renowned brands such as Chanel and Rains, as well as magazines of the likes of *Kinfolk*, *Vogue*, and *Cereal*. Frédéric's filigree line drawings seem like sketches at first sight. He focuses on the silhouettes of bodies, landscapes, architecture, and still lifes that are seductive in a minimal kind of way.

Though Frédéric had always been an artist, he had never dreamed of being one. "I didn't actively seek to turn my art into my professional life. I've always drawn and painted for my own pleasure. Up to today, my goal remains to simply express the beauty that I witness." To this day, Frédéric is still amazed by the popularity of his creations and always surprised to see the use people make of his art. "I had never thought that one day people would get tattoos of my designs. Today, there are more than five thousand throughout the world, *Self Love* being the most tattooed drawing to this day."

Recently, Frédéric's practice has begun to grow beyond drawing, from illustrations to paintings, lithographs, and, more recently, ceramics. "My favorite role is precisely not having one. This allows me to be incessantly stimulated and not dependent on any single medium."

INDEX